Black Power and White Protestants

Black Power
and White Protestants

A CHRISTIAN RESPONSE TO
THE NEW NEGRO PLURALISM

JOSEPH C. HOUGH, Jr.

New York OXFORD UNIVERSITY PRESS 1968

To Robert L. McCan,
Pastor, Colleague, and Friend

Preface

A risk is involved in writing a book about American race relations. Persons involved in the public discussion are constantly changing their positions, and old leaders are fast replaced by new ones. This raises the danger that what is being written will be dated by the time it appears in print.

Such a danger is especially immanent when the author addresses himself to a phenomenon such as "Black Power," the future definitions of which may be subject to the convulsions of a racial conflict that grows more intense each day. The factors that produce change are often irrational and hence unpredictable. The actors are often products of mass media which dispose of their creations as soon as someone more newsworthy appears on the scene.

In spite of these dangers, I am still confident that the emergence of the "Black Power" slogan as a rallying cry among American Negroes signifies something of permanent importance. In the pages that follow, therefore, I have tried to interpret "Black Power" not only as a slogan of the more militant Negro leadership but also as the *product* of many factors and the *sign* of a new situation.

"Black Power" is a product of the history of slavery and segregation in the United States. It is the product of Supreme Court decisions and congressional and Executive action at the federal level, as well as governmental action at the state and local level. It is the product of social and physical mobility occasioned by war, urbanization, and industrialization. It is the product of a changing self-understanding among Negroes and a changing of opinons among whites. It is the product of personal action and group action; of public policy and private association—all this and more forms the historical and cultural matrix in which something like "Black Power" becomes possible.

"Black Power" is a sign of a changing minority, of the pressure for a change in strategy by Negroes. It represents a demand for a new stance toward whites and a new appreciation of being black. It is a call for self-determination, equal opportunity, and full appreciation for black men in a white man's nation.

All this, I believe, is captured in the concept of a pluralistic minorty, a concept which is introduced and discussed in Chapter I. Therefore, in spite of the objections to the slogan by many Negroes, I have interpreted "Black Power" most broadly to mean the move toward pluralism that is evident in the strategy, stance, and goals of the Negro community as a whole.

Put in this perspective, the phenomenon that is signified by "Black Power" is likely to be with us for some time. Positions may change and new actors will appear, but the problems occasioned by this new phenomenon will not soon be dated.

The writing of this book was made possible by many persons. From my parents I first learned the meaning of a Christian response to persons of different color. To my teachers at Wake Forest College and Yale University I am indebted for their guidance and their encouragement of my interest in race relations. My students and colleagues at the School of Theology in Claremont, California, have been very helpful in providing dialogue and insight. My student assistant, John Hagar, and my typist, Mrs. Elizabeth Stafford, have provided much energy and help in the arduous tasks of research and proofreading of texts. President Ernest C. Colwell of the School of Theology provided a research grant that enabled me to spend a summer in Watts, Los Angeles, and Dean F. Thomas Trotter gave constant encouragement and arranged for me to have time and assistance for my writing. The Reverend James Joseph and the Reverend Speed Lees provided me with critical and sympathetic comments which helped to sharpen my ideas. Finally, I am grateful to my wife, Heidi, for her encouragement and for her forbearance and patience during the stress of writing.

Claremont, California   J. C. H., JR.
January 1968

Contents

Black Power and White Protestants

I

Introduction

In 1962, Arnold Rose wrote an introductory chapter to the twentieth-anniversary edition of Gunnar Myrdal's *An American Dilemma*. After reviewing the developments in American race relations that had occurred in the twenty years since that book was first published, Rose wrote:

> There could be no doubt that the races were moving rapidly toward equality and desegregation by 1962. In retrospect, the change of the preceding twenty years appeared as one of the most rapid in the history of human relations. Much of the old segregation and discrimination remained in the Deep South, and housing segregation with its concomitants was still found throughout the country, but the all-encompassing caste system had been broken everywhere. Prejudice as an attitude was still common, but racism as a comprehensive ideology was maintained by only a few. The change had been so rapid, and caste and racism so debilitated, that I venture to predict the end of all formal segregation and discrimination within a decade, and the decline of informal segregation and discrimination so that it would be a mere shadow in two decades. The attitude of prejudice might remain indefinitely, but it will be on the minor order of Catholic-Protestant prejudice within three decades. These changes would not mean that there would be equality between the races within this time, for the heritage of past discriminations would still operate to give Negroes lower "life chances." But the dynamic social forces

3

creating inequality will, I predict, be practically eliminated in three decades.[1]

Just two years later, Lewis Killian and Charles Grigg published a book on the basis of studies that were being carried on at about the same time Rose was writing, and near the end of the book the authors had this to say:

> Americans, white and black, may have to endure an ordeal of hatred and conflict before they ever learn to live with each other in peace. . . . The prospect is dismal; the need for a solution to the crisis in race relations is desperate. . . . Honesty compels the sociologist to admit that he cannot see the end of the road of social change; he can only warn of the steep hills and treacherous quagmires just ahead. He can foretell the changes will not come about easily and painlessly. Americans, particularly white Americans, must soon awake to the fact that the crisis in race relations is second in gravity only to the threat of nuclear war. . . . It has become painfully evident in the past few years that, unless the nation begins to take longer strides on the first mile of the long road to equality and integration, the Negro revolt will change from a nonviolent to a violent one. The white community will have to fight those Negroes who have too much spirit to submit any longer, and it will have to support with its charity those who are too apathetic to fight. The only other alternative will be increasingly repressive measures which would change the nature of the Republic and destroy the image of American democracy in the eyes of the world. There is no easy way out. The battle has been joined. The question is whether the conflict will rend American society irreparably or draw its racially separated parts together in some yet unforeseeable future.[2]

These conflicting prophecies by social scientists, who represent two differing models for understanding social change, were not merely academic matters, for it has become plain that the

1. Gunnar Myrdal, *An American Dilemma* (Anniv. Edition, New York: Harper & Row, 1964), pp. xliii–xliv.
2. Lewis Killian and Charles Grigg, *Racial Crisis in America* (Englewood Cliffs, N.J.: Prentice-Hall, Inc., 1964), pp. 128, 130, 143–4.

events of the last two years have verified the latter and con-
founded the former.

A NEW ERA IN RACE RELATIONS

Some sociologists, other than Killian and Grigg, were sensitive
to the growing signs of change. This was partly due to their
orientation to the conflict model of social change, but professionals and non-professionals alike had begun to sense rumblings underneath the liberal white-Negro coalition that had
been born with the National Association for the Advancement
of Colored People. Even more, most of us were aware of some
conflict between Negroes and *some* whites, particularly in the
South, and we had some indication that the "new Negro" of
the Martin Luther King stripe was more than a protest extension of the "old Negro." We had become accustomed to the
new militancy, but that militancy was in the context of peaceful co-existence, and the form of the militancy was such that it
could not help arousing our moral support. These men were
not talking about power conflict; they were simply demanding
that we live up to the promises we had made and that we give
them their rights.

American courts had made strides in race relations, too. Beginning with a series of court decisions around 1940, the nation
had marched toward higher and higher pinnacles of racial justice, and we had just passed the monumental Civil Rights Act
of 1964 and the Voting Rights Act of 1965. If whites had realized how stubborn the problem of segregation really was or
how deep the scars of discrimination had really penetrated,
perhaps our optimism would have been more qualified, but the
majority of us were not aware of these things, and by 1965, the
nation was exuberant about the changes that had been brought
about by the combined efforts of a sensitive court, a liberal national government, and the Negro revolution. Hence, it is really not too surprising that optimistic prophecies spoke of the
"solving" of the "American dilemma" as if it were just over
the horizon.

A careful look, however, would have revealed some ominous

signs. The pace of school integration was agonizingly slow; periodic outbreaks of rioting occurred which reflected Negro discontent; Black Nationalism was on the upsurge; and the stubborn problems of *de facto* segregation and discrimination in the northern and western states were not yielding to any solutions that had been proposed. Moreover, in the midst of the most rapid change the nation had ever experienced, Negro leaders were becoming increasingly restless because the changes were so very slow in reaching the masses of black people. Dick Gregory probably expressed the sentiments of many Negroes when he remarked: "We promise instant freedom to a foreigner, but I get mine on the installment plan." [3]

In addition, the success of the legislative programs of 1964–5 seemed to have resulted in a diminishing interest in civil rights. Whereas civil rights organizations had been engaging in sit-ins, marches, and other protests almost daily during the early 1960's, there were only a few sporadic protests by early 1966. Furthermore, the nation had turned its attention to Vietnam, and many of those who had been most active in civil rights now turned to protesting the United States policy in southeast Asia.

In the midst of all this, several important things were happening. The Student Non-Violent Coordinating Committee had begun a voter registration drive in Lowndes County, Alabama, and this resulted in the organization of an all-Negro political party.[4] One of the most active participants in this attempt at political organization was a young man named Stokeley Carmichael who subsequently emerged as the leader of SNCC.[5] Later the same month, SNCC refused to participate in the White House Conference on Civil Rights on the grounds that the United States was fighting an immoral war and that President Johnson was not really serious about civil rights. The Congress of Racial Equality delegates practically disrupted the meeting with their demand for an anti-Vietnam policy resolu-

3. *New York Times*, Feb. 12, 1966.
4. I discuss this further in Chapter II.
5. *New York Times*, May 17, 1966.

tion.[6] Then, just a few days later, Congressman Adam Clayton Powell during a speech at Howard University made his now famous call for "audacious power" on the part of Negro people.[7] In this speech, Powell asserted that of all civil rights organizations, only SNCC had avoided the "drug" of integration which had been offered by white liberals. He enumerated a list of human rights that Negroes should demand, and then declared: "To demand these God-given rights is to seek *black power* . . . the power to build black institutions of splendid achievement." [8] [Italics mine] Events soon pushed the slogan, "Black Power," into national prominence.

James Meredith's attempted march through Mississippi touched off the final arrival of the slogan. Meredith was shot by a white sniper after he had been walking for only one day. Immediately the march became a huge demonstration involving all of the civil rights organizations. Subsequently, a rally was held in Greenwood, Mississippi, on June 17, 1966. Here the "Black Power" slogan was heard over all the communications networks of the nation. Stokeley Carmichael and other SNCC workers led the demonstrators in the chant in front of television cameras. The nation knew that something different was happening in this demonstration. They could not assess the significance of the crowd's preference for "Black Power" over "Freedom Now," but as the summer passed, "Black Power" became the subject of national conversation. Gradually, some of the implications behind the words were spelled out, and the responses began to come in.

Many American whites were enraged; they could not fathom the effrontery of these long-silent people who were now challenging the whole order of power in this country. After they had been given so much by the courts and the Congress—now this. Others were startled and confused, for they felt that their presence was important to the Negroes in the civil rights

6. Ibid. May 24, 1966.
7. Ibid. May 30, 1966.
8. This quotation is from Powell's Howard University Speech, a copy of which appeared in *Harambe*, Jan. 19, 1967.

movement. They had become involved in the struggle for Negro rights even to the point of risking their own lives and the lives of their families, and it was inconceivable to them that what they heard was really true. When the slogan was repeated and sounded by an ever-increasing number of young Negro militants, the surprise and confusion began to hurt—it was the hurt of a rejected friend, and in some cases, the hurt like that of a rejected parent. Some said it was a passing thing. Others withdrew from civil rights organizations or withdrew their financial support. Still others criticized Negro leaders for their foolhardy isolationism and rampant racism.

Some American Negro leaders in the civil rights organizations responded with opposition and denunciation too. King, Wilkins, and others denounced the Black Power advocates as divisive racists and demagogues. But as time passes, more and more black people are talking Black Power and the tone of the traditional Negro leader's response is beginning to change. This does not mean that all Negro leaders have become advocates of everything that "Black Power" means to Stokeley Carmichael and other militant leaders. But there are some indications that there has been broad acceptance in the Negro community of the fact that race relations in the United States have taken a decisive turn.

Therefore, the important thing about race relations today is not the immediate response of the blacks and the whites of America to a slogan. The slogan symbolizes more than the impulsive cry of a militant Negro leader. "Black Power" is proving to have both force and endurance precisely because it functions in a unique way as a symbol of the profound changes that have been occurring in black-white relationship in America since 1900, and neither black nor white can wish it away. "Black Power" is the sign that we have witnessed the beginning of a new era in American race relations, and whether the slogan is replaced by another or not, the reality it represents is something which will be with us for some time.

SOME SOCIOLOGICAL MODELS

To assess the meaning and implications of the change in American black-white relationship, I shall draw upon a model suggested by Wagley and Harris in their book, *Minorities in the New World*.[9] The authors conducted a comparative study of six minorities in the western hemisphere: (1) the Negroes in Martinique; (2) the Negroes in the United States; (3) the French-Canadians; (4) the Jews in the United States; (5) the Indians in Brazil; and (6) the Indians in Mexico. The history of minority-majority relations was examined in the context of the peculiar history of the nation in which the groups resided. In addition, the authors attempted to assess the importance of the cultural setting and history of both groups, prior to their contact in the new world, in terms of the influence this pre-intergroup contact history had upon the shape of minority-majority relations. And finally, consideration was given to the importance of economic developments and demographic patterns in terms of the causal role they may have played in the entire nexus of factors affecting the status of minority-majority relations.

There are two very important insights in this study to which I want to call special attention. One of these is the authors' definition of a minority group. The other is the model for understanding what factors influence the pattern of the majority-minority relations.

The Definition of a Minority Group

Several important features must be considered in the definition of minority. In the first place, a minority is a social group within a larger society, but it is not necessarily a group that has a smaller membership than the majority group. The terms "minority" and "majority" refer to a power relation between the

9. Charles Wagley and Marvin Harris, *Minorities in the New World* (New York: Columbia University Press, 1958).

groups within a particular society, and the minority is weaker
and hence suffers some kinds of disabilities at the hands of the
stronger group. In contrast, the majority group has "greater
power over the economic, political, and social mechanisms of
the society," and hence is able to advance its position at the expense of the minority.[10] Second, a minority is to be distinguished from other depressed groups within a society, because
the disabilities under which they suffer are related to "special
characteristics which the minority shares and of which the majority (and often the minority itself) disapproves in some degree." Usually these characteristics are such things as language,
religion, or peculiar cultural patterns. Third, a minority is a
self-conscious group. The very characteristics that function as
badges of disability also function to give the minority an in-
group feeling, a sense of distinctiveness. The shared misery and
isolation which result from these disabilities often function to
keep the group bound together with the consciousness of common suffering.[11] Finally, minorities are characterized by the
"rule of descent" and "the rule of endogamy." By "rule of descent" the authors mean that a member of a minority group is
born into that group and he does not join it voluntarily; the
"rule of endogamy," of course, means that minorities must
marry within the group. Either or both of these rules can be
enforced by the majority or the minority or both. The majority often enforces the rules to maintain and widen the group
differences so that they may continue to exploit the minority,
but minorities may also enforce the rules to maintain their distinctiveness and to increase group solidarity.[12] To the extent
that *both* the minority *and* the majority enforce the rules,
there will be less and less possibility for intergroup mobility,
and hence amalgamation, acculturation, and assimilation may be
reduced to a considerable degree or discontinued entirely.

   Under this definition, the Negroes of the United States can
be understood as a true minority. They are identified as a sepa-

10. Ibid. pp. 4, 5.
11. Ibid. p. 5.
12. Ibid. pp. 7–10.

rate group by color—a basis for wide stereotyping in the white community and to some degree also in the Negro community. They have experienced segregation, discrimination, and persecution, and the common misery of their existence has given them some degree of in-group consciousness. Color identification precludes their opting out of the minority, and the sanctions against intermarriage have been rather rigorously enforced by the majority. This is true in spite of some racial mixture which has been the result mostly of the exploitation of Negro women by white males, and even the offspring of these clandestine affairs are "born into" the minority group. Finally, this has meant that Negroes in this country have been virtually powerless in American society until recently, and they remain a distinctly deprived minority in the present power structures.

The Socio-Cultural Factors in Majority-Minority Relations

If the Negroes are a true minority, then the race problem in the United States can be understood as a special case of majority-minority relations. Therefore the model for understanding majority-minority relations, developed by Wagley and Harris at the conclusion of their study, will be especially illuminating for our attempt to assess the meaning of the slogan, "Black Power," as a symbol of the contemporary character of American race relations.

At the outset, the authors make it clear that they understand all majority-minority relations to be special cases of intergroup conflict. Therefore, any dramatic change in race relations will mean some change in the level or form of conflict between the groups involved. To understand why conflict takes place as well as why there are differences in the level of conflict between groups at different times and in different locales, the authors have suggested two categories of "components" which must be considered—the structural components and the historical-cultural components.[13]

13. Ibid. pp. 255, 256.

The Structural Components The structural components are those aspects of majority-minority relations which are directly related to the nature of the groups as such. Since this is true, I have already introduced them during the definition of a minority group, but some further comment is still required here. The first of the structural components is *ethnocentrism*, which Wagley and Harris define as "the belief that one's own language, religion, and physical characteristics are better or more 'natural' than those of others." [14] All majority groups have some ethnocentrism, but with minorities this is not necessarily the case. Some minorities have a degree of ethnocentrism, but many of them not only are void of ethnocentrism but actually despise their own group and want to rid themselves of the identifying characteristics which signify their membership.[15] Hence it is obvious that ethnocentrism is not the same thing as the in-group consciousness already referred to in the definition of a minority group. All groups have some kind of in-group consciousness. But ethnocentrism is *pride* in one's own group and *preference* for the distinctive characteristics that set one's own group apart. Furthermore, ethnocentrism is almost always accompanied by strong negative feelings towards those groups which do not share one's own characteristics.

Closely related to ethnocentrism is the second structural component, *endogamy*, the rule that one should marry within the group. When there is a great deal of pride within the group and preference for one's own distinctive characteristics, it is obvious that the number of persons marrying outsiders will be minimal. Hence, it might be said that endogamy is simply a function of ethnocentrism. That this is not always the case with minority groups, however, is apparent from the pattern in American race relations until recently. In America, the majority enforced endogamy for purposes of exploitation, and the minority's endogamy was, therefore, simply the reflection of the white majority's practice.[16]

14. Ibid. p. 258.
15. Ibid. pp. 258–9.
16. Ibid. pp. 259–60.

The structural components, then, are extremely important
indices of the shape and character of minority-majority relations in any given place or time, for the degree of conflict that
will occur between the groups is highly related to them. It is
not likely, for example, that conflict will be very severe between groups when there are many instances of intermarriage,
and it is not likely that the ethnocentrism of two groups includes strong negative feelings against each other if such intermarriage is possible. If the reverse is true, the likelihood of
conflict is very high.

Yet, even though the structural components are important,
they alone do not shape majority-minority relations, for the
status of the structural components themselves is partly conditioned by the kind of competition that exists between the
groups for the valuables of the society in which they reside.
To understand the development of intergroup relations it is
necessary that consideration be given to those factors that
affect the competition between the majority and the minority,
for changes in these factors signal a change in the level of competition and hence may profoundly affect the shape of the
structural components as well.[17] The factors that affect the
competition between groups are included by Wagley and Harris in the second category, the historical-cultural components.

*The Historical-Cultural Components in Majority-Minority Re-
lations*   The first of the historical components suggested by
Wagley and Harris is the *adaptive capacity of the minority*.
By this is meant the resources of the cultural heritage plus the
acquired resources of the minority group which enable them to
compete effectively against the dominant majority.[18] Included
in this component would be such things as special skills, educational background, economic resources, and opportunities for
training. Even group cohesiveness and ethnocentrism might be
included as a resource for mobilizing pressure against disabilities. The second component is *the arena of competition*. This

17. Ibid. pp. 263-4.
18. Ibid. p. 264.

includes not only the valuables for which the minority and majority are competing, but those things which function in the society to facilitate or obstruct the minority's ability to compete.[19] Within this component would fall such things as the legal structures, the economic organization, and the political organization of the society. The third component is the *ideological setting*, which in some respects is part of the arena of competition. By this is meant not only the "official" equalitarian creed of the United States to which Myrdal has given so much attention, but also the attitudes of both the minority and majority toward each other.[20] A serious contradiction exists between the official position of the United States with respect to equality and the actual behavior of most whites toward the Negro, but, as we shall see later, the "American Creed" has had some function in the changing pattern of American race relations even though the contradiction remains.

All these components are very closely related. In most cases, some change in one of them will be accompanied by changes in the others. For example, significant changes in the ideological setting will put pressure upon the nation to provide more opportunities for the minority, thus raising the level of their adaptive capacity. Moreover, a change in the adaptive capacity of the minority will almost always involve some changes in the arena of competition. Furthermore, the historical-cultural components together will have some effect upon the development of ethnocentrism, and strong ethnocentrism can well function as an important element in the adaptive capacity of a minority. The entire model suggested by Wagley and Harris is cumulative in its operation, and the separate factors constantly interact with each other as causal agents determining the character of majority-minority relations. Any significant change in the pattern of intergroup relationships will involve significant changes in most if not all of these components. Therefore, if "Black Power" symbolizes some new direction in American race relations, one way of assessing the meaning of the change will be

19. Ibid.
20. Ibid. pp. 280 ff.

to determine what kind of changes have been occurring in all of the socio-cultural components of the Negro minority-white majority situation during the past several decades. This will enable us to understand why the character of American race relations has changed and how it has changed. And from this insight perhaps we can get some idea of the directions which we can expect in the intergroup conflict that lies ahead.

Minority Aims

This interest in what lies ahead for American race relations will eventually raise the question of minority aims, for as Wagley and Harris have said, "The future prospects for any minority group depend to a large extent upon the ultimate aims and goals which it holds for itself." [21] It is, of course, inevitable that any discussion of "Black Power" will involve some assessment of what specific goals the new Negro leaders want, but we shall not capture the full meaning of the change in race relations today unless these specific aims are brought together into some theoretical framework from which broader implications can be drawn.

Such a framework is provided by Louis Wirth's very excellent typology of minority aims,[22] which includes four types of minorities based upon the type of aim which characterizes them: (1) pluralistic; (2) assimilationist; (3) secessionist; and (4) militant.[23]

Essentially a *pluralistic minority* is one that seeks toleration for its distinctive characteristics from the majority, and the quest for toleration is based upon the belief that it is possible for differing cultures to exist together in some degree of har-

---

21. Ibid. p. 285.
22. Louis Wirth, "The Problem of Minority Groups," in Ralph Linton, ed., *The Science of Man in the World Crisis* (New York: Columbia University Press, 1945), pp. 347–72. This is also the basis of a very excellent discussion of minority aims in Wagley and Harris, *Minorities . . . ,* pp. 285 ff.
23. Wirth, "The Problem of Minority Groups," p. 354.

mony. The minority itself tends to concentrate on developing the characteristics that set it apart as a group, and great attention may be given to the customs, religion, manner of dress or language that is distinctly the minority's own. This is accompanied by a developing ethnocentrism by which these characteristics become no longer the signs of inferiority but the basis for group pride. Yet, one should not assume that cultural distinctiveness and majority toleration are the only aspects of pluralism, for alongside the development of cultural distinctiveness there is usually a demand for more economic and political equality in the structures of the larger society. Therefore, it is necessary that the pluralistic minority adopt some of the cultural and institutional patterns of the majority, for otherwise the society could not function at all. Still the autonomy of the group in most things is to be preserved so that the minority can be self-determining and remain distinct.[24]

Wagley and Harris note that the minority must improve its power position through legal, economic, and political means, as well as the mobilization of group unity, and there is always a chance that these efforts will backfire in the form of increased majority resistance and less toleration for the minority. In light of this, they warn that, "pluralism will always be fraught with danger and that the probable consequence of pluralistic aims is the perpetuation of some degree of conflict between the majority and the minority." [25]

In contrast to the pluralistic minority the *assimilationist minority* seeks incorporation into the dominant group. It is characterized by the desire to lose its distinctiveness so that the individual group members may participate fully in the whole life of the larger society. The minority will tend to encourage intermarriage and the emphasis upon and pride in group distinctiveness will be discouraged. The group's own cultural achievements will not necessarily become a total loss, however, for the merger of groups is always a two-way process. Both the group that is being assimilated and the group into which they assim-

24. Ibid. pp. 354–7.
25. Wagley and Harris, *Minorities* . . . , p. 288.

ilate put some of their unique stamp upon each other, and so long as the cultural traits of each are not offensive to the other, this may be a peaceful, voluntary solution of the minority problem.[26]

The problem of minorities with either pluralistic or assimilationist aims cannot be solved by the minorities alone. In both cases, the ultimate solution of majority-minority relations is heavily dependent upon the aims of the majority toward the minority.[27] This has been most obvious in the case of the American Negro. As Wagley and Harris pointed out in their study, American Negroes have long had assimilationist aims, but they have been faced with a majority that had pluralistic aims. The result has been that the Negroes have been forced to remain apart from the larger society in spite of their desire to merge with the majority. It must be borne in mind also that a satisfactory pluralistic adjustment depends heavily on the willingness of the majority to make some concessions, for the high degree of ethnocentrism which is characteristic of pluralistic minorities means that anything short of majority acceptance of the minority's distinctiveness will result in intense conflict.

The third type of minority aim is *secessionist*. By this Wirth means that neither assimilation nor pluralism are acceptable, but complete independence from the dominant group is desired. One example of this among American Negroes was the "Back to Africa" movement of the early 1900's. Finally, there is the *militant* minority, which rejects not only assimilation and pluralism but also secession. The aim of the militant minority is to overturn the entire power relation of the groups involved so that the minority group becomes the dominant group. They are characterized by the conviction that they are far superior to the existing dominant group, and hence are confident that they can overpower them. American Negroes generally have not fallen into this category. Although some of the statements

26. Wirth, "The Problem . . . ," pp. 357–8.
27. For a discussion of types of majority aims, see George Simpson and J. Milton Yinger, *Racial and Cultural Minorities* (Rev. Ed., New York: Harper & Brothers, 1958), pp. 27 ff.

of the more radical black nationalists do carry overtones of black supremacy, the aims are usually set in the context of a world-wide revolution of all colored nations to overthrow white nations.[28]

This description of minority aims never characterizes actual minority groups as a whole, partly owing to the fact that no minority group is ever unanimous in its aims at any given time. But it is also due to the fact that minority aims are dynamic.[29] Hence, one can never speak of pluralistic or secessionist minorities as if the question of aim is ever finally settled, but it is useful to employ the types to assess *directions* in which minorities seem to be moving and hence to clarify the nature of changes that are occurring. This, in turn, will give us a better vantage point from which to consider an appropriate response.

THE NATURE OF THE RESPONSE

This book is conceived as a response to the recent changes that have occurred in American race relations and there are features of the response that require some comment. For one thing, because I am a white man, the response will be from the perspective of the white community and addressed to the white community, although I hope that interested Negroes will read these pages critically and perhaps enter into dialogue with me.

I believe that this is a legitimate ordering of priorities for three reasons. First, it is not any white man's prerogative to attempt a definition of "Black Power" *for Negroes,* because one of the most important aspects of the new era in race relations is the Negro's uncompromising determination that he shall decide who he is and what he shall do. This has been made clear time and time again by Negro leaders in recent months, and whites must take it seriously. Second, if the white man cannot address the Negro community about the meaning of "Black Power,"

28. The types are introduced by Wirth, but the allusion to the American Negroes is my own. (Wirth, "The Problem . . . ," pp. 361-3.)
29. Ibid. pp. 360, 364.

he *must* address his own community. No change in race relations is ever a minority problem alone. Though the change may focus upon the minority, the majority is deeply involved in both the causes and the solution of racial crisis, and the full meaning of the changes that are now developing in American race relations will not be known until the white community has made its response. Hence, concerned whites can attempt to put that response in the context of some reason and understanding. Third, this ordering of priorities has been urged upon concerned whites by some of the new Negro leaders. For example, Stokeley Carmichael once said to a white liberal, "Your job is to understand us," [30] and he has repeatedly urged whites to turn their attention to their own communities.[31]

Another feature of my response that might require comment is the focus upon a religious institution. This certainly reflects no lack of concern about the other institutions of American society. In fact, it will become obvious in the ensuing discussion that I place a high priority upon the Christian's obligation to participate in shaping the so-called "secular" institutions of American society. Moreover, this latter statement should not be construed to mean that I think that the churches are the chief source from which the initiative in the struggle for justice will arise. On the contrary, history would lead me to expect that in general the churches will lag behind other institutions in this regard. Therefore, my reason for focusing upon the churches lies simply in my special sense of responsibility to those institutions with whom I am most closely identified and from whose faith comes the motivation for my own moral concern.

Finally, the orientation of my response specifically to white Protestantism might require some comment. At the outset, what I have said before about my focus upon the white community applies here also. While it is true that any total understanding of a Protestant response to American race relations must include the remarkable changes in the role of the Negro

30. *New York Times*, Sept. 25, 1966.
31. A speech at the University of California in Berkeley, Nov. 19, 1966.

churches during recent years, this very change has resulted in some widening of the breach between black and white Christians within Protestantism. The growing estrangement can be understood from one standpoint as a judgment upon white Protestants; but from another, it is simply a reflection of the whole change in black-white relations to which my response here is directed. In either case, it is not appropriate for me to address Negro churchmen on the subject of "Black Power." My stance as a white Protestant in relation to Negro Christians must be that of the listener who is seeking to understand.

Another reason for focusing on white Protestantism lies in the important role which white Protestants have played in American race relations in the past. For years, we have been the dominant religious group in America, and the shape of American race relations is, therefore, our own doing. In a very real sense, the history of American race relations has been our history, and the guilt of white America is our guilt. Therefore, white Protestants have a special responsibility to attempt some understanding and creative response to the present racial crisis.

I also have a personal reason for focusing upon white Protestantism. I am a white Protestant, and I have always been part of that history. Moreover, as a professor of ethics in a white Protestant theological seminary, it has been necessary for me to give my primary attention to the role of the white Protestant churches in a wide variety of social problems. This in no way implies, of course, that I do not utilize valuable insight from other religious traditions, but it does mean that I have had to give top priority to the problems and possibilities within my own religious tradition.

None of this is meant to minimize in any way the important roles that have been and are being played by other religious groups in American race relations. Jewish and Roman Catholic groups and individuals have, on many occasions, provided very excellent leadership in the struggle for racial justice. Moreover, the important advances toward racial equality in America in recent years have been markedly influenced by the *joint* efforts of representatives from all the major religious groups, both black and white. Therefore, rather than minimizing the role of other traditions, it is my fervent hope that this white Protestant response to the new developments in the Negro community can become some small part of the continuing interfaith dialogue on the problems of race relations which is so necessary if we Americans are ever to achieve racial justice.

II

Black Power: The Rise of Group Pride

One of the important variables in intergroup relations, particularly in a minority-majority situation, is the degree of ethnocentrism that is characteristic of the minority group. Ethnocentrism is the positive feeling toward one's own group and its peculiar characteristics, and it is often accompanied by negative feelings toward the out-group. Furthermore, ethnocentrism by its very definition must include strong feelings of group solidarity and mutual identification among the in-group members.

In light of this definition, it may be said that the development of ethnocentrism is relatively recent among American Negroes, and that the slogan, "Black Power," symbolizes precisely this development.

THE "SHAME" OF BEING BLACK

Some degree of group consciousness, of course, has been characteristic of American Negroes since the time of slavery. However, until very recently the character of that group consciousness, for the most part, has been negative rather than positive when it had any value content. Moreover, during the time of slavery the consciousness of group affiliation consisted of little more than the consciousness of being different from the dominant whites and of the different social roles entailed by blackness. Gradually, as the slaves became acculturated, the consciousness of being black came to mean an essentially nega-

tive evaluation of one's own group in relation to the white
group. There were certainly individual exceptions to the rule
—the Turners, the Veseys, and the Gabriels, who had a fierce
pride in their own race and who plotted and attempted revolts
against their masters.[1] A contemporary report about Vesey
will illustrate the intense pride that characterized him and
many other unnamed leaders of slave revolts.

> Even whilst walking through the streets in company with
> another he was not idle; for if his companion bowed to a
> white person he would rebuke him, and observe that all
> men were born equal, and that he was surprised that any-
> one would degrade himself by such conduct; that he would
> never cringe to whites, nor ought any one who had the
> feelings of a man.[2]

Vesey and others like him refused to accept the inferior status
ascribed to them by the white man, but they never really succeeded in exerting much influence on the Negro population at
large. Lacking in effective communication and being separated
from their common heritage by distance and time, the masses
of Negroes never moved to any appreciation of or pride in
their own group, and their own estimation of themselves fairly
accurately reflected that which the whites held for them.[3]

Another exception to the tendency of the Negroes to view
themselves negatively is to be found, to some extent, among the
"free Negroes." The best known of these men was Frederick

1. Frazier writes that these insurrections were being planned as early as
1663. He also gives a survey account of numerous slave revolts as well as
a detailed discussion of the Gabriel, Turner, and Vesey rebellions. See
E. F. Frazier. *The Negro in the United States* (Rev. Ed., New York:
The Macmillan Co., 1957), pp. 82 ff.)
2. *An Official Report of the Trials of Sundry Negroes Charged with an
Attempt To Raise an Insurrection in the State of South Carolina*, prepared and published at the request of the Court by Lionel Kennedy and
Thomas Parker, Charleston: 1822, p. 19, quoted in Frazier, *The Negro in
the U.S.*, p. 88.
3. Recent studies confirm this and demonstrate that the "mirror" mecha-
nism, i.e. Negro acceptance of white evaluation of them, still persists.
Some of these studies are discussed below on pp. 26–7.

Douglass, the Negro abolitionist, but there were numerous others who began in the early 1800's to plead the cause of the Negroes and to articulate a growing restlessness with their plight in America.[4]

The Civil War brought an end to slavery, but it did not immediately bring any change in Negro group consciousness. The old social controls of the plantation no longer defined the role of the black man, in the sense he was no longer a slave. For a time immediately following the war, Negroes enjoyed more freedom and participated more fully in the political life of America than at any previous time. But the white man was quick to erect new controls to "keep the Negro in his place." By the beginning of the twentieth century, less than fifty years after the Civil War which "liberated" the slaves, the black man was firmly relegated to his inferior role under new controls, both legal and non-legal. It was soon apparent that these new controls were not really "new," for the expectations of the whites for black people still conformed to the old "caste" system which had its roots in slavery.[5] Negroes were to "stay in their place" and any "show of arrogance" could result in severe reprisals.[6] Furthermore, laws had been enacted forcing segregation upon the Negro, and he had been completely disfranchised. He was in separate and inferior schools and used sepa-

4. Frazier, *The Negro in the U.S.*, pp. 59 ff. Cf. also Gunnar Myrdal, *An American Dilemma* (Rev. Ed., New York: Harper & Row, 1962), pp. 737–9.
5. An interesting study was made of the "caste system" in a small southern town by John Dollard. The system set whites and Negroes apart in separate castes with special rules of etiquette for Negroes and special privileges for whites. Although there was a "class system" in each of the "castes," the line between the strata in society at large was fully determined by caste. *All* Negroes, regardless of financial standing or educational background, were members of the lower caste. Further discussion of this system and its effects will follow in Chapter V, below. See John Dollard, *Caste and Class in Southern Town* (New Haven: Yale University Press, 1937).
6. "Show of arrogance" could mean anything from failure to say "Yes, Sir" to a white, or failure to tip the hat to a white man, all the way up to being argumentative. Negroes were actually lynched for such minor breaches of the informal laws of etiquette.

rate public facilities.[7] And the Negroes' acquiescence was symbolized rather graphically in a speech made by Booker T.
Washington at Atlanta, Georgia, in 1895. There he laid out his
oft repeated formula for racial harmony in the words, "in all
things that are purely social we can be as separate as the fin-
gers, yet one as the hand in all things essential to mutual progress." [8] Soon after that speech, in 1896 the Supreme Court of
the United States placed the stamp of legality upon the system
of segregation in the *Plessy* vs. *Ferguson* decision.[9] And the nation was back to "business as usual."

In all of the strife and anguish of the Reconstruction and its
aftermath, it could not be said that the black man was ever
without some form of race consciousness. He was forced on
every hand to recognize his differences from the white man.
Race was the ever-present undercurrent of every encounter
with the white man. It was the subject of jokes; it determined
opportunities; and it placed a constant burden of anxiety and
fear upon the Negro masses.[10] It was even implicit in the Negroes' relationships with each other and white stereotypes of
the Negro were used as terms of abuse by black against black.
In a word, every moment of the black man's life was shaped by
his racial identity. He was, indeed, forced to be conscious of
race, but what his blackness meant and how it functioned was
determined not by him but by the white man.[11]

The effect of all this upon the Negroes was to make them

7. Frazier, *The Negro in the U.S.*, pp. 123–62. An excellent historical ac-
count of this period of the establishment of segregation is contained in C.
Vann Woodward, *The Strange Career of Jim Crow* (New York: Oxford
University Press, 1957 Ed.). pp. 49 ff.

8. Quoted in Frazier, *The Negro in the U.S.*, p. 162.

9. 163 U.S. 537, 1896. The opinion argued that segregation did *not* imply
inferiority. It was *only* because Negroes interpreted it that way that the
argument could be made. This was *precisely* the point the opinion
missed. Negroes *did* interpret it that way. Therefore, *Plessy* vs. *Ferguson*
added more support for the Negro's negative self image. For a further
discussion of this case see Chapter III, pp. 63–4 of this book.

10. See, for example, Robert Coles, "It's the Same, but It's Different," in
Talcott Parsons and Kenneth B. Clark, eds., *The Negro American* (Boston: Houghton Mifflin Co., 1966), pp. 260 ff.

11. Myrdal, *An American Dilemma*, pp. 758, 759.

apathetic and whimsical about their position. Released from slavery amid promises of new freedom only to be reduced to a pernicious inferior position by the whites again, they became disheartened and disillusioned. Subjected daily to an etiquette system that implied servitude and forced repeatedly to listen to harangues about their racial inferiority, it was inevitable that individual Negroes began to believe what they heard and to see themselves in the image mirrored by the whites. Black people began to accept their own inferiority and to live on the white man's terms. Hence, the "race consciousness" of the Negro up through the early 1900's was largely the consciousness of being black and all that this meant in a white-dominated society. It was not anything remotely resembling racial pride or identification with a racial tradition.[12]

The legacy of the Negroes' acceptance of negative feelings about themselves as a group is still with us. Three relatively recent studies spanning two decades serve to illustrate this point.

In the first place, James A. Bayton found in his study of 100 Negro college students in 1941 that more than half of his subjects accepted typical white stereotypes of the Negro as objectively true. Furthermore, more than 60 per cent of them accepted the superior stereotypes of the whites such as "intelligent," "industrious," and "scientifically minded."[13]

A second study conducted by Kenneth Clark and Mamie Clark during 1940–41 is even more revealing.[14] The Clarks' study included 253 Negro children. Slightly more than half were students in segregated nursery schools and public schools in the South. The others were students in racially mixed north-

12. Frazier, The Negro in the U.S., pp. 530, 531. As noted earlier, there were some exceptions. What is expressed here was characteristic of the majority of the Negroes.
13. James A. Bayton, "The Racial Stereotypes of Negro College Students," The Journal of Abnormal and Social Psychology (Vol. 36, 1941), pp. 97–102.
14. Kenneth B. Clark and Mamie P. Clark, "Racial Identification and Preference in Negro Children," in Society for the Study of Social Issues, Readings in Social Psychology (New York: Henry Holt and Company 1947), pp. 169–78.

ern nursery schools and public schools. The subjects were shown four dolls which were identical except for color. Two of the dolls were white with blond hair and two were brown with black hair. The dolls had no clothes except white diapers.

The children were asked to respond to several requests that would indicate their awareness of racial identification, their own self-identification and their scale of preferences. Seventy-two per cent of the children were able to distinguish racial differences. Sixty-two per cent identified themselves with the colored doll. But the majority of the children *preferred* the white doll and *rejected* the colored doll. Their rejection of the brown doll and their own identification with it caused rather severe reactions in some of the children. Some of them broke down and cried when confronted with the question of self-identification. Others tried to rationalize by saying such things as "I burned my face and made it spoil," and "I look brown because I got a suntan in the summer." [15]

A third kind of finding is that reported by Lee Rainwater from his study of a Negro family. When the family quarreled, the terms of derision hurled at each other were usually preceded by the word "black." Rainwater concludes his discussion of the meaning of blackness to the Negro in the ghetto with the suggestion that Negro children are exposed to a variety of experiences which bring home to them the conception of themselves as weak and debased persons.[16]

These studies could be augmented by numerous others reporting similar findings, but they suffice to make the point clear. The black man's own estimation of himself is still partially the product of his perception of the white man's estimation of him, and hence his group identity or race consciousness is cast for him in predominantly negative terms.[17] This negative type of

15. Ibid. p. 178.
16. Lee Rainwater, "Crucible of Identity: The Negro Lower Class Family," in Parsons and Clark, *The Negro American*. pp. 189 ff.
17. C. S. Johnson, *Growing Up in the Black Belt* (Washington: American Council on Education, 1941); M. Seeman, "A Situational Approach to Intergroup Negro Attitudes," *Sociometry* (Vol. 9, 1946), pp. 199–206; Marian R. Yarrow, ed., "Interpersonal Dynamics in a Desegregation Pro-

race consciousness was certainly characteristic of the majority of Negroes until at least the turn of the century.

THE HERALDS OF CHANGE

Beginning with the early 1900's, however, this characteristic began to be modified. The race consciousness of the Negro began to develop into true ethnocentrism, and it is the gathering momentum of this development that is symbolized by the call for "Black Power." [18]

It is extremely difficult to date precisely the beginning of something as nebulous as a "change in group consciousness," but certain movements signal changes which have finally emerged.

We have noted previously that there were free Negroes who participated in the abolition movement. Certainly among these remarkable men were those who took pride in their racial identity and who had very deep feelings of solidarity with all members of their race. Moveover, the emerging Negro literary movement and the so-called "Negro Renaissance" sparked a new pride in being black.[19] Among Negro intellectuals, the name of W. E. B. Du Bois is especially worthy of note. Du Bois

cess," *Journal of Social Issues* (Vol. 14, 1958), pp. 3–63; Catherine Landreth and Barbara C. Johnson, "Young Children's Responses to a Picture and Inset Test Designed to Reveal Reactions to Person of Different Skin Color," *Child Development* (Vol. 24, 1953), pp. 63–80; Mary Goodman. *Race Awareness in Young Children* (Cambridge, Mass.: Addison Wesley, 1952); and J. K. Morand, "Racial Perception by Nursery School Children in Lynchburg, Virginia," *Social Forces* (Vol. 37, 1958), pp. 132–7. All of these are cited in Thomas F. Pettigrew, *A Profile of the Negro American* (New York: D. Van Nostrand Co., Inc., 1964), p. 8. Pettigrew points out that the Negro reaction should not be surprising in light of the vast number of psychological studies which demonstrate the relationship between the *role* one plays and his self-identity. (Ibid. p. 5, especially the references in Footnote 1.) See also, Kenneth B. Clark, *Dark Ghetto* (New York: Harper & Row, 1965), pp. 63 ff.

18. There were many factors which played a role in changing the race consciousness of the Negro such as migration, war, urbanization, etc. These factors will be discussed in Chapter III.

19. Frazier, *The Negro in the U.S.*, pp. 506–9.

was the leader of a group of northern Negroes who challenged the compromise of Booker T. Washington. Du Bois accused Washington of putting the onus for the black men's condition upon them, and implied that he was undercutting their efforts to attain some kind of equal life chances in America. In 1905, Du Bois and his followers organized a movement designed to become a national protest organization. However, the movement never really got under way, and by 1910 it had ceased to function. Yet, among Negro intellectuals, Du Bois had a profound influence, so much so that Ray Stannard Baker observed in 1908 that nearly all Negroes of intelligence were followers either of Du Bois or Washington.[20]

To be sure, the influence of these men and movements extended far beyond their apparent circle of influence, and the protest they raised gave new hope to the Negroes and a new pride in being black. Yet none of them were successful in capturing the imagination of the Negro masses. It remained for an intense and energetic Jamaican to fan the flames of negritude[21] sufficiently to claim the attention of large groups of American Negroes.

Marcus Garvey was more than a man. He was an astounding phenomenon.[22] Arriving in New York in March 1916 as an unknown Negro visitor, he was able in a period of ten years to organize the largest mass movement of black people in the history of the United States. His business and organizational accomplishments alone were enough to assure him a place in history,[23] and he possessed the charismatic gifts that soon estab-

20. Myrdal, *An American Dilemma*, pp. 742 ff. The Niagara movement eventually merged with the NAACP.
21. Colin Legum, *Pan Africanism* (Rev. Ed., New York: Frederick A. Praeger, 1965), pp. 95-7, for a discussion of the meaning of "negritude." It means generally a new self-consciousness of the Negro and pride in his past. "Black Power" is really a popular version of this.
22. The background reading which I have done for the discussion of Garvey was E. D. Cronon, *Black Moses* (Madison: University of Wisconsin Press, 1962).
23. Among his various accomplishments, the organization of the Universal Negro Improvement Association stands at the zenith. The grandeur and pageantry of the convention meetings commanded world-wide Negro

lished him as a leader among his own race. However, it is the pervading theme of all his activity that is of interest for our understanding the rise of the American black man's ethnocentrism.

The very title of Garvey's organization, "The Universal Negro Improvement Association," suggests his passion. Garvey was a "race man," that is, his aspirations were for the Negro; his identity was black and he was very proud of that fact. The constant theme of his newspaper, *Negro World*, was the beauty of blackness and pride in being black.

> Garvey exalted everything black and exhorted Negroes to be proud of their distinctive features and color. Negroid characteristics were not shameful marks of inferiority to be camouflaged and altered; they were rather symbols of beauty and grace.[24]

Garvey utilized his own unique understanding of history to build hero images for Negroes. He accused the white man of distorting history in order to subdue the blacks, and predictably his fires of negritude carried with them overtones of hostility toward and deprecation of whites. He delighted in pointing out that black people had developed advanced civilizations before the European whites emerged from primitivism. The whites were, in fact, a much lower breed than the blacks who themselves were the descendents of the proudest and noblest race on earth.

> When Europe was inhabited by a race of cannibals, a race of savages, naked men, heathens and pagans, Africa was peopled with a race of cultured black men, who were masters in art, science and literature; men who were cultured and refined; men, who, it was said, were like the gods.

participation and the attention of the whole world (Ibid. pp. 62–5). Although the Black Star Steamship Line was not a financial success, it *was* something of a feat. In addition he founded two newspapers, one of which had a circulation of over 200,000, and a monthly magazine. He developed a chain of co-operative grocery stores, a restaurant, a steam laundry, a tailor and dressmaking shop, a millinery store, and a publishing house. (Ibid. p. 60.)
24. Ibid. p. 174.

> Even the great poets of old sang in beautiful sonnets of the
> delight it afforded the gods to be in companionship with
> the Ethiopians. Why, then, should we lose Hope? Black
> men, you were once great; you shall be great again. Lose
> not courage, lose not faith, go forward.[25]

Garvey did not limit himself to history. He also called for a
complete reorientation of Negro religion. With the assistance
of the Reverend George A. McGuire, Garvey began to urge
the Negroes to forget white gods and think of God in black
terms. The sufferings of Christ symbolized the sufferings of the
black races for Garvey, and by 1924 at the *Fourth International Convention of the Negro Peoples of the World,* the
leaders of Garvey's new "Black Religion" were urging the
worship of a Negro Christ.

As important as the reorientation of history and religion
were, perhaps the most prominent example of Garvey's affirmation of negritude was his program to encourage Negroes to return to Africa.

> A great independent African nation was the essential in-
> gredient in the Garvey recipe for race redemption and he
> was earnestly convinced that Negroes needed the dark
> continent to achieve their destiny as a great people.[26]

Garvey never really intended that the "back to Africa" movement should result in all American Negroes leaving their country. What he did want, however, was a strong African nation,
buttressed with the talent of American Negroes, which would
serve as an inspiration for black people all over the world and
which would be a powerful prestige symbol for the black man
as he attempted to recover his proper place in the world. He
had no illusions about the possibilities for black people in a
country dominated by whites. He was convinced that the black
men could only gain respect and justice when he became strong
enough to challenge whites with power. This could never happen in America, and, therefore, the only answer to the Negro's

25. Marcus Garvey, *Philosophy and Opinions of Marcus Garvey,* 2 vols.
(New York: University Publishing house, 1923), Vol. I, p. 77; quoted in
Cronon, *Black Moses,* p. 176.
26. Cronon, *Black Moses,* p. 183.

problem was for him to organize his own state and to become a superior nation among nations.

Garvey was also very cynical about the "white man's love." He was convinced that the whole notion of love for the black man by whites was simply a convenient device to keep Negroes in America where they could conveniently be exploited. Therefore, it was not the so-called "liberal" who was the "friend" of the black man, but rather the Bilbo's and the Klansmen who helped to drive home the necessity for an all-black nation as the only alternative for freedom from the white man's victimization. This led him to the ill-fated courtship of American white racists. He echoed their fears of intermarriage between the races, and he sternly warned both blacks and whites against the "evil" effects of amalgamation and assimilation. He was especially vehement in his denunciation of W. E. B. Du Bois and the National Association for the Advancement of Colored People. Garvey argued that these people were really enemies of the black man, bent on assimilation and amalgamation of black people and hence the destruction of their uniqueness and their honor. In opposition he argued, "To be a Negro is no disgrace, but an honor, and we of the U.N.I.A. do not want to become white." [27]

This kind of approach to the problem of the Negro in America kept Garvey in trouble with Negro intellectuals from the start. And the antagonisms of the Negro intellectual community together with legal and financial difficulties finally led to Garvey's failure. He died in 1940 in London, a forgotten man. The details of Garvey's descent from power and his disappearance from the American scene need not concern us here.[28] What is important for my purpose is some evaluation of the general response of the black people of America to Garvey's clear appeal to Negro ethnocentrism.

27. Garvey, *Philosophy and Opinions*. Vol. II, pp. 325–6; quoted in Cronon, *Black Moses*, p. 193.
28. Cronon gives a detailed discussion of Garvey's successes and failures which is extremely interesting, but it is not important for my purposes here.

It was once asserted that no more than half a dozen educated Negroes in America were genuinely interested in Garvey's scheme.[29] This is certainly not true, but it is true that Garvey found very powerful opposition among Negro leaders. The Negro press was at first skeptical and later vehemently critical, especially Cyril Briggs, editor of *Crusader*, who took delight in exposing Garvey's variety of difficulties. Other Negro leaders, such as Dr. Robert W. Bagnall, A. Philip Randolph, Chandler Owen, and William Pickens, repeatedly challenged Garvey and impugned his motives. Especially did they emphasize Garvey's flirtations with the Ku Klux Klan and his financial problems. Even the Reverend James Eason, who earlier was a leader in the Garvey movement, became one of his most severe critics. Eason shared what was probably the main concern of all the Negro intellectual leadership. He was fearful that Garvey's patent black nationalism and the "back to Africa" emphasis he gave to that nationalism would impair the efforts of Negro leadership to encourage the masses to solve the problems at home. The opposition reached a peak in January 1923, when a group of eight prominent Negroes sent an open letter to the New York State's Attorney protesting the delay of Garvey's trial and condemning Garveyism as a hate fanaticism composed mostly of "Negro sharks" and "ignorant Negro fanatics."[30]

In light of this chorus of opposition it might appear that Negroes in general rejected Garvey's attempt to instill racial pride and preference into the hearts of American black people. That this is not the case is evident upon some closer examination of the response to Garvey. At the outset, it should be noted that the major point at issue between Garvey and Negro leadership was his "back to Africa" scheme. Very few Negro leaders, in reflection upon Marcus Garvey, rejected his aim of restoring race pride and group solidarity. Such men as Du Bois, James Weldon Johnson, and Benjamin Brawley note with pride and sympathy Garvey's role in inspiring pride in race and deter-

29. John G. Van Deusen, *The Black Man in White America* (Washington: Associated Pub., 1944), p. 331, cited in Cronon, *Black Moses*, p. 208.
30. Cronon, *Black Moses*, pp. 105–11.

mination for self-improvement. And several students of Negro history have linked Garvey to the rise of the contemporary Negro protest.[31]

The response of the masses of black people to Garvey is difficult to measure because of the unreliability of the statistics of Garvey as well as those of his critics. It is possible, however, to get some indication of his impact by reviewing some important events in the rise of Garveyism and by noting some pertinent facts very briefly.

In the first place, it is certain that the U.N.I.A. had branch offices in Chicago, Philadelphia, Cincinnati, Detroit, Washington, and Boston, in addition to the New York organization. Nearly all these chapters had at least 5000 members. Even Garvey's enemies concede that he might have had 30,000 members in his organization, and W. E. B. Du Bois, one of his sternest critics, later conceded that Garvey might have had up to 80,000 followers. Garvey's friends made estimates of his following which ran as high as 4,000,000, but these are seen by most observers to be highly exaggerated. It does seem reasonable, however, to concede Garvey's claim that he had by far more members in his organization than all other American Negro organizations combined.

Membership figures alone cannot tell the whole story. There is absolutely no way to measure the support that was given to Garvey by millions of silent Negroes who responded warmly to Garvey's glorification of blackness as some grounds for hope. What we do know is that the U.N.I.A. convention of 1920 was one of the most spectacular events of the year. On the night of August 2, 25,000 black people gathered in Madison Square Garden to hear Garvey, and the whole world began to take notice. We do know that the maiden voyage of the Black Star Line was cheered from 135th Street pier by literally thousands of enthusiastic Negroes. We do know that Garvey's newspaper, *Negro World*, reached a circulation of 200,000. We do know that when he was finally deported, hundreds of

31. Ibid. pp. 212 ff.

New Orleans Negroes gathered at the pier to hear him speak.[32]

All of this certainly indicates that Marcus Garvey is the first pinnacle of the rising in-group consciousness and the new pride of the black man. Perhaps very few American Negroes took seriously Garvey's proposed program for the black man's redemption including his "back to Africa" emphasis. But they did hear with eager attention his message of the glory and the goodness of being black, and it is this which is the important contribution of Garvey to American Negroes. As Cronon put it in his study concluded in 1954:

> Marcus Garvey is gone and with him many of the more spectacular yet ephemeral aspects of his colorful movement, but the awakened spirit of Negro pride that he so ardently championed remains an important legacy to the Negro people.[33]

Whatever the uncertainties might be about the total number of Garvey's following, he marks an important step in the developing group consciousness of the black people of this country. His was the first mass appeal to the Negro to be proud of his blackness and to hold his head high. He gave new impetus to the black man's determination to participate as a man in the formation of his society and to share as a human being in the goods of his society. The wide acceptance of his appeal is a strong indication that the Negroes as a group were on their way toward a new positive race consciousness by the middle of the 1920's, and also an indication of the growing solidarity they felt with other blacks, both in the United States and abroad.

It was noted earlier that the rise of ethnocentrism includes a growing racial pride and racial solidarity. It was suggested also that growing ethnocentrism *may* include increasing hostility toward the out-group. Whether ethnocentrism includes hatred of the out-group depends a great deal on the manner in which the out-group and in-group have been related historically. For

---

32. The statistical material on Garvey's following is taken from Cronon, *Black Moses*, pp. 45, 62–5, 142, 204–7.
33. Ibid. p. 201.

example, Wagley and Harris call attention to the fact that the differences between the levels of interracial hostility in Martinique and in the United States can be accounted for partially by reference to the Civil War and the Reconstruction experiences of the United States. Manumission was accomplished rather smoothly in Martinique in comparison to the bloody struggle that accompanied emancipation in the United States.[34] The institutional forms of white hostility that grew out of these experiences have plagued the nation in the form of segregation and discrimination for more than one hundred years. The rationalizations were buttressed by theological and biological arguments, both of which spoke eloquently of the white man's contempt for the black man.[35] Therefore, any attempt on the part of the black man to develop pride in his own identity was destined to clash head-on with the ideology of the dominant group that thinks and acts as if the black man is irrevocably inferior.

The white man's attitude toward the black man is not merely supported by rationalizations. Racists have long pointed to the persisting poverty, crime, ill-health, low educational standards, and other indices of Negro deprivation as concrete evidence of his inferiority. What happens is represented rather graphically by Myrdal's model of the "vicious circle." [36] White racist "mythology" supports the view of the Negro as inferior. This in turn results in discriminatory behavior, which is justified by reference to the lower position of the Negro in society caused by discrimination. This lower position also makes possible the persistence of the "myth" in spite of scientific evidence to the contrary. The only way to counter racial oppression, then, is to break into the circle at some point and reverse the movement.

By and large, American Negroes have attempted to concen-

34. Wagley and Harris, *Minorities* . . . , pp. 276–7. See also, Donald Pierson, *Negroes in Brazil* (Chicago: University of Chicago Press, 1942).
35. Examples of these rationalizations abound. For one of the worst see Charles Carroll, *The Negro a Beast* (St. Louis: American Book and Bible House, 1900).
36. See Myrdal, *An American Dilemma*, pp. 75 ff. Myrdal also refers the reader to his methodological comments in Appendix 3 on pp. 1065 ff.

trate on the objective indices of discrimination by demanding a better competitive position in terms of equality under the law and equal opportunity. This has meant, of course, that the level of competition for valuables between whites and blacks has risen markedly as the blacks increase their efforts to attain better life chances in American society. That this competition has resulted in increasing hostility on both sides is hardly surprising. Recent studies have confirmed that intergroup competition is always accompanied by rising hostility.[37]

In light of these observations, it would be expected that developing Negro ethnocentrism would include some measure of hostility toward the out-group. The clashing of ideology and the heightening of competition are frustrating beyond description to a group which is forced to compete on the white man's own terms. And the object which is the seat of frustration is relatively easy to identify—it is "The Man," "Whitey."

It is precisely this hatred of the white out-group that is characteristic in the second pinnacle of the developing Negro ethnocentrism, the Black Muslim movement.[38] The movement had its beginning almost immediately after the decline of Marcus Garvey. The hope and the protest raised in the masses of Negroes which had been inspired by Garvey was receding, and the weight and despair of the depression years was upon the nation. It was in this soil that the movement took root. A man named W. D. Fard came to Detroit in 1930 and began to teach the faith. Many who heard him were formerly Garvey's followers, and they responded once again to the familiar words about the nobility of being black.[39] However, under Fard's leadership, the Muslims never became a truly mass movement.

37. Muzafer and Carolyn Sherif, *Groups in Harmony and Tension* (New York: Harper & Brothers, 1953); Muzafer Sherif, D. J. Harvey, W. R. Hood, and Carolyn Sherif, *Intergroup Conflict and Cooperation: The Robbers Cave Experiment* (Norman: University of Oklahoma Press, 1962).

38. C. Eric Lincoln was probably the first to coin this descriptive term. His book, *The Black Muslims in America*, is one of the best studies of the movement (Boston: Beacon Press, 1961). See also, Louis Lomax, *When the Word Is Given* (New York: Signet Books, 1963).

39. Lincoln, *The Black Muslims*, p. 66.

Until the emergence of Elijah Muhammed, the movement never had more than 8000 members. But Muhammed has appealed to the masses. Utilizing the press and a trained cadre of ministers, he spread the word of black supremacy and white degradation to the black masses. By 1961, according to C. Eric Lincoln, the movement had more than 100,000 members with more being added every day.[40]

Much of the Black Muslim teaching [41] is similar to that of Garvey. There is the emphasis upon the goodness of being black. The Negroes have not been able to appreciate their blackness because they have been kept in mental slavery by whites, and their leaders have betrayed them by submitting to whites. Nevertheless, the black people are the descendents of the "Original Man" who is the creator of the universe and the father of all nations. The white man is a rather late arrival in the world who represents decadence and deterioration of the human race. The black man, on the other hand, is the direct blood descendent of the Original Man, and hence is the "sacred vessel of the Temple of God." He is hope of the world, and unless black people heed the call to know true blackness, all is lost, for the white man is incapable of leading the human race to redemption.[42]

Alongside this glorification of blackness there is a strong emphasis on the demonic character of whiteness. The white man is the white devil, and the sin of the Negro leadership of America has been their teaching the Negroes to love the white man. White Christianity comes in for a special indictment, because it has been the chief tool for keeping the Negro subservient. Nor is Negro Christianity spared. Some of the most virulent attacks by the Muslims have been upon Negro Christian preachers who are so busy currying favor with whites that they never get around to helping the black man in his attempts to gain justice. Any show of "love" for whites or any co-operative "association" with whites is roundly condemned by the Muslims

40. Ibid. p. 106.
41. The teachings are from a booklet by Elijah Muhammed, *The Supreme Wisdom*, cited in Lincoln, *The Black Muslims*, p. 68.
42. Ibid. pp. 68–76.

precisely because it can only mean further poisoning and the ultimate deterioration of the pure black man.

From what can be discerned in Muslim statements, their concrete goals flow directly from these teachings. Above all else, the Muslims stress black men's self-reliance and mutual responsibility. The ideal is a unity of all black men everywhere in a fight for freedom. Whites will surely oppose these black men, and so they should be prepared for conflict, and some of them for death.

In order to keep the black race free from the degradation of whites, the Muslims also want racial separation. To seek integration is stupid, because the white man will never share his wealth with the Negroes at large. They will, of course, allow a few individuals (Negro leaders) to share some of the goods of society, but only to seduce them and use them as instruments to keep the black men as a group under control. *All* personal relationships with whites must be broken, and above all, it is inconceivable that intermarriage should take place. Mixture can only weaken the strong black men, and without it the degenerate whites will perish.[43]

Although economic and political separation are not necessarily immediate goals, these two are ultimate goals for the Muslims. They have instituted "buy black" campaigns, and Malcolm X, a leading Muslim spokesman, made it quite clear at the Muslim convention in 1960 that the Muslims also want a territory of their own in which they can be self-determined and separated completely from the whites.[44]

The Black Muslims, like the Garvey movement, are a mass movement. Their appeal is geared to the huge Negro populations in the urban areas who are frustrated and cut loose from familiar moorings. To make this appeal the Muslims offer what Lincoln has called a "rebirth."

> The true believer who becomes a Muslim casts off at last his old self and takes on a new identity. He changes his name, his religion, his homeland, his "natural" language, his moral and cultural values, his very purpose in living. He is

43. Ibid. pp. 76–80.
44. Ibid. pp. 84–97.

no longer a Negro, so long despised by the white man that he has come almost to despise himself. Now he is a Black Man—divine, ruler of the universe, different only in degree from Allah Himself. He is no longer discontent and baffled harried by social obloquy and a gnawing sense of personal inadequacy. Now he is a Muslim, bearing in himself the power of the Black Nation and its glorious destiny.[45]

The revaluation of one's own self and his group; the feeling of strong identity with black men everywhere; the devaluation of the out-group, the white world—these are the marks of the Black Muslim movement, and they are concrete illustrations that what was begun by Garvey was continuing and looming as a very important factor in intergroup relations in America.

BLACK POWER: THE PRIDE OF BEING BLACK

The third pinnacle of the rising ethnocentrism of American black men is the product of a rather unique merging of the streams of Elijah Muhammed and Marcus Garvey. Malcolm X's father was a Baptist preacher who was a Garvey organizer and who was very much caught up in the Garvey dream. Malcolm himself was, until his defection, a rising star in the Black Muslim movement of Elijah Muhammed.[46]

Malcolm's early activities as a Muslim minister (he rejected Lincoln's "Black Muslim" title) [47] gave evidence that he was in the main stream of the teachings of Elijah Muhammed. So great was Muhammed's impact upon Malcolm that he worshiped his teacher, and his supreme interest was to remain true to the teaching in his own proclamation. The themes were the familiar lines of black nobility together with the denunciation of the "white devils" who had enslaved and brainwashed the black man until he accepted the white man's own estimate of

45. Ibid. pp. 108–9.
46. All the material on Malcolm X is taken from his autobiography which was compiled by Alex Haley (*The Autobiography of Malcolm X*, New York: Grove Press, Inc., 1964).
47. Ibid. pp. 247 ff.

him. The black man should never expect the white man to help him, but rather he should develop his own institutions and organizations in order to gain self-respect.

Malcolm was especially vehement in his denunciation of the "white press" which he felt distorted what he said and continually harassed him with tricky questions. Nor were "Negro leaders" spared. He referred to these "leaders" as those black men who are trying so hard to be white that they do not have time to worry about what it is to be black.[48] He referred to the March on Washington as the "Farce on Washington," which was but one more example of how the white man takes some black men and brings them into his yard—out of the fields. In Washington the "Big Six" were brought into the "big house" for a conference. The "Big Six" were joined by four religious leaders who now became the "Big Ten" and what started as a grass-roots, spontaneous black protest became "integrated" and amounted to little if anything at all.[49]

This evaluation of the March on Washington is but one major example of Malcolm X's strong opposition to movements that supported integration. For him, integration was the white man's way of allowing a few black men in the "goodies" in return for the services of the "integrated" blacks in keeping the black masses hypnotized into inaction with talk of "progress." For black men to support integration is nothing short of madness.[50]

Malcolm was especially disparaging of blacks who accept Christianity.

> Brothers and sisters, the white man has brainwashed us black people to fasten our gaze upon a blond-haired, blue-eyed Jesus! We're worshiping a Jesus that doesn't even look like us! Oh yes! Now just bear with me, listen to the teachings of the Messenger of Allah, The Honorable Elijah Muhammed. Now, just think of this. The blond-haired, blue-eyed, white man has taught you and me to worship a

48. Ibid. p. 243.
49. Ibid. pp. 279 ff.
50. Ibid. pp. 245–6.

white Jesus and to shout and sing and pray to this God
that's his God, the white man's God. The white man has
taught us to shout and sing and pray until we die, to wait
until death, for some dreamy heaven-in-the-hereafter, when
we're dead, while this white man has his milk and honey in
the streets paved with golden dollars right here on this
earth! [51]

The necessity for black men to reject Christianity and come to
the true religion of Islam is a recurring theme, and Malcolm
confidently predicted the end of Christianity because it does
not have the resources to save civilization.

One finds very few kind words for white liberals in Malcolm's writings either. He was constantly repeating the charge
of hypocrisy toward those who claim to "love" the black man,
but who do not really want him to be human. In fact, he
thought more highly of the white southerner than of the
northern liberal because the white southerner was at least honest. He made the same sort of distinction between presidential
candidates Barry Goldwater and Lyndon Johnson, preferring
the "dangerous wolf" to the "smooth sly fox." [52]

It was about 1962 when Malcolm began to sense that something was wrong between him and Elijah Muhammed. Recurring reports of immorality at the Chicago mosque had dis-
turbed Malcolm X and he had confronted Elijah Muhammed
with these reports. Finally, his "chickens come home to roost"
statements at the time of the assassination of President Kennedy in November 1963 was the occasion for his being "si-
lenced" by orders of Elijah Muhammed for a period of ninety
days. Malcolm X submitted and still no breach came. Gradually, however, Malcolm began to get intimations that his death
was being plotted by the Muslims, and before the end of 1963
he announced an open break with Muhammed. Following this
break he made a pilgrimage to Mecca and then a trip to Africa,

51. Ibid. p. 220.
52. Ibid. pp. 276, 373 ff.

where he was hailed as a great black spiritual leader, and he returned a man of international importance.[53]

It soon became apparent that the break with Elijah Muhammed was not merely a personal thing, but rather that it represented some important new directions in the vision of Malcolm X. In the first place Malcolm began to think more in terms of a broad interfaith organization of black men that was to be oriented toward some kind of solution of the economic and political sickness of the black man. He also was concerned about the spiritual sickness of the black man, and he felt that the return to Islam, the indigenous religion of Africa, was the answer to that problem. However, increasingly he thought more in terms of economic organization and the power of political organization. He was convinced that the black men of America now have the potential for political power which in turn can help to bring them economic power. It was toward these goals that black men now needed to turn their attention.[54]

The trip to Mecca, especially, had an important effect on Malcolm's view of the white devil. He became convinced that some whites, perhaps many of them, were sincere in their concern over racial injustice. Moreover, he was perfectly willing to have them work to help the black men in their struggle for racial justice. Malcolm even dreamed of an organization that might include coalitions of concerned whites and blacks which could overthrow the essentially racist institutions of America and hence save the nation from certain destruction. However, it was clear that now was *not* the time for whites to join the black movement. That could come only after the blacks have recovered their self-respect by their own efforts. Blacks first would have to learn to do for themselves, and then, perhaps, the vision of a brotherhood of men mutually respecting each other might become a possibility. Yet, the Muslims *had* been mistaken, and Malcolm confessed that he had been brainwashed

53. For a detailed discussion of these events by Malcolm himself, see Ibid. pp. 288–363.
54. Ibid. pp. 312 ff.

to such an extent that he could not make the proper distinctions between the inherent racism of white institutions and the genuine concern and brotherliness of individual whites.[55]

The trip to Africa increased his sense of global identity with the black man. Everywhere black men are struggling to achieve self-respect, and Malcolm began to identify himself more and more as an Afro-American in recognition of the importance of the African roots of the American blacks.[56]

Malcolm's amanuensis, Alex Haley, notes two other apparent changes in his thinking. In the first place, Malcolm changed his view on racial intermarriage. Alongside his emerging vision of brotherhood came an emphasis on the common humanity of all men. Hence, intermarriage was a matter of personal choice rather than a matter of racial purity. Second, Mrs. Martin Luther King reported that Malcolm had expressed to her his desire to "help" in what King was trying to do. He thought that perhaps his presence and his teaching would make it easier for King to make headway in his drive for black equality.[57]

In summary, the break with Elijah Muhammed culminated in a rather dramatic move away from hatred of whites toward a critique of American institutions that Malcolm saw to be inherently discriminatory. Increasingly, he refused to categorize all whites as "devils" and began to make distinctions between the good and the bad. This was accompanied by a growing moderation of his opposition to integration, until at his death, Malcolm might not have been far from the aims of the "Big Six" he so roundly condemned for their "Farce on Washington." Finally, Malcolm increasingly began to give attention to an organization of black men of all faiths which would concentrate on the development of political and economic power so that the American black man could bargain for and win his place in the American dream of equality for all men.

The untimely death of Malcolm X at the hands of assassins

55. Ibid. pp. 332 ff.; 362 ff.; 429.
56. Ibid. especially p. 363.
57. Ibid. pp. 424, 427.

deprived the Negro community and the nation of a creative young leader, and cut short Malcolm's dream for the future of race relations.[58] However, his influence is very much alive in the Black Power movement. Not only is his name invoked in admiration, but some of his ideas have become main themes in the developing concept of Black Power.

One good example is Stokely Carmichael, the man who first gave national prominence to the "Black Power" slogan. At the beginning of his rise to leadership, he had already picked up Malcolm X's emphasis on the need for black men to organize. Before his election as chairman of the Student Non-Violent Coordinating Committee in May 1966, Carmichael began to organize the black people of Lowndes County, Alabama. He found in Lowndes County the picture that has been all too familar to southern Negroes for years. Here they lived in shabby housing; they did not vote; they were excluded from employment in the industries and were mostly poor tenant farmers. They were scared, and constant intimidation kept them in a state of fear-induced apathy. Therefore, even though blacks outnumbered whites in Lowndes County by four to one, whites effectively maintained control and continued to discriminate against black people in every facet of local government.

Carmichael was determined to see this changed. He set out to register the black voters and to organize them into an effectively functioning political group. Through his efforts and those of other SNCC workers, the Lowndes County Freedom Organization was formed, whose symbol was a black panther.[59]

In the context of Lowndes County, "Black Power" meant black political power popularly based and effectively functioning to change the status of the black people and to ease the oppressive economic and social conditions under which they lived. Throughout the period of organization, the constant

58. Malcolm was shot and killed on February 18, 1965, while speaking in New York City.
59. See Andrew Kopkind, "The Lair of the Black Panther," *The New Republic* (Vol. 155, Aug. 13, 1966), pp. 10 ff.

theme was the necessity for black people to act on their *own* behalf without white help; to force concessions rather than to ask for them.

Soon after the "Black Power" slogan came to the attention of the nation, Carmichael spelled out some of the themes that he saw as central to the new stance.[60] In the first place, Black Power represents a pride in being black.

> Now there's one modern day lie that we want to attack . . . and that is the lie that says anything all black is bad. Let's make that our major premise. Anything all black is bad. Minor premise, or particular premise: I am all black. Therefore . . . I'm *never* going to be put in that trick bag. I'm all black. And I'm all good.[61]

Closely related to this pride in being black is a second theme, the recovery of the African heritage of the Negro as a basis for pride in being black. The history, the art, the music, styles of dress, and even hair styles must reflect a change in the Negro's understanding of his identity from a badge of shame to a mark of distinction.[62]

The recovery of African identity not only functions as a basis for pride, it also involves an identification of the American Negro with the interests of other black people all over the world. Carmichael said, "We articulate that we therefore have to hook up with black people around the world, and that hook up is not only psychological but becomes very real." [63] This would mean questioning United States foreign policy with respect to black nations and demanding that this nation cease to exploit them. It would mean a demand from Negroes that American foreign policy should be shaped as much by opposition to racism as it is by opposition to communism.[64]

A third theme of Black Power is the emphasis upon Negro self-determination, including the development of Negro-owned

60. *New York Times,* July 3, 1966, Sec. IV, p. 3.
61. Carmichael, "Speech at Berkeley," Nov. 19, 1966.
62. *New York Times,* July 3, 1966, Sec. IV, p. 3.
63. "Speech at Berkeley," Nov. 19, 1966.
64. Ibid.

business enterprises and political control of Negro communities [65] Basically this is a strategy to increase Negro power in
order to crack the cycle of deprivation that is the lot of the
black people in America. Carmichael is convinced that the political parties of the nation do not meet the needs of black people precisely because they are dominated by whites, and he apparently has little hope that either the Democrats or the Republicans will ever really allow the Negro voice to have any significant weight. Only a unified Negro political organization
with an economic base of Negro-owned commercial enterprises
can function to provide the Negro with a proper degree of self-
determination.

Even this strategy, however, is closely connected with pride
in being black, for, as Carmichael has pointed out, it is difficult
to develop self-esteem without self-determination.

> It is clear to me that we have to wage a psychological bat-
> tle on the right for black people to define their own terms,
> define themselves as they see fit and organize themselves as
> they see fit. . . . The fact is that all black people often
> question whether or not they are equal to whites because
> every time they start to do something white people are
> around showing them how to do it. If we are going to elim-
> inate that for the generations that come after us, then
> black people must be seen in positions of power doing and
> articulating for themselves.[66]

This connection between group pride and group power is extremely important for Carmichael. It reflects his basic concern
with the problem of full humanity for Negroes in the larger
society. As long as Negroes remain dependent upon whites,
their aspirations for freedom and their personal identification
will be cast in terms that are characteristic of the white community. In this way, whiteness becomes identified with those
things that are valued, and blackness will continue to function
as a disvalue in the Negro's own psyche. Therefore, the problem of self-acceptance will continue to be an insurmountable

65. *New York Times,* July 3, 1966, Sec. IV, p. 3.
66. "Speech at Berkeley," Nov. 19, 1966.

obstacle for individual Negroes in their psychological development, and their own self-image will continue to be something less than fully human.

It is on this basis that Carmichael's opposition both to integration and to white participation in Negro-based organization is to be understood. Under present conditions, integration simply perpetuates the Negro negative self-image, and any white participation in Negro-based organizations too easily becomes a reminder of a former dependency.[67]

In general terms, then, it is clear that Carmichael is in agreement with the later developments in the thought of Malcolm X, but his interpretation of Black Power has focused especially upon the profound psychological problem of Negro self-understanding which is the result of years of white prejudice and discrimination. All that he says and proposes as strategy is finally based upon his determination to develop group pride in the distinctiveness of being black.

Another of the leaders in the Black Power movement is Ron Karenga. Karenga, who lives in Los Angeles, is the head of an organization called "US," and like Carmichael, he is dedicated to developing a new pride in being Negro and to the development of Black Power. Somewhat in contrast to Carmichael, however, Karenga emphasizes strongly the need for the black people to become *culturally* distinct as a basis upon which to function politically and economically as a unified group. He argues that the whole problem of Negro identity and pride is dependent upon the American Negroes' recovery of their *African* heritage, and this heritage will form the basis upon which the Negro community can give distinct shape to its own institutions. In other words, if the Negro community is to develop the self-determination and self-respect which is meant by Black Power, Negroes must engage in a cultural revolution.

Karenga suggests seven aspects of this cultural revolution. In the first place, the black man must develop a *mythology*. The myth is to be based on black values which can give pride to the black people. It will be a myth which describes the superior

67. Ibid.

qualities of being black, one which gives to the black man a sense of being a chosen people.

Second, the black man must develop a *history* which will be a continuation of mythology down to the present. At present the black man has no heroic images. His only heroes are supplied to him by a white man's history which ignores black people. It is neither Thomas Jefferson nor George Washington who is the hero of the black people. It is a man like Malcolm X who affirmed his blackness and stood courageously in the face of white attacks. It is not a Negro like Senator Edward Brooke of Massachusetts, says Karenga, who is elected by whites, represents whites, and thinks white. The hero is the black man who thinks black and who acts black. The new history will also determine the dates of festivals. The festival days will no longer be Christmas and Easter and the Fourth of July, but rather the dates of significant events in the rise of the American black man.[68]

Third, the black man must develop *social organization*. Presently, the community is disorganized and the men are psychologically emasculated. The restoration of the male as head of the family is one of the primary tasks, and the organization of the community to lift itself toward "separate and equal" status in America is the prime target.

Fourth, the black man must develop *political organization*. There is no place for him in either the Democratic party or the Republican party. The Republicans at least have the virtue of being honest. They tell the black man that they have nothing for him. The Democrats really mean the same thing, although they can be seductive to the black man because of their professed "love" for him and their alleged "liberal" leanings. All this means is that they "love" to keep him quiet and that they are "liberal" about him living in someone else's neighborhood. There is no place, therefore in either party for the black man, and he must organize his own.

Following political organizations, Karenga suggested that the

68. One of them is to be the date of Malcolm X's death. (All of the material here is from a lecture by Karenga at Pomona College in Claremont, Calif., on Feb. 16, 1967.)

fifth facet of the revolution must be *economic organization.*
This organization will be based on models of economics derived from the "mother country," Africa, and it will not be
capitalistic. He sees the pattern to be one of economic coopera-
tives organized by, owned by, and staffed by black men who
will have as their goal, not profit, but service to the community
of black people.

A sixth facet of the black power revolution will be the development of *creative art, literary and music forms* that are distinctly the forms of expression suitable to the black man.
Karenga especially challenges black college students to be active in this phase of the revolution, to create the standards of
black beauty, and to interpret the "soul" of black men.

Finally, the development of the "soul" of the black man
must be accompanied by education which will create and support a *black ethos.* This ethos is the matrix in which the black
"soul" (the feeling of being black) will come alive. It will be
formed by rational reflection upon the traditions and myths of
black people to give them a sense of what it means to be black
and to establish a solidarity of blackness in which the possession of "soul" is a source of great pride.[69]

Karenga has attempted to initiate this cultural reform by
developing a center for instruction in African culture at his
Los Angeles headquarters. There he teaches African history,
African mythology, and other courses designed to inform the
students about the nature of their African heritage. He also
places a great deal of stress upon hair styles and manner of
dress, and has even introduced instruction in the Swahili language.

The response to Karenga's attempt at "Africanizing" the Negro community has not been very enthusiastic, and other
Negro leaders have shown no signs of emulating his strategy.
Still, Karenga's program is very indicative of the strongly ethnocentric character of the Black Power movement, and while
most Black Power leaders will probably stop short of the kind

69. Ibid.

of total orientation toward Africa that Karenga characterizes, all of them are attempting in some way to tle the distinctiveness of black people in America to their African heritage.

It is important to note that beyond the special emphases of Black Power leaders, they all seem to be agreed upon the focal point of strategy for the present. It is to be *political organization*. As I noted before, Carmichael began his career as a political organizer in Alabama, and he has repeatedly called for black political organization in his speeches. Ron Karenga also puts special emphasis upon the need for political organization, and it is highly significant that he, along with other Negro leaders in the Los Angeles area, has recently formed a California Black Panther Party, thus adopting in their name the symbol of Carmichael's all-Negro "Lowndes County Freedom Organization." [70] Furthermore, Congressman Adam Clayton Powell, who was one of the early advocates of Black Power, certainly gave a distinctly political meaning to the term. I have already referred to the speech Powell gave at Howard University in May 1966 in which he called for audacious black power to change American life. In that speech Powell urged that blacks mobilize and focus their power on the development of black institutions "of splendid achievement," such as black universities and black businesses. In addition, he called for more black politicians to engage in shaping the future of American political life.[71] In July of 1966, Powell elaborated further on the nature of the Negro's political aspirations by stating that he foresaw the development of black enclaves in every major city in the United States which would be governed by black men.[72]

I shall discuss the emphasis upon politics in the Negro community at large in Chapter IV, but the point here is that the

70. This was reported in the *Los Angeles Times*, Feb. 20, 1967.
71. *Harambe*, Jan. 19, 1967.
72. *New York Times*, July 19, 1966, p. 22. Political self-determination within black communities was also a major theme of the Black Power Conference held in Newark, N.J., in July 1967. (See *New York Times*, July 24, p. 1.)

Black Power movement as such places a very high priority on political organization in its over-all strategy for developing Negro group pride.

Alongside this positive development of ethnocentrism, the Black Power leaders also manifest the negative aspect, that is, hostility toward the majority, or "out-grouping." At least Karenga and Carmichael are opposed to intermarriage.[73] All of them are opposed to integration,[74] and there is a strong undercurrent of anti-white feeling. Although Malcolm X, Carmichael, and Karenga, in contrast to the Black Muslims, do try to distinguish between white men and the corrupt institutions that whites have developed, one has the feeling that all whites are suspect. At best, only a very few could possibly prove themselves to be human by joining in the struggle for reform. It is very clear, however, that whatever "joining" that will be done by whites will be strictly on the Negroes' terms, and there are strong indications that the Black Power leaders see the primary function of "good" whites to be that of addressing the problems of racist ideology and institutions within their own communities.[75] Though all of this points toward some kind of separation on a wide scale, it is important to note that it does *not* mean either the "Back to Africa" strategy of Garvey or the strategy of the Black Muslims to develop all-Negro states.[76] It is not clear just what form the separation will take, but Powell's suggestion of all-Negro enclaves in the cities, referred to above, may be some clue.

73. The only apparent exception among those I have discussed is Malcolm X's later view that intermarriage is irrelevant. I do not know Powell's view on this matter.
74. Powell has called integration "a drug"; in his Howard University speech he criticized most civil rights organizations for being taken in by the "phony integration line." (*New York Times,* July 19, 1966, p. 22, and *Harambe,* Jan. 19, 1967.)
75. This was a major theme of Karenga's speech at Pomona College (Feb. 16, 1967) and of Carmichael's speech at the University of California in Berkeley (Nov. 19, 1966).
76. Carmichael has stated this clearly (*New York Times,* July 3, 1966, Sec. IV, p. 3.) as has Karenga ("Speech at Pomona," Feb. 16, 1967).

This "out-grouping" of whites is probably reflected also in the diminishing confidence which Black Power leaders have in white institutions. Carmichael seems certain that whites cannot make their own democracy work, and he is also sure that they will resist the Negro's strategy for himself. It is not surprising, therefore, that he is convinced that some heightening of conflict is inevitable between whites and blacks. Karenga thinks that all social change is accompanied by conflict and what the black men want is a *very radical* social change. In light of this, the "cultural revolution" is a preparation for black men to give them strength for the conflict that must come.[77] The events of summer 1967, however, should not lead American whites to construe that the conflict that is to come will necessarily be planned violent uprising. In spite of the violent overtones of the public speeches of Carmichael and Karenga, as well as H. Rap Brown (now head of SNCC) and other militant leaders, my own conversations with some Negro militants indicate that the possibility of planned violence in this country is more or less tied to the flexibility or the inflexibility of white men in their response to change.

Here it is especially important to distinguish between spontaneous eruptions of mass frustration and what some Negro leaders have called "creative violence."[78] On the one hand it seems likely that spontaneous outbreaks of violence will continue to erupt in American cities where Negro aspirations have been frustrated and their hopes disappointed. But there is little

77. This is also the theme of the excellent study by Killian and Grigg in which it is argued that no longer is the model of Negro-white relationships the peaceful co-operative accommodation model of Myrdal and others like him. What Killian and Grigg foresee is an indefinite period of intensifying racial conflict. (Killian and Grigg, *Racial Crisis in America*, pp. 130 ff.)
78. There has been a good bit of conversation in the Los Angeles Negro community about the notion of "creative violence." The concept is probably derived from Frantz Fanon's *The Wretched of the Earth* (New York: Grove Press, 1963). See especially pp. 55 ff. where he discusses the "operative role" of violence for nations engaged in revolution against colonial regimes.

evidence yet that Negro leadership, apart from a few extremists, is relying on "creative violence" as a first line of strategy. It is insisted, of course, that Negroes will defend themselves when they are attacked violently, and that the defense will be in kind.[79] And so there is little hope that a response of force alone will ever solve the problem of ghetto violence.

What all of this means seems reasonably clear: America must change. To do otherwise is to face the destruction of democracy, for no matter who "wins" such violent confrontations, either widespread destruction or repression by force will raise serious questions about the viability of the American democratic experiment.

The Black Power movement, then, like the Garvey movement and the Black Muslims, is a clear example of fierce pride in the distinctiveness of the Negro group as well as negative feelings toward the out-group, the whites, and in spite of the differences between the Black Power leaders and the earlier ethnocentric leaders, they remain part of a total movement which seems to be symbolic of certain important changes in the entire Negro community. This does not mean that these men alone were responsible for the change, but their emergence as leaders is an indication that something has been happening to the self-understanding of the Negro community which is finding expression in their particular brand of charisma. The leader in each case became the catalyst which crystalized the "happening" and gave it form. The result has been a history of developing Negro ethnocentrism that is gaining momentum rapidly throughout the Negro community. In other words, what Wagley and Harris have labeled the "structural" components of majority-minority relations have undergone significant alteration, from the side of the minority, and this is a strong indication that we have a new situation in American race relations.

79. This was the main theme of the remarks by James Meredith in the August 21, 1966, session of NBC's "Meet the Press." Carmichael seconded his remarks enthusiastically. (*Transcript*, Washington, D.C.: The Merkle Press, pp. 20–23.)

III

The Context of Black Power

Black Power as such is only one of the ethnocentric movements that have appeared among American Negroes throughout their history, but, as we have seen, it is part of a total movement which began around 1900 and which was geared primarily to the masses. Furthermore, there are indications that the Black Power movement as the most recent development in the history of Negro ethnocentrism, is attracting a wider interest than any of the other phases of the movement. Therefore, I have argued that one significant meaning of Black Power is the change it symbolizes in the structural components of majority-minority relations, at least within the minority itself.

It must be remembered, however, that all of the socio-cultural components suggested by Wagley and Harris are inter-related, and changes in one of the components will almost always be accompanied by changes in the others. Hence, it is not appropriate to think of the structural components alone as causes of changes that occur in the broad picture of majority-minority relations. On the contrary, changes in the structural components are usually accompanied by, and in many cases, preceded by changes in the historical-cultural factors. It is my thesis, therefore, that Black Power is not only a sign of developing ethnocentrism, but that it is also both the sign and product of important changes in the whole nexus of historical and cultural factors that are the context of Negro group consciousness.

In this chapter, then, I shall turn to a discussion of some of the major events and developments in the United States as a whole which form the context of Black Power, and I shall conclude by assessing them in terms of the historical-cultural components suggested by Wagley and Harris.[1]

THE GREAT MIGRATION

Most of the factors that form the context of the rise of "Black Power" are so well known that they require only limited comment here. This is especially true of what Myrdal has called "The Great Migration," which began around 1915.[2]

The migration has been purely internal, of course, but it does represent a very distinct movement of Negro people. It was both a northern and a western movement as well as an urban movement. Negroes by the thousands moved out of the South and off the farm into the northern and western urban centers. For example, in 1910, about 9 per cent of the Negroes in the United States lived in the northern and western states. By 1940 this had risen to 21 per cent.[3] Moreover, during this same period, the combined Negro populations of New York, Chicago, Cleveland, and Pittsburgh increased from about 2.5 per cent to 8 per cent.[4] This trend continued from 1940 to 1960. According to the census of 1940, 55 per cent of the non-white population of the United States, resided in rural area, and more than 70 per cent of the non-whites were living in the South. By 1960, however, 72 per cent of the non-whites were living in urban areas

1. Chapter I of this book, pp. 13–14.
2. Myrdal, *An American Dilemma*, p. 183. See also Frazier, *The Negro in the U.S.*, p. 192. For a contemporary study that discusses both migration out of the South and into the central cities, see Karl and Alma Taeuber, *Negroes in Cities: Residential Segregation and Neighborhood Change* (Chicago: Aldine Publishing Company, 1965). See also the excellent article by Philip Hauser, "Demographic Factors in the Integration of the Negro," in Parsons and Clark, *The Negro American*, pp. 71–101; and "The Negroes in the United States," U.S. Department of Labor, Bureau of Statistics, Bulletin No. 1511, June 1966, pp. 5–15.
3. Myrdal, *An American Dilemma*, p. 192.
4. Ibid.

and more than 40 per cent were living in the North and West.[5] The migration to very large metropolitan centers continued also,[6] but what is even more important, the Negro population within the large cities tended to congregate in the central cities. The pattern was for a "Black Belt" to develop in the core of the central city and move outward.[7] As a result, in every major city in the United States today there is a huge Negro ghetto, some of which are now international bywords such as Harlem, Southside Chicago, and Watts.

At the present time, there is little reason to believe that the "Great Migration" will either diminish or cease. In fact, the indications are that it will continue apace.[8]

Generally speaking, the migration has had two kinds of results. On the one hand it has provided the Negro with the entrance into a new world. Legal segregation did not exist in the North and West. This meant that a vast range of public facilities and political opportunities were open to the Negro as he moved out of the rural South. There was also a demand for labor in the rapidly industrializing cities of the North so that the Negro began to diversify his occupational types. In short, the

5. U.S. Bureau of the Census, 1960. See Taeuber and Taeuber, *Negroes in Cities*, pp. 1 ff.

6. Thomas F. Pettigrew, *A Profile of the Negro American*, p. 180. In 1910 no city in the United States had as many as 100,000 Negroes and only 8 had more than 50,000. By 1960 *18* cities had more than 100,000 and New York City had over 1,000,000. Though this reflects the general urbanization of the total American population and the increase in over-all population to some extent, if the present trends continue, non-white population will constitute the majority of metropolitan population in a few decades.

7. Occasionally, there will be Negro enclaves scattered throughout the city, but this is not the general rule. (See Morton Grodzins, "The Metropolitan Areas a Racial Problem," in Earl Raab, ed., *American Race Relations Today*, Garden City, N.Y.: Doubleday, 1957.)

8. See Ben J. Wattenberg and Richard M. Scammon, *This U.S.A.* (Garden City, N.Y.: Doubleday, 1965), p. 300. Matthews and Prothro found that at least 33 per cent of the southern Negro college students in their sample plan to live outside the South in the future, and nearly 40 per cent of those who will leave the South plan to go to the Pacific Coast, *mostly to Los Angeles*. See *Southern Politics* (New York: Harcourt, Brace and World, Inc., 1966), p. 447.

new life out of the South provided the Negro not only with new physical mobility but with social mobility as well. Many Negroes were able to penetrate successfully into the pattern of living characteristic of the American middle class. This mobility, when added to the exercise of the rights of a citizen, created a new independence and new self-respect in the Negro group as a whole.

On the other hand, there was a growing feeling of solidarity and a deepening sense of community developing in the concentrations of Negroes in the large cities.[9] The mere proximity of so many Negroes enabled the group to grasp for the first time something of the political potential of the thousands of people like themselves, and their potential is not unknown to white politicians. Perhaps even more important, however, was the sense of shared misery that bound Negroes together and turned their attention more and more to common problems. While the opportunities of the North were much better at the outset than those of the South, still more and more Negroes moved into the ghettos, and the problems of living in the cities became more and more oppressive. Thus, ghetto life set the problem of discrimination in the context of Negro solidarity and interdependence. This, in turn, laid the foundation for a new sense of group identity and an increasing concern with the common problems that affected the lives of all black people.

THE WORLD WARS

Another factor in the changing context of Negro-white relations has been the involvement of the United States in two ma-

9. An interesting and informative study of Negro ghetto life in Southside Chicago was published in 1945 by Drake and Cayton. An updated revised edition was published in 1963. (St. Clair Drake and Horace R. Cayton, *Black Metropolis*, New York: Harcourt Brace and Co., 1945.) The story here is much the same as that of other cities (Ibid. pp. 755–6). See also Robert C. Weaver, *The Negro Ghetto* (New York: Harcourt Brace and Co., 1946). A very excellent book about ghetto life and its effects upon Negroes is Clark, *Dark Ghetto*, mentioned earlier. For further insight

jor wars. One of the effects of the wars, of course, was to speed the process of migration and thus accelerate some of the effects occasioned by Negro population movement into the urban North. The pressure of war created more jobs, and the need for military personnel expanded the labor market considerably. Negroes who were already moving out of the South responded with even greater speed to this new stimulus, and they enjoyed more job choice and income than at any time in their history.

In addition to this, Negroes by the thousands enlisted in the armed services.[10] Though largely confined at first to labor battalions, black men were gradually formed into fighting units and finally began to fight alongside white men. Some of the Negro units had distinguished combat records and some of the men developed intense pride in this fact. Moreover, many more black men traveled widely to different parts of the world, and they discovered that discrimination against Negroes was not nearly so blatant in some other countries as it was in the United States. These experiences naturally did not make them likely candidates for a return to the old roles of submissiveness and inferiority. They came home from the war for democracy determined to have more democracy at home.

Experiences like these which began in World War I increased in World War II. More than a million Negroes enlisted in the armed services. They fought not only in black units, but in-

into ghetto life, the following are excellent sources too: Claude Brown, *Manchild in the Promised Land* (New York: The Macmillan Co., 1965); and Frazier, *The Negro in the United States*, pp. 229 ff. and 289 ff.
10. For a study of Negro experience in the armed services, see S. J. Scheenfeld, *The Negro in the Armed Forces* (Washington: Associated Publishers 1945). See the brief references in J. H. Franklin, "The Two Worlds of Race: A Historical View," in Parsons and Clark, *The Negro American*, pp. 59 ff.; Myrdal, *An American Dilemma*, pp. 419 ff.; and Eli Ginsberg and Alfred S. Eichner, *The Troublesome Presence* (Glencoe. Ill.: The Free Press, 1964), pp. 279–80. The experiences in the armed forces continue to be important; see Rupert Emerson and Martin Kilson, "The American Dilemma in a Changing World: The Rise of Africa and the Negro American," in Parsons and Clark, *The Negro American*, p. 645.

creasingly they fought alongside white men in some units. Those who enlisted no longer submitted happily to the segregated structures of the military, but fought discrimination and segregation from the beginning of the war period. Moreover, World War II, even more than World War I, was conceived by the nation to be a war for democracy, and in addition it was a struggle against the most vicious form of racism ever to appear on the earth. Having fought racism as an enemy on behalf of one's country Negro veterans understandably were not content with a return to the structures of segregation at home, and the return of the veterans brought with it an inevitable rise in Negro restiveness.

Related to the experience of Negro soldiers during the wars, but perhaps even more important, is what Myrdal calls "an opinion explosion." [11] During both wars the people were told repeatedly that they were fighting for the ideals of democracy, such as liberty and equality against totalitarian and racist regimes that would enslave the world. The result was a literal ground swell of democratic sentiment that pervaded both black and white communities. The barrage of wartime propaganda had its effect upon the Negroes themselves. After all, they were fighting and working for democracy, and many of them could see less and less reason why they should not enjoy its fruits in their own communities. Moreover, the anti-racist overtones of American war propaganda certainly made it easier for Negro leaders to press for reform at home. And within the white communities this same "opinion explosion" meant an increasing revulsion against the excesses of racism and a greater tension in the consciences of white men who had long given only lip service to the "American Creed" of equality and liberty. As a re-

11. Myrdal, *An American Dilemma*, p. 1032 ff. This is a term for the event of mass opinion change. Myrdal thinks that as the pressure of inconsistency between ideals and practices increases, individual moral personalities change to conform to the ideals. This can happen as a result of some precipitating event raising the importance of ideals (such as the war against Naziism). The cumulative effect of such changes among individuals constitutes a public opinion change—an "opinion explosion."

sult, the demands of Negro leaders began to meet an increasingly receptive white audience.

THE RISE OF AFRICA [12]

In the wake of World War II, events were set in motion that have brought into being a huge number of new nations. Nearly all of these new nations are populated by and led by non-whites, and the majority of them are black nations emerging out of the colonial empires that had been established in Africa. One important indication of the scope of this development is the rapidly changing character of the United Nations. As Emerson and Kilson point out:

> At the end of 1945, the U.N. had fifty-one members, of which six were located in the Middle East, four in Africa (including Egypt), and three in Asia. Twenty years later the total had soared to one hundred fifteen, among which the Africans numbered thirty-six, the Asians fifteen, and the Middle East eleven.[13]

This rise to prominence of the African nations has begun to be the basis for a new Negro pride in his cultural and historical heritage. Of course, the interest in Africa among American Negroes is not new. Garvey, Du Bois, and other Negro leaders and intellectuals have all confessed a profound interest in the African roots of the American black man.[14]

More and more the Negro leaders have found the masses receptive to their identification of the Negro with his African homeland and its heritage. As Karenga put it:

> A Negro is from nowhere. You call a man from Germany a German-American; a man from Japan a Japanese-Amer-

12. Throughout this section I lean heavily on the excellent article by Emerson and Kilson, "The American Dilemma . . . ," in Parsons and Clark, *The Negro American.*
13. Ibid. p. 631.
14. See Harold R. Isaacs, *The New World of the Negro American* (New York: The John Day Co., 1963), pp. 105 ff.

ican, and a man from Mexico a Mexican-American. The so-
called "Negro" if he is from anywhere is from Africa. If
he lives in the United States he is an Afro-American.[15]

This does not mean that the American Negro is becoming African, but it does indicate that they are rethinking their identity
as American Negroes in light of their African roots.

The new emphasis upon the African heritage seems also to be
accompanied by an increasing identification of the American
Negro with the world-wide struggle of colored people in their
effort to achieve freedom from the dominance of white nations.
This began as early as the Italian attack on Ethiopia. In some
American Negro communities it probably lies behind much of
the recent criticism of American policy in Vietnam.[16]

The changing self-consciousness of American Negroes is not
the only effect of the rise of Africa. As the affairs of the United
States are more and more entwined with the politics of Africa,
it becomes increasingly necessary that this country be alert to
the problem of discrimination within its own borders. Africans
also identify with American Negroes, as do all other colored nations. They are, therefore, very sensitive to the failure of this
country to deal with discrimination against Negroes within its
own borders. Both mass communication and rapid world-wide
transportation are intensifying these foreign policy problems
daily. Police dogs in Birmingham made the front pages of newspapers in Accra, Elizabethtown, Jakarta, and New Delhi, and
Negro leaders can easily tell the story of their plight in America
in person only a few hours later. All this makes the United
States position in the world more directly dependent upon its

15. Karenga, "Speech at Pomona College," Feb. 16, 1967.
16. Drake and Cayton, *Black Metropolis, pp.* 89, 760–61; Frazier, *The Negro in the U.S.,* pp. 703–5. See also, Louis Lomax, *The Negro Revolt*
(New York: Harper & Row, 1962). This was published as a paperback by
Signet Books in 1963. The reference here is to that edition, pp. 257–63. The
recent attack on American policy in Vietnam by Negro leaders is an indication that the identification is not only with Africa but with other
colored nations as well. (Carmichael, "Speech at Berkeley," Nov. 19,
1966.)

own domestic life, an especially sensitive development for national politicians.

THE CHANGING LEGAL CONTEXT

To this new international situation and to the changed public climate in America, the domestic legal machinery has responded amazingly. It is no accident that nearly 90 per cent of all Negroes interviewed by the Brink-Harris Poll in 1963 definitely felt that the federal government had been the most helpful agency in improving their lot.[17] The Supreme Court of the United States had completed two decades of effective undermining of the legal structures of segregation and the new administration was actively supporting new civil rights legislation. In addition to this, some states had already moved ahead in imaginative ways to strike down the structures of segregation within their own borders. This whole complex of government action is surely one of the most important factors in that changing context of black-white group relationship which is the backdrop of the Black Power movement.

The changes in the legal structure of the nation in regard to the Negro have been, to a large extent, owing to decisions by the Supreme Court. The scope of these decisions can best be understood by considering a landmark decision by the Court just prior to the twentieth century, *Plessy* vs. *Ferguson*.[18]

The issue in the case was segregation on railroad passenger cars. Plessy, the plaintiff, who was part Negro and part Caucasian, had taken a seat in a car reserved for white persons only. He was forcibly removed from the car and placed in jail, being charged with violating an 1890 statute of Louisiana prohibiting persons of one race from occupying cars designated for the use

17. William Brink and Louis Harris, *The Negro Revolution in America* (New York: Simon and Schuster, 1964), pp. 131-2.
18. 163 U.S. 537 1896. For the following discussion of Supreme Court action, I have relied somewhat on the excellent collection of cases in Joseph Tussman, ed., *The Supreme Court on Racial Discrimination* (New York: Oxford University Press, 1963).

of persons of another race. In his petition Plessy had argued that this action violated his rights which were secured under the Thirteenth and Fourteenth Amendments.[19] With respect to the Fourteenth Amendment, the Court declared:

> The object of the amendment was undoubtedly to enforce the absolute equality of the two races before the law, but in the nature of things, it could not have been intended to abolish distinctions based upon color, or to enforce social, as distinguished from political, equality, or a comingling of the two races upon terms unsatisfactory to either. . . . We consider the underlying fallacy of the plaintiff's argument to consist in the assumption that enforced separation of the two races stamps the colored race with a badge of inferiority. If this be so, it is not by reason of anything found in the act, but solely because the colored race chooses to put that construction upon it.[20]

The equality provided in the Fourteenth Amendment, therefore, was construed to allow a "separate but equal" interpretation, for the Court did not believe that separation was in any way inherently unequal. In other words, the *Plessy* decision announced to the nation that segregation according to race was legal.

Within three years after the *Plessy* vs. *Ferguson* decision, the Supreme Court was tested again.[21] The Court fairly consistently held the line, however, up until 1940. Beginning in 1940, the Court cut away at the *Plessy* vs. *Ferguson* ruling in a series of moves that has profoundly changed the whole setting of Negro participation in American society. The following brief survey of some of these moves is, of course, not comprehensive,

19. Ibid. pp. 65–6.
20. Ibid. pp. 68, 73.
21. *Cummings* vs. *Board of Education*, 175 U.S. 258, 1899. This was followed by *Berea College* vs. *Kentucky*, 211 U.S. 45, 1908. The Court had already ruled before *Plessy*, however, that Negroes could not be excluded from juries (*Strauder* vs. *West Virginia*, 100 U.S. 303, 1880) and that local ordinances could not be administered in such a way as to deny the rights of racial groups, in this case, Chinese. (*Yick Wo* vs. *Hopkins*, 118 U.S. 356, 1886.)

but it will give some idea of the momentous changes that were involved.

For example, the rights of Negroes to participate as jurors in the trial process has been repeatedly affirmed. As early as 1880, in *Strauder* vs. *West Virginia*, the Court had held that the trial of a Negro by a jury from which Negroes were excluded was unconstitutional. This ruling has been upheld and expanded by a series of cases beginning in 1940.[22] Furthermore, the voting rights of Negroes have been upheld against the various "white primary" devices as well as against racial gerrymandering.[23]

The court has also struck at discrimination in public accommodations and travel, including both segregated seating on public conveyances as well as segregated terminal facilities.[24] Moreover, the court has resisted all attempts to bar Negroes from participating in legitimate bargaining sessions on behalf of labor.[25]

Free speech for Negroes and Negro organizations has been affirmed and protected in a series of decisions dating from 1957. The NAACP has been under repeated attack from southern states in an attempt to silence them by various means. Beginning in 1957 with *NAACP* vs. *Alabama*,[26] the Court has repeatedly resisted every attack on the right of the NAACP to operate in all lawful ways uninhibited by discriminatory laws.[27]

Perhaps one of the most insulting devices perpetrated upon Negroes to keep them segregated was the so-called "restrictive

---

22. *Strauder* vs. *West Virginia*, 100 U.S. 303, 1880; *Smith* vs. *Texas*, 311 U.S. 128, 1940; *Patton* vs. *Mississippi*, 332 U.S. 463, 1947; *Cassell* vs. *Texas*, 339 U.S. 282, 1950; *Avery* vs. *Georgia*, 345 U.S. 559, 1953.

23. See, for example, *Smith* vs. *Allwright*, 321 U.S. 649, 1944; *Terry* vs. *Adams*, 345 U.S. 461, 1953; and *Gomillion* vs. *Lightfoot*, 364 U.S. 339, 1960.

24. *Morgan* vs. *Virginia*, 328 U.S. 704, 1946; and *Boynton* vs. *Virginia*, 364 U.S. 454, 1960.

25. *Steele* vs. *Louisville and Nashville Railroad Company*, 323 U.S. 192, 1944; *Railroad Trainmen* vs. *Howard*, 343 U.S. 768, 1951.

26. *NAACP* vs. *Alabama*, 357 U.S. 449, 1957.

27. *Bates* vs. *Little Rock*, 361 U.S. 516, 1959; *Louisiana* vs. *NAACP*, 366 U.S. 293, 1960.

covenant," by which property owners in an area could legally prohibit the sale of property to Negroes by other property owners in the same area. In 1948, the Court ruled that these offensive devices were not enforceable in the courts.[28]

In all these rulings and others like them, the Court had been slowly chipping away at the blanket "separate but equal" ruling of *Plessy* vs. *Ferguson,* but it was over the matter of segregated education that the final blow was struck. The rumblings began at least as early as 1938. In *Missouri ex. rel. Gains* vs. *Canada,* the Court ruled that a state was required either to provide a Negro law student with educational facilities that were of a quality equal to the white law school, or else they were to admit students of all races to the facilities that were available. It did not matter that the state of Missouri planned better facilities for Negroes or that excellent facilities were available to Negroes in neighboring states. Each state had to provide equal facilities for the Negro citizens within its borders.[29] This was followed by similar rulings in cases involving Oklahoma and Texas.[30] Then, in 1950, the Court ruled that once a Negro student was admitted to an educational institution, he could not be given unequal treatment.[31] In these cases, the Court made it clear that "separate but equal" meant that if the separation in fact meant unequal, then the separation was unconstitutional.

It was not until the famous *Brown* vs. *Board of Education* decision, however, that the "separate but equal" doctrine was overturned.[32] In this 1954 case involving the segregation of public schools in Kansas, South Carolina, Virginia, and Delaware, the Court delivered the *coup de grâce* to *Plessy.* In the words of the opinion:

> We conclude that in the field of public education the doctrine of "separate but equal" has no place. *Separate educa-*

28. *Shelley* vs. *Kraemer,* 334 U.S. 1, 1948.
29. 305 U.S. 337, 1938.
30. *Sipuel* vs. *Oklahoma,* 332 U.S. 631, 1948, and *Sweatt* vs. *Painter,* 339 U.S. 629, 1950.
31. *McLaurin* vs. *Oklahoma State Regents,* 339 U.S. 637, 1950.
32. 347 U.S. 483, 1954.

tonal facilities are inherently unequal. Therefore, we hold to the plaintiffs and others similarly situated for whom the actions have been brought are, by reason of the segregation complained of, deprived of the equal protection of the laws guaranteed by the Fourteenth Amendment.[33] [Italics mine]

The *Plessy* vs. *Ferguson* ruling was dead. No longer were Negroes to be subjected to inferior facilities under the court of law. Discrimination and segregation could now exist only in ill-defined and subtle ways. There is, of course, still very much discrimination and segregation, but it no longer extends to the highest laws of the land. The courts finally extended Constitutional rights to all during the historic decades of the 1940's and 1950's.

The Supreme Court is not the only governmental agency that has been important in the changing legal context of Negro-white relations. Beginning in 1957, the Congress of the United States has taken giant strides to ensure that the Negro's rights are protected by law. In the 1957 bill Congress gave the Justice Department some limited power in preventing local registrars from interfering with Negro voters.[34] The 1957 bill also established a special civil rights division in the Justice Department.[35] The record of convictions was not especially impressive, and so in 1960, Congress passed another bill strengthening the previous one by adding federal referees to whom appeals against discrimination could be made. This bill also empowered the Justice Department to institute suits.[36] In spite of the fact that the long years of silence were broken by the 1957 and 1960 actions of Congress, it was not until 1964 and 1965 that the high point of congressional activity finally came. In two comprehensive bills, Congress struck hard at the persisting patterns of discrimination in American life, and in spite of the fact that some of the gains would be felt at some levels only in the distant future, it was clear that the mind of the national legislative body

33. Tussman, *The Supreme Court* . . . , p. 42.
34. *Public Law 85-315,* 85th Congress, Sept. 9, 1957, Pt. IV, p. 4.
35. Ibid. Pt. I, p. 1.
36. *Public Law 86-449,* 86th Congress, May 6, 1960.

had been spoken in no uncertain terms.[37] Segregation and discrimination have no legal standing in the American democracy of the future.

Alongside the action of the Court and the Congress has been some vigorous Executive action. This is not to say that the Presidents of the United States have been innovators in the legal struggle against segregation and discrimination. It is to say that during the 1940's, 1950's, and 1960's the Executive branch has certainly supported the other branches. In some particular cases, it was true that the Congress responded to the strong urging of Presidents who were committed to civil rights. In addition to any role the President might have played in the legislative process, some Executive orders have been rather dramatic steps in the attack upon the structures of discrimination. Franklin D. Roosevelt's order banning discrimination in hiring in the war industries and by consent of Fair Employment Practices Commission, Harry Truman's order ending discrimination in the armed forces, and Dwight D. Eisenhower's call for troops in the Little Rock crisis are all cases in point. The initiative of Presidents Kennedy and Johnson is so well known that little comment is required. Suffice it to say that 1960 marked a new point in the initiative of the Executive branch on behalf of civil rights, and that initiative as yet shows little sign of waning.

The direct action against racial segregation and discrimination is not the only important governmental activity in the changing context of intergroup relations in the United States. Though more difficult to assess, the vast number of New Deal programs under Roosevelt and the social welfare programs of all kinds under Kennedy and Johnson have most certainly had a profound effect upon the status of the Negro and his competitive position in America today. One has but to mention the programs for education, social security, medical care, unemployment assistance, and the War on Poverty to make the case. Since Negroes have constituted a major portion of the dis-

37. *Public Law 88-352*, 88th Congress, July 2, 1964; and *Public Law 89-110*, 89th Congress, Aug. 6, 1965.

possessed in our economic system, programs aimed at eradicating poverty and providing for more equal opportunity for all
Americans at the lowest economic levels are bound to have an
exaggerated effect upon the Negroes themselves. In a real sense,
the government attack upon the problem of equal opportunity
for Negro citizens began with Roosevelt's New Deal. Whatever
might have been Roosevelt's personal views on the matter, his
years in office certainly must occupy a place of high priority in
any assessment of American governmental action against discrimination. The same must also be said of the various aspects of
the legislative program of Johnson's Great Society.

It is not only the federal government that has been active in
eradicating legal discrimination in America. For example,
though the record of the agencies is not impressive, Illinois,
Wisconsin, and Michigan had passed FEPC laws by April 1964.
And as early as 1958, New York had passed a law prohibiting
racial discrimination in most categories of housing. Several
other northern states followed suit.

The impact of all this government action upon the competitive position of the Negro has been impressive. There has unquestionably been much "progress" in the battle against discrimination as the legal props to segregation continue to fall.

LABOR UNIONS

Closely related to governmental activity in the field of civil
rights and social welfare has been the activity of the labor
unions. The story of labor and the Negro is highly mixed. On
the one hand, the national organizations of Congress of Indus-
trial Organizations and American Federation of Labor moved
early to facilitate the clearance of Negro workers for war industries. It must be noted, however, that these moves were
largely in response to government pressure, especially Executive
Orders 8802 and 9346 under Roosevelt. Moreover, local unions
have consistently impeded the upgrading of Negroes in employment and resisted efforts of Negroes to join the union on a desegregated basis. This has been especially true of the important

International Association of Machinists.[38] Nonetheless, by 1954, the combined AFL-CIO national leaders had proclaimed the ultimate objective of eliminating racial discrimination not only from the labor movement but from the nation as a whole.

In the past three decades, an enormous number of studies have been done of the notion of race and the problem of prejudice. The studies of race have completely undercut the fantastic racial mythology which emerged in support of white dominance. Today it has been conclusively demonstrated that the race of a person has nothing to do with his mental, moral, physical, or artistic ability.[39] Though there are certainly differences between whites as a group and Negroes as a group, these differences are clearly not to be attributed to any innate racial characteristics. As a result, it has been increasingly the case that neither the white man nor the black man really believes any "natural" or "theological" rationalization for segregation and discrimination against the Negro.

Alongside these studies of racial beliefs and racial differences there have been studies which have uncovered the real reasons for segregation and discrimination. Psychologists have discovered that problems of frustration and aggression as well as problems in the whole psychological developmental process are significantly related to negative attitudes toward Negroes and

38. See Robert C. Weaver, *Negro Labor* (New York: Harcourt Brace and Co., 1946).
39. Ashley M. Montague, *Man's Most Dangerous Myth: The Fallacy of Race* (New York: Columbia University Press, 1942); Ruth Benedict, *Race: Science and Politics* (New York: Modern Age Books, 1940); Franz Boas, *Race, Language and Culture* (New York; Harper & Brothers, 1935); Otto Klineberg, *Race Differences* (New York: Harper & Brothers, 1935). For a summary statement, see Simpson and Yinger, *Racial and Cultural Minorities*, pp. 59–68. A thorough critique of the use of the Bible to support segregation is contained in Everett Tilson, *Segregation and the Bible* (Nashville, Tenn.: Abingdon Press, 1958).

other minority groups.[40] Historical and comparative studies of
the development of minority situations have demonstrated the
significance of social, economic, and demographic factors in the
development of patterns of segregation and discrimination.[41]
Experimental studies in the nature of group formation and the
maintenance of group solidarity as well as intergroup competition have thrown a great deal of light upon the process by
which groups influence individual attitudes and behavior.[42]
These findings indicate that prejudice against the Negro is the
product of very complex factors operating both in the dynamics of group action as well as individual psychological development among whites. Furthermore, these studies have exposed
the utter fallacy of supposing that the discrimination of whites
against the blacks is the product of the Negro's natural inferiority.

This has had the effect of undercutting the position of the
white man who had assumed that what he did to the Negro was
only "natural," and in fact for the Negro's own good. No
longer could literate whites rest easily with this kind of rationalization. The possible effect upon the Negro was to release him
from belief in the myths that the white man had taught him
about himself. While the results of these studies have not fil-
tered through to the masses of Negroes yet, they will assume
greater and greater importance for the Negroes' understanding
of themselves as the educational level of the non-white population of America continues to rise. This will only add to the im-

40. John Dollard, Neal E. Miller, Leonard W. Doole, O. H. Mowrer, and
Robert Sears, *Frustration and Aggression* (New Haven: Yale University
Press, 1939); T. W. Adorno, *et al.*, *The Authoritarian Personality* (New
York: Harper & Brothers, 1950). Bruno Bettelheim and Morris Janowitz,
Social Change and Prejudice (Glencoe, Ill.: The Free Press, 1964), relates
psychological factors to social and economic conditions in the prejudice-
producing nexus. For a summary of various understandings of the nature
of prejudice, see Gordon Allport, *The Nature of Prejudice* (Garden
City, N.Y.: Doubleday and Co., Inc.), Chapter 13, pp. 201 ff.
41. An example is Wagley and Harris, *Minorities* . . . ; see also Frazier,
The Negro in the U.S.
42. Sherif and Sherif, *Groups in Harmony and Tension.*

pact of the new ethnocentrism as the basis for Negro determination to live with the white man on the Negro's terms.

RELIGION

The scientific studies of race have contributed in an important way to the changing role of religion in American race relations, for they have at least cut the intellectual ground out from under "theological" and "biblical" rationalizations for segregation and discrimination. Today, no person in the religious community with any intelligence can take seriously the old arguments about the inferiority of the Negro.

In spite of this, the changes in the white religious communities have been largely ideological, and action does not yet, for the most part, keep pace with the theological emphases on the universalism of God's love, man's natural rights as revealed in the natural law, and brotherhood. Since I shall discuss this in some detail with respect to white Protestantism in Chapter VII, I shall not labor the point here.

In spite of the "action gap" in the white religious community as a whole, it must be noted that religious leaders in the white community have recently begun to support the Negro struggle for justice, and there have been some creative and daring experiments in interracial co-operation developed under the sponsorship of religious institutions. Moreover, a substantial portion of the financial support for civil rights organizations has come from persons in the white religious community who have been motivated by their understanding of the ethical implications of their faith.

These developments have certainly had some effect on the changing ideological climate in America, but by far the most remarkable change in the religious community has occurred in the Negro churches. The churches have always played an extremely important role in the life of the Negro community.[43]

43. See E. F. Frazier, *The Negro Church in America* (New York: Schocken Books, 1963).

For a number of years they were practically the only kind of social organization available to Negroes, and the church was the one place where, on occasion, Negroes could come out of the hostile white world, gain strength from their togetherness, and find grounds for new hope.[44] In spite of the changing character of American society, the church still functions in this way for a large number of Negroes, especially those of the alienated lower class who are the majority of blacks in the United States.

Recently, however, there has been an important change in the character of many Negro churches' witness to the gospel. Prior to the "Negro Revolt" of the 1950's and 1960's, the hope that was preached in the Negro church was of a distinctly other-worldly character. This is reflected in the songs that were sung and the sermons that were preached. The Negro church offered a religion for oppressed people who saw no deliverance from their oppressors, and whose strength to continue to exist in the world of segregation and discrimination was renewed by a hope for a better time some day in heaven. This is no longer the gospel of many Negro churches, for the message preached in many of them today is distinctly "this-worldly." In the South especially, and elsewhere to a lesser extent, the Negro churches have become centers for protest against segregation and discrimination.

The best example of the new emphasis in the Negro church was the gospel which Martin Luther King introduced to his Baptist congregation in Montgomery, Alabama.[45] The story of how that church became the center of "realized eschatology" that focused upon concrete social problems of the Negro is too well known to require repeating here. Suffice it to say that the Montgomery experience was a sign that a new stance and a new theology had come to the Negro churches, and these churches clearly represent the most significant aspect of the role of religion in the changing context of race relations in the United States. Negro churches repeatedly became centers of the civil

44. Ibid. pp. 44 ff.
45. Martin Luther King, *Stride Toward Freedom* (New York: Harper & Row, 1958).

rights protest, and out of their membership has come much of the leadership in contemporary civil rights organizations.

THE CIVIL RIGHTS ORGANIZATIONS

The inclusion of the civil rights organizations as one of the factors in the changing context of American race relations is not meant to imply that the role of these groups has been a minor one. Nor is it meant to imply that they are in any way ancillary to the main stream of black nationalism. On the contrary, still today the vast majority of Negroes apparently rate the leaders of the civil rights organizations at the top of the scale of Negro group leadership.[46] There is good reason for this. The dramatic work of Martin Luther King in Montgomery, Alabama, signaled the beginning of the most widespread mobilization of support for the rights of Negroes in the history of this country. Less dramatic, but perhaps more important in the long run, has been the persistent and patient work of NAACP lawyers who have fought the issues of segregation and discrimination through the highest Court in the nation. If it is true that "the greatest movement toward black nationalism has invariably come at moments of high expectations among Negroes that change will occur," [47] then it can be said that more than any other factor, the civil rights organizations have laid the groundwork for the rise of ethnocentrism among American Negroes, for their efforts have been extremely important in making changes occur.

Kenneth Clark has pointed out that the "civil rights movement" is as old as slavery in the United States:

> From the beginning, the essential conflict of the civil rights movement was inherent in the contradiction between the practical economic and status advantages associated with

46. Martin Luther King, Roy Wilkins, Whitney Young, and Thurgood Marshall all ranked *far* ahead of Carmichael and Muhammad in the 1966 *Newsweek* survey. (*Newsweek*, Aug. 22, 1966, p. 34.)
47. Emerson and Kilson, "The American Dilemma . . ." in *The Negro American*, p. 639.

slavery and racial oppression, and the Judeo-Christian ideals of love and brotherhood and their translation into the democratic ideology of equality and justice.[48]

In this sense the civil rights movement is not coterminous with civil rights organizations. It was the movement that, in fact, impelled the creation of civil rights organizations in order to provide the "necessary machinery, organizations, and leaders" to channel the movement and guide it in effective methods to eliminate racial oppression.[49] Some background on the leading organizations in the movement will help to clarify their role in the changing context of race relations.

The National Association for the Advancement of Colored People

The NAACP was actually founded in 1909.[50] Among its founders were some members of the group known as the "Niagara Movement" which included W. E. B. Du Bois. Du Bois, more than any other single person, shaped the stance and strategy of the NAACP at its beginning. It was characterized by a new militance which brought Du Bois into conflict with the more moderate Booker T. Washington. Du Bois eschewed any compromise of his human dignity, and he refused to make adjustments in the name of practicality.[51] The NAACP was interracial from the beginning and thoroughly committed to the view that change in the status of the Negro could be brought about within the framework of American democracy. As a result the organization has concentrated largely upon the legal system of the United States with the objective of including the Negro within the rights guaranteed to him by the Constitution

48. Kenneth B. Clark, "The Civil Rights Movement: Momentum and Organization," in Parsons and Clark, *The Negro American*, p. 595. I rely on this article, and Louis Lomax's, *The Negro Revolt* for this section.
49. Clark, "The Civil Rights Movement," *The Negro American*, pp. 597–8.
50. Ibid. p. 599.
51. Ibid. pp. 598–601.

as a citizen of the United States of America. The work of the NAACP and the NAACP Legal Defense and Education Fund are common knowledge.[52] Their most dramatic victory was the *Brown* vs. *Board of Education* decision [53] but they were also successful in cases striking down a wide variety of discriminatory legal barriers to full Negro citizenship.

Today the NAACP continues to flourish in spite of mounting criticism within the Negro community. Through research, lobbying, legal assistance, and formal protest through legal and other governmental channels, the NAACP continues its pressure upon the structures of segregation. It has been and will continue to be an important arm of the total civil rights movement in the United States.

The Urban League

The Urban League, organized in 1910, had as its object the facilitation of the southern Negro worker's entry into the industrialized cities of the North. Formed just before the "Great Migration" began to crest, it did an enormous amount of work in finding jobs for the Negroes moving into the urban centers. Increasingly, however, the role of the League is being redefined under the leadership of Whitney Young, Jr. Today, the League is focusing upon the Negro family as a unit, and in line with its past history as a "go-between" organization is attempting to bring social services to the Negro family to help overcome the disintegrative forces that have such a stranglehold on this primary institution in the Negro community. Young's vision is not limited to this, however. He sees beyond "one-shot" remedies to a vast program of assistance to the Negroes to enable them to break out of the cycle of deprivation and oppression once and for all. His vision is of a comprehensive program of internal "aid to underdeveloped people" as a compensation for centuries of discrimination. Under his vigorous leadership it is possible

52. Established in 1939, the Fund became a separate organization in 1955. (Lomax, *The Negro Revolt*, p. 121.)
53. 347 U.S. 483, 1954.

that the Urban League may again emerge as a potent factor in the Negro community.[54]

The Congress of Racial Equality

The Congress of Racial Equality (CORE) was organized in 1942 under the leadership of pacifist members of the Fellowship of Reconciliation. They began as a small group and remained so until after the initial impact of the Negro Revolt of the late 1950's. The early activities of the group were confined to non-violent forms of protest such as "sit-ins" and a 1947 "Freedom Ride." In 1961, CORE burst into the headlines. Under the leadership of James Farmer, who had just resigned as program director for the NAACP to assume the post of director of CORE, the now famous "Freedom Rides" of April and May 1961 were planned and executed. These rides demonstrated the tense situation of the South and the intransigence of southern authorities in their refusal to enforce what were now federal court rulings about interstate travel. Perhaps more than any single other event, these bus rides convinced the nation that more had to be done "to secure these rights." [55] Since the rides, CORE's membership has increased markedly, and the organization has continued its direct action approach. The recent leadership change from Farmer to Floyd McKissick is probably an indication that not only will direct action be the *modus operandi* of CORE in the future but also that the organization will become more and more militant.[56]

54. Clark, "The Civil Rights Movement," *The Negro American* pp. 601 ff.; Lomax, *The Negro Revolt*, pp. 224–35.
55. The words in italics are the title of the 1957 report of the President's Commission on Civil Rights. For an account of the "Freedom Rides," see Anthony Lewis, *Portrait of a Decade: The Second American Revolution* (New York: Random House, 1964), pp. 87–93. See also Lomax, *The Negro Revolt*, pp. 144–59.
56. McKissick is very close to Carmichael in his stance. (See NBC "Meet the Press," Sunday, Aug. 21, 1966, [*Transcript*].) The recent resignation from CORE by Lillian Smith was accompanied by her testimony that the new leadership was increasingly anti-white. (A quotation of parts of her

The Southern Christian Leadership Conference

The SCLC *"is* Martin Luther King." [57] This organization grew out of King's successful boycott of the segregated bus system in Montgomery, Alabama. This organization shares the non-violent approach to direct action that was characteristic of CORE in its earlier development, and it is also shaped by King's own allegience to the philosophy of love for the enemy as part and parcel of the protest strategy. King's strategy also includes the pattern of focusing upon specific concrete issues in a particular locale, and part of his strength lies in his charismatic power that tends to mobilize large numbers of Negroes and to involve them directly in protest action. As yet, the strategy has not passed the test of intransigent and subtle problems characteristic of the ghettos of the northern cities. As Clark points out, the method of non-violence and love for enemies is most effective in arousing the conscience of the nation when non-violent protest is opposed by blatant hatred and cruelty. Therefore, even though King is rated by rank and file Negroes and Negro leaders as the most important figure in the civil rights movement,[58] it remains to be seen whether his own strategy will be effective in the changing setting of the civil rights struggle.[59]

The Student Nonviolent Coordinating Committee

SNCC began in the wake of the non-violent protest of the SCLC. It was organized by a group of young Negro students at Shaw University in Raleigh, North Carolina, in 1960. The organization grew out of a "sit-in" by several students in Greens-

letter to Floyd McKissick appears in the unpublished convocation lectures of Albert Manley, delivered at Spelman College, Atlanta, Georgia, Sept. 22 through Oct. 6, 1966, Lecture II.)

57. Clark, "The Civil Rights Movement," *The Negro American*, p. 612. For a full account of the Montgomery experience, see Martin Luther King, *Stride Toward Freedom*.

58. *Newsweek*, Aug. 22, 1966, p. 34.

59. Clark, "The Civil Rights Movement," *The Negro American*, pp. 612–15.

boro, North Carolina, earlier that same year. What Lomax has called the "second major battle of the Negro revolt"[60] was similar both to CORE and SCLC in its method, but it was considerably more defiant than King and came to represent more of a mass movement than CORE. The "sit-in" began when four college freshmen from North Carolina Agricultural and Technical College walked into a Woolworth's lunch counter and sat down for service. When service was refused, they refused to move. Soon hundreds of other students rushed downtown to join the protest. What began with these four students soon became a nationwide movement involving not only thousands of Negro college students but other Negroes and whites as well.[61]

SNCC with its predominately youthful base and leadership was impatient with negotiation and litigation. They set about direct political action by identifying with the Negroes of the South, even to their manner of dress. They are confident and militant, and although they do not reject white participation in their activities, neither do they feel any special gratitude to those whites who join them. The view of the SNCC leadership is that the reform of American democracy is clearly the responsibility of all Americans, but they are beginning where they think the reform must begin—with the mobilization and organization of Negroes into a potent and viable political organization.

SNCC continues to focus upon political organization and it became clear that with the election of Carmichael as its leader that the organization was moving more and more toward the mainstream of a strongly ethnocentric black nationalism. Though SNCC still has white workers in its organization, it is increasingly difficult for whites to exercise any leadership, and for some it is difficult to work at all.[62]

60. Lomax, *The Negro Revolt*, p. 133.
61. See Glenford E. Mitchell and William H. Peace III, eds., *The Angry Black South* (New York: Corinth Books, 1962); and Merrill Proudfoot, *Diary of a Sit-In* (Chapel Hill, N.C.: University of North Carolina Press, 1962).
62. This last statement is based upon a recent conversation with a white SNCC worker in the southern part of Georgia.

Certainly one significant thing about SNCC and SCLC is that they were the first southern-based mass protest organizations on behalf of Negro rights. Since the time of Booker T. Washington the pattern of interracial adjustment had been accommodation from the side of the Negro, but with the rise of King and the student movement, that day of passive acquiescense, long since gone from the North, disappeared also from the South.

CONCLUSION

In conclusion, it will be useful to assess the impact of all these factors in terms of the historical-cultural components of majority-minority relations. In the first place, it is unquestionably the case that there has been a change in the *adaptive capacity* of the Negroes in the United States. The Negroes of the 1960's have more education, better health, more occupational diversification, more money, and more political power than at any time in the history of the United States.[63] This means that the Negro's competitive position has undergone a marked change for the better since 1900, and this is clearly reflected in the accelerating pace which has characterized the improvement of his position in the 1950's and 1960's.

None of this, of course, has erased the "color gap" in the opportunities in America today. In fact, if the improvement in Negro opportunities, owing to urbanization and the migration out of the South, is taken into account, it does not appear that the actual "color gap" has been narrowed very significantly.[64] For example, it is still true that the white high school dropout will earn more than a Negro high school graduate, and a white high school graduate will earn more than a Negro college gradu-

63. For a summary statement, see Rose, "Postscript Twenty Years Later," in Myrdal, *An American Dilemma,* pp. xxvii–xlv.
64. See the excellent articles by Rashi Fein and Daniel P. Moynihan. (Rashi Fein, "An Economic and Social Profile of the Negro American," in Parsons and Clark, *The Negro American,* pp. 102–33; Daniel P. Moynihan, "Employment, Income and the Ordeal of the Negro Family," in Parsons and Clark, *The Negro American,* pp. 134–59.)

ate.[65] The percentage of substandard dwellings among Negro households is actually increasing. More than 40 per cent of all Negro children live in poverty homes, and about 40 per cent of them live in overcrowded residential areas.[66] The Negro child has only one-half as great a chance of completing high school, one-third the chance of becoming a professional man, and one-seventh the chance ever to earn $10,000 per year as does his white counterpart. Furthermore, the danger of his becoming unemployed is almost twice as great.[67] He still votes less and attends inferior schools. In short, in spite of the great gains of the last five and one-half decades, the Negro still lags far behind his white fellow citizens in terms of his life chances and competitive ability. When this has been said, however, we can return to the previous statement that the Negro has marked improvement in those indices which point to adaptive capacity.

One other thing should be mentioned here. Wagley and Harris have indicated that one of the chief problems of the American Negro in developing his adaptive capacity has been the lack of ethnocentrism. Hence, if our thesis about the rise of ethnocentrism is correct, this is simply one more indication that the adaptive capacity of the Negro in America is improving rapidly.[68]

In the second place, my sketch of the factors in the changing context of intergroup relations has demonstrated a significant alteration in the *arena of competition*. For one thing, the Negroes have changed their place of residence from the South to the North and West and from the farms to the cities. Moreover, it is clear that the massive attack on the legal barriers to integration in the South and in the United States as a whole have changed the conditions under which Negroes and whites compete. Especially the various branches of the federal government have made giant strides toward the "equality before the law"

65. Wattenberg and Scammon, *This U.S.A.*, p. 282.
66. U.S. Dept. of Labor, Bureau of Statistics, Bulletin 1511, June 1966, p. 41.
67. Lewis, *Portrait of a Decade*, pp. 10–11.
68. Wagley and Harris, *Minorities . . .* , p. 270.

that was guaranteed to all citizens of the nation by the Four-teenth and Fifteenth Amendments. And here, too, the new pride in being Negro and the change in white attitudes toward the Negro are factors in the shifting conditions of competition.[69]

The change in attitudes, however, really belongs to the third historical-cultural component suggested by Wagley and Harris, the *ideological setting*. There has been no basic change in the democratic creed since the founding of the nation, but there surely has been a profound change in the conscience of many Americans about the gap between creed and deed. I have already referred to Myrdal's concept of an "opinion explosion." It is useful to recall the concept here, for it rather accurately describes what has been happening in the minds of Americans both black and white. The impact of war propaganda gave impetus to the change, especially the propaganda of World War II directed against racism. In addition, labor groups and religious groups have propounded the equalitarian dogmas with increasing fervor; and finally, Negroes themselves have been increasingly resistant to the rationalizations about their own inferiority. All of this has meant a virtual explosion of equalitarian ideology that is surely more widespread in American democracy than ever before. The country as a whole may not have been ahead of the Supreme Court, but the Court was surely expressing the opinion of many Americans when they finally decided that separation meant unequal and overturned the *Plessy* decision.

The foregoing discussion, then, makes it clear that there have been marked changes in all of the historical-cultural components of majority-minority relations during the last six decades, and within the Negro community these changes have occasioned high hopes and heightened expectations. It is a mistake, however, to read the response of the Negroes simply as hope and

69. Paul B. Sheatsley, "White Attitudes Toward the Negro," in Parsons and Clark, *The Negro American*, pp. 303–24. The post-"Black Power" attitudes may represent retrenchment, however. (See the poll reported in *Newsweek*, Aug. 22, 1966, p. 34.)

expectation. The real gains among Negroes unfortunately have been confined to a fairly narrow and select group within the Negro community, the "talented tenth," the middle class. The group that Pettigrew has called the "other Negroes," [70] the poor, the ghetto residents, the 70 per cent mass of black people, have not seen much evidence of concrete gains. Hence, at the same time that rapid changes in the context of American race relations have created the conditions for the developing Negro ethnocentrism, it may well be that the disillusionment caused by unfulfilled expectations among the masses of Negroes is shaping the character of that ethnocentrism. This is surely true of the strain of ethnocentrism represented by the Black Power movement.[71] Therefore, if Black Power is the product of these changes in the sense that the changes have made Negro group pride more possible, it is even more the symbol of the restlessness and impatience of the Negro masses with the slow pace of change in America. As such, it is an ominous warning that the great changes of the 1940's, the 1950's, and the 1960's have not been sufficient, and the emphasis on political power that characterizes Black Power reflects both the disillusionment of Negroes with the American political process and a determination to accelerate and shape the changes that are to come.

70. Thomas F. Pettigrew, "Complexity and Change in American Racial Patterns: A Social Psychological View," in Parsons and Clark, The Negro American, pp. 352–3.
71. This became clear in Chapter II.

IV

Black Power and Civil Rights:
Trends in Negro Leadership

In the preceding chapters, Black Power has been interpreted as both the symbol and the product of broad changes in American race relations which have been developing since about 1900. This should not be construed to mean that I believe that the entire Negro community is now enthusiastically committed to the entire ideology and strategy of men like Stokeley Carmichael and Ron Karenga. On the contrary, there is a tremendous amount of diversity among Negro leaders today on tactical as well as ideological questions, and that very diversity is indicative of the vitality of the Negro community as a whole. In recent years, however, there does seem to be a discernible trend among Negro leaders toward a more ethnocentric stance. Moreover, there are signs of growing unanimity on strategy and aims. In both cases, the Negro leadership is focusing upon themes that are remarkably similar to those which characterize the Black Power leaders, and it is in light of this that I have interpreted Black Power as the sign of a new situation in American race relations.

In this chapter, then, I shall discuss the changing patterns of Negro leadership in general; the nature of the current leadership crisis; and some of the trends in stance, strategy, and aims that constitute the "new era" in race relations.

THE CHANGING PATTERNS OF LEADERSHIP

Diversity in Negro leadership is not a new thing. An early example of the debate over strategy and aims was the three-sided controversy between Washington, Du Bois, and Garvey. Washington, it will be recalled, was the champion of the strategy of accommodation. His view was that the Negro's best strategy, and perhaps his only possible strategy, was to work within the biracial setting of white-black separation to improve himself and to train himself to enter the labor market at the level of skilled workmen. Washington did not challenge the structures of segregation as such, but emphasized the necessity for improving the Negro's chances within the institutional patterns that had emerged and had been sanctified by *Plessy* vs. *Ferguson*. Du Bois denounced this strategy with vehemence. He would countenance no compromise with his dignity and his status as a human being. To him, the forced separation of Negroes and whites meant only the pernicious inference of Negro inferiority. Negroes should demand their full rights as citizens of this country and they could not rest until the barriers of segregation were struck down to allow free movement and assimilation of the Negro into the mainstream of American society as equals to whites. Du Bois and others like him scoffed at Washington's appeal to realism and patience. To them, these were mere subterfuges to cover an inexcusable timidity.

At the same time, Du Bois denounced Garvey as a buffoon, a charlatan, and a fraud. He accused Garvey, by insinuation, of all manner of conniving to extract funds from unsuspecting Negroes, and he was especially contemptuous of Garvey's "back to Africa" theme. Du Bois argued that the American Negro is an American and he should concentrate upon the kind of strategy that would enable him to assume his rightful place in this society. "Back to Africa" strategy cut directly across Du Bois's strongly assimilationist aims and tended to give aid and comfort to the very kind of whites whom Du Bois thought should be the focal point of the Negro attack.

It is important again to remember that it was *not* Garvey's ethnocentrism that offended Du Bois, but his strategy, and it is clear that Garvey's militant stance and his championing of distinctly Negro interests were much more palatable to Du Bois than the Booker T. Washington package of accommodation.

The picture here is instructive. There is Du Bois the militant, Du Bois the assimilationist, opposed to Washington the accommodator and Garvey the separatist. It is instructive because it is illustrative of the types of leaders that have appeared dominant in the history of the Negro group.

Daniel Thompson, in his book, *The Negro Leadership Class*, has developed a typology of Negro leadership which is useful as a heuristic device for understanding what options have appeared historically for Negro leadership. The author, in his study of New Orleans Negro leadership, found that there were three patterns of leadership: the "Uncle Tom" pattern; the "racial diplomat" pattern; and the "race man" pattern. The *"Uncle Tom"* pattern of Negro leadership was characteristic of the post-slavery and post-Reconstruction South. Negro leaders of this era were apparently happy with the system of segregation—at least they had to operate as if they were. Their lives were geared to currying favor with the whites so that they could, in turn, deliver favors from the white community to the Negroes. These favors then acted as the means by which they wielded power in the Negro community. As a result, the Negro leader in this pattern spent his efforts meeting the expectations of the whites and he never publicly questioned the validity of his second-class citizenship. His power was derived, and whether he represented any choice of the Negro community mattered little. The Negroes as a group represented no power base at all, and the only meaning of power was white favor. Therefore, even those Negroes who did not like their subservient position saw that the only way they could make any gains was to conform to the leadership pattern expected by the whites.

The second pattern of Negro leadership, the *"racial diplomat,"* represents a change in Negro perspective and tactics. Unlike the first type of Negro leader, the racial diplomat refused to accept the segregated world of second-class citizenship. He was concerned with the need of the Negroes for equal rights and dignity, but he never expressed his position purely in terms of specifically Negro interests. Rather, he was concerned to express the needs of his own group in the context of the needs of the entire community for the better things in life. The stance of these leaders was that of inter-racial co-operation for those who were at the lower end of the social and economic scale of America. The races were to co-operate for the common good of the whole American society.

The *"race man"* pattern of leadership does not accept any part of the biracial system as right. He is the avowed enemy of all forms of second-class citizenship for Negroes and sees himself specifically as the champion of Negro interest. Yet, Thompson's "race man" type is not a racist. He sees himself as first an American and then as a Negro. Yet he does demand the full and complete rights of American citizenship for Negroes and is ready through all forms of legal and direct action to destroy the system of segregation that denies the Negro his rights. According to Thompson, the "race man" with his pride in his "Negro-ness" and his militant advocacy of Negro rights is the new leader of the Negro community. At the present time, no pattern of leadership is remotely acceptable to the Negro community which does not specifically identify itself as peculiarly Negro in interest and avowedly at war with discrimination. It is the change to the "race man" in the leadership pattern of the Negro community which Thompson thinks is the basis of the current crisis in race relations.[1]

Like all typologies, the types do not readily lend themselves to specific application. Yet, it seems fairly safe to say that we can place the change from "Uncle Tom" to the "racial diplomat" somewhere in the early 1900's as the new leaders like Du Bois began to attack the leadership of Booker T. Washington. The change from the dominance of the "racial diplomat" pattern to the "race man" pattern came about forty-five years la-

1. Daniel Thompson, *The Negro Leadership Class* (Englewood Cliffs, N.J.: Prentice-Hall, Inc., 1963), Chap. 5, pp. 58–79.

ter. No single man represents the change, but Martin Luther King certainly was one of the heralds of change, and the emergence of James Farmer into leadership of CORE was another indication. Yet before King or Farmer, NAACP leadership had begun direct attacks upon the legal structures of segregation, and they were becoming more and more militant.

Thompson's typology, then, illustrates what has been happening in Negro leadership patterns over the last six decades. In general there has been a move toward more and more militance in the pursuit of rights and more and more concentration upon the specific needs of the Negro group. By 1962, the top leadership had moved completely away from Washington to the stance of Du Bois. The old image of the co-operative accommodating man had given way to the daily newspaper pictures of new militant and determined leaders leading their people in marches and rides to freedom. Young Negroes were sitting-in, kneeling-in, lying-in, and marching. The race was on the move and the marchers were in a determined mood.

THE PRESENT CRISIS IN NEGRO LEADERSHIP

The fact that most Negro leaders today are either the "race man" type or close to it does not mean that the leadership crisis is over. In fact, the sharpness of the public debate between organizations and leaders of SNCC, CORE, SCLC, NAACP, and the Urban League might seem to indicate even more of a division in the Negro community than before. This division is occasioned by the emergence of the new leader discussed in the first chapter of the book, and this leadership is causing a crisis within Thompson's "race man" type.[2]

As we have seen, there has been, at least since the 1920's, a growing fringe of Negro leadership who have focused upon the glory of being black. This pattern of developing Negro ethnocentrism has spawned leaders who are not only concerned with the interests of the group, but who think it is necessary that Negroes struggle for their rights almost entirely on their own.

2. Ibid. p. 59, note 4. The author took no account of black nationalism.

Moreover, there is a strong undercurrent of separatist ideology which carries with it strong anti white sentiments. These young leaders, like Garvey, see themselves primarily as Negroes and only secondarily as Americans. They are convinced that America is a white man's country and that the Negro's real allies are all the other colored nations in the world who are struggling to overthrow white oppression. Though none of the new leadership advocates Garvey's "back to Africa" strategy, they do have their own version of the same idea. Negroes must look back to Africa for the foundations of a new sense of identity and a new cultural milieu. And it is the "motherland" that will also provide the prototypes for the new Negro institutions.

Over against this "fringe" leadership is the "race man" type represented by King, and to some extent, Wilkins and Young. These men are also concerned with distinctly Negro rights and primarily Negro interests. Yet, their concern with black interests does not lead them to be anti-white, nor does it require them to look to Africa for the development of new institutions.

When the Black Power leaders began to emerge into prominence, the response of the "race men" was antagonistic. Martin Luther King has been an especially vocal critic of the new leadership. He has attacked their racism, arguing that black supremacy is as evil as white supremacy. From his point of view, the Negro community must not succumb to the temptation to return ideology in kind, and he is fearful that their emphasis on self-defense in opposition to non-violence will lead to violent confrontations between Negroes and whites. He is also very sensitive to the fact that the emphasis on exclusive Negro power will tend to alienate white support and force the Negroes to go it alone.

> It [black power] connotes black supremacy and an anti-white feeling that does not or should not prevail. It leaves a feeling that the Negro wants to go it alone, which he cannot do. . . . My problem with SNCC and CORE is not their militancy; I think you can be militantly non-violent. It's what I see as a pattern of violence emerging and their

use of the cry Black Power which falls on the ear as racism in reverse. . . . I cannot agree with the teaching of de-
fensive violence. . . . We do not need to have a program
for defense. The line of demarcation between defense and
aggressive violence is too thin.[3]

Roy Wilkins is even more decisive in his indictment of the
trends he sees developing under the impetus of Black Power
leadership. He has charged that SNCC is divisive and is attempting to undermine the efforts of the NAACP. He has
hinted that the Black Power leaders have created a split in the
aims and goals of Negro organizations that may result in
NAACP's going its separate way. Finally, he feels reasonably
certain that the organizations that follow the Black Power line
are doomed to failure.

> We venture the observation that such a posture could
> serve to stir counter-planning, counter action, and possible
> conflict. Moreover in attempting to substitute for derelict
> law enforcement machinery, the policy entails the risk of a
> broader, more indiscriminate crackdown by law officers
> under the ready-made excuse of restoring law and order.
> . . . No matter how endlessly they try to explain it, the
> term black power means antiwhite power. . . . It has to
> mean going it alone. It has to mean separatism. Now sepa-
> ratism . . . offers a disadvantaged minority little except a
> chance to shrivel and die. . . . It is a reverse Mississippi, a
> reverse Hitler, a reverse Ku Klux Klan. . . . We of the
> NAACP will have none of this. We have fought it too
> long.[4]

One real point at issue among Negro leadership is obviously the
question about the participation of whites in the struggle for
Negro goals. A newspaper account rather nicely pictured the
situation by referring to the debate over the role of the white
liberals in the march to Jackson during early June 1966. That
march had its beginning in the pilgrimage of James Meredith.

3. *New York Times,* July 6, 1966, p. 15, and July 9, 1966, p. 8.
4. Ibid. July 6, 1966, p. 14. See also, July 8, 1966, p. 1.

When Meredith was shot down by a white sniper, hundreds of Negroes continued the pilgrimage.

Observing the debate over white liberal participation, the writer noted that King and the SCLC continually expressed gratitude to white northerners for their participation. SNCC leaders were wondering aloud whether whites should be permitted in the march at all. McKissick welcomed white participation, but he insisted that all the decisions about policy and aims be made by Negroes. Finally, Roy Wilkins and Whitney Young refused to support the march at all because they thought its anti-Johnson overtones might impair their relationship to President Johnson and liberal congressmen.[5]

These organizations represent several concepts of strategy that point to varying degrees of dependence upon white support. There is the *legal strategy* represented by Wilkins and Young which depends heavily on the machinery of American governmental institutions. For this strategy to be effective, it is obvious that the support of powerful white judges and law-makers is crucial. Moreover, the support of a large number of whites in forming a liberal coalition on Negro rights must be attempted in order to ensure the continued co-operation of the Congress. Should whites withdraw support and form political coalitions that for various reasons are hostile to Negro demands, this strategy would be seriously hampered if not defeated entirely.

King's strategy is direct action to mobilize the Negro masses on specific issues and to arouse the conscience of liberal whites. King is very cognizant of the fact that it is the *moral power* of an aroused white America in support of black direct action that brings about change. As a result, King, while not so directly dependent upon white support to bring about specific changes, does depend upon the marshaling of white support in order to extend his influence to issues of broad importance and to bring about any sweeping changes in the structures of discrimination.

5. Ibid. June 12, 1966, p. 1.

McKissick is in a very ambiguous position. On the one hand, he is a vigorous advocate of black leadership and black self-determination. He is convinced that any changes in American society must come about through black political organization. Yet, his organization, CORE, depends heavily on whites for financial support, and has traditionally included white leaders and members.[6] Therefore, McKissick stands squarely in the middle. While advocating black political and economic organization, he eschews the more blatantly anti-white statements that have been attributed to some of the other Black Power leaders. In spite of this, however, he shows a special sensitivity to the charges of King, Wilkins, and others.

> Black power is no mere slogan. It is a movement dedicated to the exercise of American democracy in its highest tradition; it is a drive to mobilize the black communities of this country in a monumental effort to remove the basic causes of alienation, frustration, despair, low self-esteem, and hopelessness. Black power is not black supremacy, does not mean the exclusion of white Americans from the Negro revolution, does not advocate violence and will not start riots.[7]

Carmichael's stance, of course, is even more ethnocentric than that of McKissick. He clearly believes that the only hope for Negroes is for them to organize effectively the masses of black people into a united political front and to strengthen the black economic base in this country. The Negro will never really be equal until he has self-determination, and this means that he must develop a political organization based upon intense in-group loyalty. The vicious psychological circle of inferiority can never be broken until the Negro has pride in his blackness, and if this involves the rejection of whiteness, it is exactly what Carmichael would expect in the context of white racism that he thinks is rampant in America. If this scares white men and they

6. About 80 per cent of CORE's financial support is from whites. (*Newsweek*, Aug. 22, 1966, p. 34.) By the end of July the financial contributions to CORE had dropped almost 50 per cent from their high level in preceding years. (*New York Times*, July 25, 1966, p. 1.)
7. *New York Times*, July 8, 1966, p. 16.

pull out—Carmichael's response would probably be, "Let them!" To him this would only prove that even liberal whites are unwilling to allow Negroes to have full self-determination and self-respect. If whites become more recalcitrant, Carmichael would see this only as proof that the so-called liberal support of Negroes is tenuous at best and is really a thinly veiled form of white condescension.

The younger militants focus more on the psychological problem of racial discrimination. They believe that Negro dignity can come only when Negroes have enough power to demand reform for themselves. Continued dependence upon white good will and support can only weaken the Negro in his attempt to develop a position of strength, and any alliances with whites other than from a position of strength are meaningless. Whites continue to pull the strings and Negroes will continue to move only as directed by the white power holders.

Even if the Black Power leaders are still open to strategy other than planned violence, it must be noted that there is an air of resignation about the intransigence of white institutions that is so pronounced as to make violence almost unavoidable. And in spite of his disclaimer of absolute anti-white sentiments, Carmichael's tendency to focus upon the racist character of all white institutions seems to bring the cause of the blacks and hatred of whites in very close proximity. Finally, as we have noted in the second chapter, some sort of separatism seems to be a part of the strategy of the younger militants. Although this does not mean emigration nor does it mean strict geographical separation, the emphasis upon the need for a new cultural milieu for black men certainly does seem to imply the separation of large Negro communities from whites in the huge urban centers of the country—and this time by Negro choice instead of white residential discrimination.

THE IMPACT OF BLACK POWER

What this new crisis means for Negro leadership today is not altogether clear. King seems to think that the Black Power leadership does not reflect any sizable segment of Negro opinion.

His view was strongly supported by the results of the 1966 *Newsweek* poll of the Negroes on the matter of leadership. According to this poll, Martin Luther King remains far ahead of any other Negro leader in popularity. King was approved by 88 per cent of the Negro rank and file and 87 per cent of the Negro leadership group. With the rank and file, Roy Wilkins also maintained his following, but the new militants had significant followings too. Charles Evers was approved by 54 per cent and both Carmichael and McKissick were approved by 19 per cent. The younger militants showed even sharper gains among the sampling of Negro leaders. This group gave a 68 per cent approval to Evers, and McKissick and Carmichael both received more than 30 per cent approval from those polled. This was accompanied by a significant drop in the popularity of Roy Wilkins. Furthermore, although nearly 60 per cent of the Negroes favor the method of non-violence and only 5 per cent favored the black nationalists, at least 25 percent do favor the idea of Black Power and among the younger and lower income Negroes, 31 per cent favored the idea. Still, 64 per cent of the rank-and-file Negroes opposed strictly black organization as did 74 per cent of the leadership. Moreover, 81 per cent of Negroes favor continued collaboration with whites. The picture that emerged from the poll led the analysts to conclude that while Black Power as a slogan does have appeal to Negroes, neither its program nor its leaders have captured much of a following.[8]

But perhaps the polls do not tell the whole story. It appears that there *are* significant changes brewing in the mood of the Negro community, and that a major shift has occurred over the last two or three years. Moreover, this change in mood and strategy seems to reflect a growing influence of the Black Power ideology throughout the Negro community.

Essentially there is an increasing emphasis upon the necessity for blacks to organize and act for themselves, and this is apparently accompanied by a diminishing role for white liberals in Negro strategy. For example, it is utterly clear that with the election of Carmichael as head of SNCC in May 1966 and the election of Floyd McKissick as head of CORE in March 1966, two of the "mainstream" civil rights organizations moved dramatically toward an ideological stance that is more sharply ethnocentric than had previously been the case.[9] As a result it is becoming increasingly difficult for whites to participate in the leadership of these organizations.

The SCLC under the leadership of Martin Luther King was really the first mass-based civil rights organization. King has long been committed to the strategy of direct action, but he has consistently welcomed white support in his demonstrations. Recently, however, there have been some indications that King may be moving more toward a black "in-group" emphasis.

When King moved out of the South into the Chicago ghetto, he encountered a new but even more difficult kind of resistance. In contrast to Southern officials, the Chicago mayor and other officials welcomed him to the city. Mayor Richard J. Daley even sent out a fact sheet showing what his administration had already done.[10] King's strategy, as we have said before, depends on contrast—the contrast between non-violent protesting Negroes and violent recalcitrant white officials. When officials offer protection against the howling mobs, the contrast is less effective, and the search begins for more immediately effective means of action. This might explain why King joined forces with the Black Muslims in Chicago to organize rent strikes, but King's *own words* spoke of the necessity for *Negroes* to unite in search of solutions for mutual problems.[11]

He also agreed later that what the Mississippi Negro needed most was to transform his powerlessness into economic and political power.[12]

By August 1967, King was sounding even more militant in his

9. McKissick's understanding of "Black Power" differs only slightly from that of Carmichael and Karenga. (*Transcript,* "Meet the Press," Aug. 21, 1966, pp. 18–19.)

10. *New York Times,* March 24, 1966, p. 33.

11. Ibid. July 25, 1966, p. 18.

12. Ibid. June 20, 1966, p. 17.

approach to change in American society. In a speech delivered in Atlanta, Georgia, King revealed that he planned to disrupt the functioning of cities in order to create a non-violent confrontation between Negroes and the federal government. Even though King offered this suggestion specifically as an alternative to violence, it is obvious that even widespread non-violent disruption of cities represents a considerably more militant stance than orderly marching protests.[13]

Still it must be remembered that King has remained critical of what he calls "black supremacy" sentiments in the statements of Carmichael and other more militant leaders. He is certain that Negroes want to get into the mainstream of American life and that the separatist leanings of Carmichael and others do not represent the leanings of American Negroes.[14]

With respect to some second-level leaders in SCLC, however, the Black Power "line" is more evident. It was reported that King's Chicago staff sounded "more and more like SNCC and CORE workers." [15] Furthermore, the Reverend James Bevel, a top SCLC aide, sounded all the familiar Black Power themes in a discussion on the campus of Pomona College early in 1967.[16] His appeal was to the necessity for black people to gain power through their own efforts in order to secure their rights against a recalcitrant white society.

What is true of the SCLC is also true of the older civil rights organizations to some degree. The Whitney Young who proposed the so-called "Domestic Marshall Plan" certainly reflects much more militance than the Whitney Young who had formerly led the Urban League to concentrate on welfare services to the Negro family. Young does not countenance any talk of separatism either, but he is increasingly focusing upon distinctly

13. Ibid. Aug. 16, 1967, p. 1.
14. Ibid. May 28, 1966, p. 1.
15. "Violence in the City," *The New Republic* (Vol. 155, nos. 4, 5), July 30, 1966, p. 6.
16. "Urban America: Crisis and Opportunity," A Conference at Pomona College, Claremont, California, Feb. 23–5, 1967.

Negro problems rather than general problems in society.[17] This would certainly mean that he has moved out of the "racial dip-lomat" classification into the "race man" classification.

Roy Wilkins of the NAACP certainly remains close to the "racial diplomat" pattern. However, in a speech at the NAACP convention in July 1967, Roy Wilkins defended the role of mili-tance in the Civil Rights movements.

> In spite of their raucous activity, shoddy techniques and over-simplification of complex issues they have shaken up Negroes and whites, both of whom badly needed the treat-ment. Their service outweighs their disservice.[18]

While this statement by no means indicates a militant stance on the part of Wilkins, it certainly expresses much more sympathy for the new militance than his previous public utterances had evidenced.

Local NAACP leadership reflects outright militancy. By Feb-ruary 1966, a *New York Times* writer could comment that "ex-perts in racial relations considered it significant that the top positions of the NAACP's largest state organization have re-cently been entrusted to a younger and more aggressive man." [19] The militance of Charles Evers, state director of the NAACP in Mississippi, is well known. These cases could probably be duplicated at the local levels of leadership throughout the coun-try, and the message has found its way even to the top echelons of NAACP leadership.[20]

17. For example, Young's testimony before the House Committee on Education and Labor, April 14, 1964, as reported in Francis Broderick and August Meier, eds., *Negro Protest Thought in the Twentieth Century* (New York: The Bobbs-Merrill Co., Inc., 1965), pp. 83-90.
18. *New York Times*, July 11, 1967, Sec. I, p. 15.
19. Ibid. Feb. 21, 1966, p. 42.
20. At a conference on "The Tragic Gap," the new impatience and mounting disillusionment with legal remedies were noted by Jack Green-berg. (*New York Times*, May 17, 1966, p. 21.) In addition, it was reported by persons who attended the Black Power Conference from Negro organi-zations in Watts that all of the mainline civil rights organizations sent representatives to the Conference which was held in Newark in July 1967.

Two other groups in which the change is visible are the Negro literary community and the Negro clergy. With respect to Negro literary circles, one could cite the names of Ralph Ellison and James Baldwin especially, but for purposes of contrast it is instructive to compare articles by Langston Hughes, a figure in the "Negro Renaissance," and John Killens, a contemporary Negro novelist.[21] The article by Hughes appeared in *The Nation* in 1926, and Hughes urged that Negroes cease to think badly of blackness and to concentrate on the contributions made by black men to American culture. Killens, in contrast, not only argues for pride in being black but reflects a basic contempt for whites. No longer is the writer making an appeal to the nation to tolerate blacks and to recognize their contributions. He appeals only to blacks to see themselves as they are and denounces those who try to be like whites. From apology to fierce pride and contempt for white values—this is the change in stance and mood that occurred during the span of only three and one-half decades.

Negro clergymen, in a statement issued on July 31, 1966, had this to say about "Black Power":

> As black men who were long ago forced out of the white church to create and wield "black power," we fail to understand the emotional quality of the outcry of some clergy against the use of the term today. It is not enough to answer that "integration" is the solution. For it is precisely the nature of the operation of power under some forms of integration which is being challenged. . . . We understand the growing demand of Negro and white youth for a more honest kind of integration; one which increases rather than decreases the capacity of the disinherited to participate with power in all of the structures of our common life. Without this capacity to *participate with power* —i.e. to have some organized political and economic strength to really influence people with whom one interacts—integration is not meaningful. For the issue is not one

21. Included as selections in Broderick and Meier, *Negro Protest Thought* . . . , pp. 91–7, 348–57.

of racial balance but of honest interracial interactions. For this kind of interaction to take place, all people need power, whether black or white.[22]

The remainder of the statement is conciliatory but firm. It is clear that there is no marked disapproval of the basic ethnocentrism that is the core of "Black Power." Yet this power is to be used to create a stronger America in which all can live together as one. The response is especially significant in light of the fact that it represents the clergy's concern with the here and now—a marked contrast to the caricature of Negro clergy as purveyors of a heavenly dream. It is significant too because it focuses upon the basic premise of Black Power leaders that integration is irrelevant and that Negroes *as Negroes* must organize to gain power.

In addition to the indices we have already mentioned, there is the growing unanimity of mood among the masses of Negroes that crops up in many ways.[23] Perhaps the best example of this growing single-mindedness of the developing ethnocentrism was

22. *New York Times,* May 31, 1966, Sec. E, p. 5.
23. Examples abound. Dick Gregory: "If Americans want law and order without justice, they are going to have to have one cop per Negro in America." (*New York Times,* Feb. 12, 1966, p. 56.) Lincoln Lynch, Associate Director of CORE: "We need black people to stand on their own two feet. . . . History has shown that if you're really depending on the vast majority of whites to help, you're really leaning on a broken reed." (*New York Times,* June 22, 1966, p. 24.) Gloria Laney, Field Secretary for SNCC at an N.Y.U. lawyers' seminar: "Today most of us have come to the conclusion that integration is not meaningful . . . what we decided to do was to move into communities and build up political, cultural and economic strength." (*New York Times,* June 5, 1966, p. 75.) James Phipps, a Mississippi Negro, denounced the white man's government and praised Jomo Kenyatta. (*New York Times,* Feb. 7, 1966, p. 1.) Thomas Jones, a Civil Court Judge in New York: "Negro people are angry. . . . I'm angry too." (*New York Times,* Feb. 5, 1966, p. 17.) Ruth Goling, Asst. to Brooklyn Borough President, Abe Stark: "We've got to have something concrete now, not tomorrow, yesterday." (Ibid.) The police commission in Los Angeles tried to hold a conference with Negro leaders. The meeting was thrown into a fist-shaking uproar over the failure of the commission to invite black nationalist leaders. (*New York Times,* June 12, 1966, p. 85.)

the response of the Negro community to the "Adam Clayton Powell Affair." Negro politicians, men in the street, organization heads and clergymen all raised their voice in one mighty protest of the censure and unseating of Powell by his fellow Congressmen. Whatever the other issues might be, the issue that was most clear to them was that one of their own had been singled out for what they considered to be very harsh treatment in the highest law-making body in the land, simply because he was black.[24] In this case it was almost with one voice that the Negro community had spoken, and the speech was clearly a manifesto on the disillusionment of Negroes with white allies and the need for Negroes to mobilize their own power to counter the new forms of discrimination that cannot be solved in alliance with the enemy.

What all this seems to indicate is a growing consensus among American Negroes that is compatible to a greater extent with Black Power strategy than had previously been the case. The consensus includes agreement that Negroes must rely more and more on their own initiative and their own leadership and organizations to reach the goals they have determined for themselves. The extent to which liberal whites can be included in the "Negro Revolt" is still a very much debated issue, but the move toward more reliance on in-group identity and effort is common to nearly all of the Negro leaders. Furthermore, the consensus seems to include some general agreement on the matter of strategy. Negroes must turn their attention to the very important tasks of political and economic organization. Again, the question as to whether this organization is to be done with a view toward participation in America's traditional two-party system or whether it should be an effort to organize an all-Negro third party is still open.[25] But there is no disagreement about the

24. See *East Harlem Protestant Parish Special Report*, April 1, 1967.
25. The meeting in Los Angeles on Feb. 19, 1967, to which I have already referred, and the recent moves of Negro leaders in response to Powell's ouster all indicate that a third party is certainly a possibility. (See David Welsh, "South: Election Night in Lowndes County," *Ramparts* (January 1967), pp. 12 ff.)

need for Negroes to turn their attention to grass-roots organization. As Bayard Rustin has put it, the civil rights struggle has
moved from "protest to politics," and this marks a very important shift of strategy in itself.[26]

The shift in strategy among all civil rights groups has an important bearing upon the understanding of Black Power. If
there is an emerging consensus on strategy in the Negro community as we have described it, then it is also true that the term
"Black Power" is coming to mean the political organization of
the Negro community. Whatever else is involved in future
black-white relations in America, this much is certain: Blacks
are determined to get more power and to exercise power more
effectively. This means that the future of American race relations is interwoven with the dynamics of power in intergroup
relations.

Hubert Blalock suggested an excellent theoretical model for
understanding the components of power that are integral to
minority-majority relations.[27] This will enable us to see more
clearly what might be involved in the Negroes' quest for power
and what some of the consequences might be.

Blalock first distinguishes between what he calls power potential and power exercise. To avoid confusion he suggests that
power potential be referred to as *resources* and power exercise
as *power*. Obviously, the degree to which one can exercise
power is dependent upon the resources for power at his dis-
posal, but this is not the only variable in power. The other variable is *mobilization*, or getting the resources into action. This
has to do with the degree of unity, motivation, and strategy that
is available to the power agent in a given situation. In any given
majority-minority relationship, then, there will be at least four

26. See Bayard Rustin, "From Protest to Politics: The Future of the Civil
Rights Movement," *Commentary* (Vol. 32, no. 2), February 1965, pp.
25–31.
27. This is material from an unpublished discussion of Blalock's theoretical model. Professor Blalock has indicated to me that further discussion
of the model will appear in his forthcoming book. (Hubert Blalock, Jr.,
Toward a Theory of Minority Group Relations (New York: Wiley,
1967), Chapter 4.)

power variables which function to determine the ratio of power between the two groups—minority resources, minority mobilization, dominant resources, and dominant mobilization.

Blalock then utilizes these variables to construct a theoretical model relating these variables to inequality, segregation, and overt conflict, and a copy of the finished model appears below.

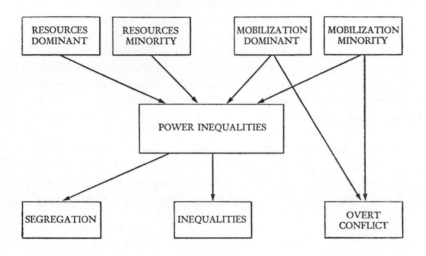

Power Variables and Dependent Variables

From this model it is apparent that there are two ways in which a group may get more power. They might increase their resources or they might raise the level of mobilization within the group. Furthermore, the model clearly shows that power inequality is directly related to the structures of discrimination and segregation. Therefore, if the goal of a group is to remove discrimination and segregation, the power balance must be altered. Either one's own power must be increased or the opponent's power must be decreased.

In the third chapter I indicated that the resources of the Negroes in the United States have been immeasurably strength-

ened. In comparison with the early 1900's the Negroes have better education, better jobs, more money, and a fantastically im-
proved legal situation today. In spite of these new resources,
however, the Negroes are sorely limited in comparison to
whites. Furthermore, it is becoming more and more obvious
that even the accelerated pace of change over the past two and
one-half decades is not sufficient to counter the growing despair
of the Negro masses, nor have the strategies used really cracked
the tough problems of *de facto* segregation, such as inferior
schools, poor services, high unemployment rates, and other indices of ghetto deprivation. With all the support of white liberals in the changes of the 1950's and 1960's, the life chances of
the majority of Negroes in the United States not only lag behind those of whites but actually lag further behind than they
did in 1950 in many cases. Negro leaders, therefore, have rightly
recognized that the most promising avenue for further alteration of the structures of discrimination in the United States is
mobilization of Negro power. If they are successful in multi-
plying the mobilization component in the power model, it
would appear that their actual share of power will be increased,
and hence it would be more possible to realize group aims.

In order to mobilize Negro power, the leadership must counter the pervading sense of inferiority and futility that is characteristic of the outlook of so many of the people in the Negro
ghettos. In other words, before the apathy of American Negroes can be overcome, black people must be convinced that
they are really equal to whites and that something can be done.
Hence there have been appeals to Negro history and to the
goodness of being black along with the constant reassurance
that something indeed can be done if Negroes unite and work
together, and as a result, there does appear to be a heightened
interest in power politics in the Negro communities. The appeal
to black unity has always been successful in arousing a Negro
following, and it has apparently lost little of its appeal today.

On the basis of the Blalock model, then, the Black Power
strategy that seems to be agreed upon by the majority of Negro
leaders should be successful in altering the balance of power and

ultimately in changing the persisting patterns of segregation. White power leaders will be forced to negotiate with Negro power, and the concessions made will not be defined solely in white men's terms. When the Negro has his share of power, the changes will be dictated by what the Negro demands, at least in part, and this should bring him significantly closer to his goals.

Yet, the model also suggests that there is danger in the mobilization of power. There is always the possibility that any mobilization of power by the minority will be countered by mobilization in the dominant group, and the straight lines from the mobilization variables to overt conflict clearly indicate that rapid or intense mobilization may create heightened opposition and intense conflict. It is not difficult to follow some of the implications here. White liberal support has been an important Negro resource in the past. If conflict becomes overt or violent, the Negro may suddenly realize that the increase in mobilization has been accompanied by a decrease in this resource. Moreover, a high degree of mobilization may actually result in Negroes refusing white help.

The question then becomes: Can Negro leaders persist in the mobilization of Negro power and at the same time hold their resources constant? In other words, can the Negro be politically competitive with the whites and still co-operate with some whites? Unfortunately, although Negro leaders seem determined that it can and will be done, recent studies of in-group formation do not augur well for the future.

Muzafer and Carolyn Sherif conducted an experiment involving boys at summer camp. The boys were divided into two groups, the Red Devils and the Bull Dogs, and they were immediately directed into a whole series of competitive situations. As soon as the groups were formed, their friendship preferences began to be determined by group membership. Old friendship patterns disappeared and the circle of friends was confined to the in-group members. When competition was introduced into the group relationship the in-group members began to develop strong out-group stereotypes of the members of the opposing group. Such names as "dirty rats," "cheaters," and other "bad names" were consistently applied to the opposing groups. Under the stress of sustained competition, the opposing groups actually began to attack each other's dining tables and living quarters.[28]

Although the study was made under very carefully controlled conditions which only simulated actual group formation and conflict, it does offer some very helpful insight into the problem before us here. The study gives strong indications that the process of in-group formation under the stress of continuing competition tends not only to result in unifying the in-group, but also seems necessarily to involve a growing antipathy for the opposing group members. This means that it is highly likely that the division of the "groups" in America into black and white under the broad competition for all kinds of power and goods is likely to increase the "in-group" ties of both whites and blacks. It indicates also that as the competition continues and takes on more overt forms, the result will be a growing anti-white sentiment among Negroes and a growing anti-black sentiment among whites.

This, then, is the dilemma of Black Power. On the one hand, all the Negro gains in the past several decades have been the result of Negro-white co-operation at all levels of organization and participation. Civil rights organizations have succeeded in mobilizing Negroes and liberal white support to bring about broad changes in the legal structures of the United States. On the other hand, the growing expectations and impatience of Negroes together with increasing white resistance seem to dictate stronger pro-Negro organization and more direct competitive strategy at all levels of the operation of democracy. This, in turn, seems to carry with it the heightening of conflict which is dissipating much white support. At the same time, the appeal to a uni-racial assault on discrimination heightens Negro ethnocentrism and anti-white feelings, thus narrowing the possibilities of white participation, even to those whites who remain willing to participate.

It appears that Negroes are determined to move ahead in a uni-

28. Muzafer and Carolyn Sherif, *Groups in Harmony and Tension.*

racial assault on the structures of discrimination, and white resistance seems to be mounting.[29] Even liberal whites appear to
be withholding financial support in the hopes of "slowing
down" the increasingly ethnocentric and militant movement in
civil rights organizations.[30] This is really a futile gesture, however, for no Negro leader now has even a remote chance of
mobilizing black support if he allows whites to control him with
purse strings, and there is no indication that this will change.
Indeed, if I read the signs correctly, white resistance simply
increases the Negroes' conviction that they must mobilize their
own group, and this means that it is very likely that there will
be an increase in the number of Negro leaders who take a militant stance.

Therefore, the prospects for *broad* interracial co-operation
are very dim indeed. The combined effects of the increasingly
ethnocentric stance of the Negro community and their strategy
shift from protest to politics mean that American black-white
relations have definitely moved from an era of accommodation
and interracial co-operation to an era of intensifying racial conflict.

THE NEW NEGRO PLURALISM

It has become clear that Black Power is much more than a
brainchild of Stokeley Carmichael or Adam Clayton Powell,
and it is no mere slogan that will pass away in time. Black Power

29. Some indications are the increasingly ugly mood of whites in the face
of the demonstrations in the northern and border cities (e.g. Chicago and
Louisville); the recalcitrance of Alabama before recent government directives for desegregation of schools; the "George Wallace phenomenon"; and the recent moves to repeal the Rumford Act (Fair Housing)
in California. There are dozens of others, but these suffice to make the
point. The book by Fred Powledge entitled *Black Power—White Resistance: Notes on the New Civil War* (New York: World Publishing Co.,
1967), appeared too late to be included in the text, but it does give a
very disturbing picture of the white response to Negro militance.
30. *New York Times*, July 25, 1966, p. 1. All civil rights organizations
have experienced a drop in financial contributions, and these have largely
come from liberal whites.

signifies the reality of change in the Negro community. As such
it is a developing ethnocentrism which is transforming Negro
group consciousness, and it represents a focus upon Negro
unity. Furthermore, it is a strategy for social change that focuses upon political organization. Perhaps in broader perspective, however, it is most useful to think of Black Power as rep-
resenting a change in minority aim. This will enable us not only
to understand more clearly what *has* happened in the Negro
community, but it may shed some further light on the possibilities for the future.

To understand what kind of change is involved in the minority aim of American Negroes today, I return to Louis Wirth's
typology which was discussed in the Introduction.[31] It will be
recalled that Wirth suggested a fourfold typology of minority
aims: (1) pluralistic; (2) assimilationist; (3) secessionist; and
(4) militant. At the outset, we can eliminate the secessionist
and militant aims from consideration. It is evident that by far
the majority of Negroes reject the Black Muslim program for
separate Negro states, and the Garvey "back to Africa" emphasis has been transformed into a slogan for cultural renewal.
Moreover, even the most militant black nationalists probably do
not think in terms of a take-over of the United States. As Adam
Clayton Powell put it recently, "Black Power does not by any
means suggest the black people will take over the whole
nation." [32] This means that the minority aim for the Negroes in
the United States is either assimilationist or pluralistic.

It is important for the sake of clarity to recall the chief
difference between these types of aims. The pluralistic minority
generally seeks toleration of its differences by the dominant
group, but the toleration sought is not to be based on condescension but upon the fullest measure of equality in all matters
of culture and power. On the whole, pluralistic minorities reject
the idea of intermarriage, and intimate social intercourse with
the dominant group is discouraged. In other words, when a
minority begins to develop a pluralistic aim, they are character-

31. See Chapter I of this book, pp. 15–18.
32. *New York Times*, July 19, 1966, p. 22.

ized by extreme ethnocentrism, and this goes hand in hand with demands for economic and political equality.

In contrast, the assimilationist minority seeks full incorporation into the larger society. The goal is full acceptance by the dominant group and ultimately merger into the total society. Assimilationist minorities do not disapprove of intermarriage and the merger of culture is seen as desirable and wholesome.

It is important to remember that the assimilationist aim in the minority is heavily dependent upon the good graces of the dominant or majority group. Assimilation presupposes that the dominant group either desires, or will at least allow, increasingly social intimacy and racial amalgamation. An assimilationist minority is doomed to frustration unless the majority's "conscience" drives them to accept assimilation. Therefore, as long as assimilation is the aim of the minority, the racial problem is a majority problem, or as Myrdal put it, in the context of American race relations, it is peculiarly a white man's problem.

The persistence of the pluralistic minority aim also rests somewhat upon the flexibility of the majority in its aims. As Wirth has pointed out, a strongly pluralistic minority will be driven in the direction of secession or militance if its aim is frustrated.[33] Yet, the alternatives of secession or militance, while very costly to the minority, may be too costly for the majority also. Hence, the problem of race relations may be removed from the level of appeal to the majority conscience to the level of ultimatum based upon the majority's own self-interest.

On the basis of their studies of minorities in America, Wagley and Harris typed the aim of the American Negro minority as assimilationist.[34] They were a group cut off from their historical heritage, and the only culture they knew was white culture. They were slaves and they were taught that they were inferior. Later they were freed only to be segregated and to become the victims of discrimination. Therefore, the only way up and out of misery was to merge with the whites, and Negro aspirations were cast in that direction.

33. Wirth, "The Problem of Minority Groups," in *The Science of Man* . . . , p. 364.
34. Wagley and Harris, *Minorities* . . . pp. 291-2.

All of the new developments I have discussed to this point, however, indicate a change from the Negro assimilationist aim. The strategy of power politics requires mobilization and that mobilization rests upon the development of a stronger Negro ethnocentrism. Ethnocentrism under the pressure of power competition involves increasing antipathy toward the out-group. In light of this, one would certainly expect that the interest in merging with white society will continue to diminish within the Negro group. At the same time, there will also be a new appreciation of the glory of being black; a developing interest in the historical heritage of the Negroes which is rooted in Africa; and increasing demands that the contributions of the Negro heritage to American culture be fully appreciated.

These developments have resulted in a decreasing emphasis upon integration, understood as racial balance, as a "cure-all" for the American dilemma, and there will be increased pressure for separation by the Negroes themselves. However, the separation is seen as the base for new power to demand equality in all things cultural and political. Negroes are not counting on white consciences any more, nor will they accept white condescension. The full measure of human equality is the minimum they demand.

Therefore, the new stance and strategy indicate that a movement toward pluralism is under way, and hence the crucial problem for American race relations is no longer the gap between segregation and the "American Creed." As Kenneth Clark has said, "the new American dilemma is the dilemma of power," [35] and the prospects for solving that dilemma without severe conflict are not very bright. Whatever is the final outcome of pluralism, it will mean dramatic social change and a heightening of conflict,[36] and men of good intention will find themselves increasingly frustrated as many of the old patterns of interracial co-operation disappear.

35. Kenneth Clark, "The Dilemma of Power," in Parsons and Clark, *The Negro American*, p. xi.
36. Wagley and Harris, *Minorities* . . . , p. 288. The authors think that a pluralistic solution of minority problems almost always perpetuates and intensifies conflict.

Finally, it is well to bear in mind that a minority aim is never a static or unanimous thing. Therefore, what I have said here is descriptive of *directions* only. When this qualification is made, however, it can be said with confidence that in the minority as a whole there has been a change in aim, and today white Americans face a new Negro pluralism.

V

The Ethical Dimensions of
the New Negro Pluralism

This interpretation of Black Power has now assumed several dimensions. From one standpoint, Black Power represents a contemporary manifestation of a highly ethnocentric strain of Negro leadership, including such men as Stokeley Carmichael, Malcolm X, and Ron Karenga. It is not possible, however, to understand this movement apart from the context in which it developed. Hence, another dimension of my interpretation of Black Power has been some discussion of the historical and cultural changes in America, of which Black Power is both a symbol and a product. In a third dimension, I have interpreted Black Power as a symbol of very important changes within the *total* Negro community as such. Enlarging the focus to include widely representative Negro leadership, I have described the changes that have occurred in stance and strategy which constitute what I have labeled a "new era" in American race relations. Then, on the basis of Louis Wirth's typology, I interpreted the whole picture of change as the development of a new Negro pluralism.

In this chapter, I shall give some attention to the demands and the goals of the new Negro pluralism. Here and there in the discussion, some of the Negroes' demands have, of course, become quite clear. But as a final dimension of my interpretation of Black Power as a minority development, I want to set these demands in the context of what I believe to be the broad ethical implications of the new Negro pluralism.

Essentially, the new Negro pluralism is seeking equality, and this is in keeping with the whole equalitarian movement that is going on in the United States today.[1] It is not surprising, then, that Negro goals are focused upon two dimensions of equality which are integrally related, political equality and equality of opportunity, both of which have been part of the American dream for some time. But the goals of Negro leadership today cannot be understood fully, unless one is aware of the overriding importance of the limitations of the total group status of the Negro people.

Throughout the history of this nation, black people have been able to hope for only a limited version of the American dream. The upward movement of the black man has been always determined by the abiding fact of "caste" which has been institutionalized in legal and less formal ways. What the new pluralism wants is an end to this limitation, and this is what makes the quest for political equality and equality of opportunity take on new meaning. I shall, therefore, begin with a discussion of the problem of caste limitations on the Negro and then proceed to discuss the traditional goals of Americans as they are modified by the demand for eradication of caste in American society.

THE PROBLEM OF CASTE

The American "color-caste system" originated on the plantations of colonial America. Black men came to this country, for the most part, as property, and at no time was there any widespread move to affirm their equal humanity, nor was there much pressure to accord to them equal rights. As long as black men remained property, the whole issue of equal rights could not arise. Even the Constitution did not view them as fully human when determining the population count.

We have already noted that the Civil War and Reconstruction did not really do much immediately to alter the status of the Negro *vis à vis* whites. Some individuals, it is true, rose rapidly

1. See Alan P. Grimes, *Equality in America* (New York: Oxford University Press, 1964).

to places of prominence, but the end of Reconstruction found both legal and social controls established that perpetuated the caste system. Negroes were kept "in their place" because they were inferior—and many argued that they should be kept "in their place" because God had willed it that way.[2]

The "caste" system that emerged was the subject of a study done by John Dollard in the middle 1930's which documented the caste character of the position of the Negro in a number of ways.[3] Dollard discovered that there was an ideology upon which the separation of blacks and whites was based, one which consigned the Negro to an inferior rank among humans and attributed to him a series of very definite stereotypes. Moreover, there was a well-established and universally practiced "etiquette system" which defined behavior for the black and the caste members and which outlined the privileges that the caste system assigned to both groups. Within both castes there was a fairly well developed class system as well. This meant that within the caste there was considerable leeway for upward mobility on the part of individual Negroes, but that mobility never was conceived as reaching beyond the well-defined behavioral patterns of the caste system, and the most educated and qualified Negro had to "keep his place" or face severe reprisals. Outside the caste structures there was little legal protection for Negroes and occupational diversity was allowed only insofar as Negroes developed parallel occupational diversification to that of whites in order to serve the needs of the Negro community.

What this meant was that the worth of whites and the opportunities of whites were considered on one scale and the worth of Negroes and their opportunities were considered on quite another. Negro worth and opportunity could never really be compared to those of whites, because the caste system made these comparisons impossible. Even though some Negroes had better opportunity than others, some had better self-evaluation than others, and some were permitted more entree to the white world than others, the color line generally held fast. There was

2. See Carroll, *The Negro a Beast*.
3. John Dollard, *Caste and Class in Southern Town*.

an upper limit to the Negroes' aspirations and accomplishments which was determined simply by virtue of their being black.

Now the developments of the last three and a half decades have certainly done much to undermine the particular form of caste structure that Dollard discovered. The Negro movement into the North where there were no legal caste distinctions and the changing of national legal structures have cleared away most of the formal caste structure of this nation. But unfortunately new forms of caste limitations have emerged to perpetuate the limitation upon Negro aspirations and opportunities. The most obvious of these has been the development of ghettos in the urban centers of this country. We have already noted that a great proportion of Negroes in the United States today live in these ghettos and that the signs point toward a continuation and acceleration of ghetto development.

What makes this a problem even for the separatists among the new Negro leaders, is that ghetto life is almost always synonymous with deprived life. Ghettos have poorer housing, poorer education, less employment, more crime, poorer health and recreational facilities, and poorer public services. Hence it is not the separation that makes the ghetto the contemporary caste device, but rather the oppressive conditions of ghetto life that create apathy, despair, and indifference among the Negro people who live there.

This means that soon the majority of black people in the United States will not only be separated physically from whites, but that they will be effectively confined in an informal caste-like situation that sets the patterns of behavior for its members and sets the limits upon their aspirations and accomplishments as effectively as the older formal and informal structures that have done the job since the time of slavery.

Of course, the increased mobility of large numbers of Negroes cannot be ignored entirely. It is true that Negroes today have better housing, better education, and better jobs than ever before. But I have already indicated that this is rather meaningless when one puts beside the gains of Negroes the gains of whites in comparable periods. The "color gap" is still there, and we have already noted that some experts think that it is, in fact, widening. Thus, the indices we have mentioned are strong indications that the Negro's caste status persists, and that the circle of caste still coincides with the circle of black color.

Precisely because the Negro's caste position depends to a great measure upon color for identification, it has been impossible and remains difficult for him to be assimilated into the mainstream of American institutions. This is why it makes no sense at all to compare the problem of the Negro with the problem of non-colored minorities. The one thing that cannot be removed by acculturation is color, and it is color, not culture, that sets the American Negro apart from his white fellow citizens.[4]

The effects of this caste system are obvious from the discussion in the previous chapters. The pervading fact of caste lies at the base of both the Negroes' own identity problem and the objective indices of segregation and discrimination. The "vicious circle" of caste has kept the Negro low in all the measures of opportunity, and it has ensured that only a few, if any, did well. The etiquette and ideology of the caste system have been constant reminders that his white counterparts regarded his failure not as their doing, but due to the Negro's own imcompetence and inherent inferiority. And Negroes have tended to accept that image of themselves.

Until the present time the only avenue up and out of caste has been assimilation into white society. This has included both the acquisition of white characteristics and the elimination of Negro ones, and large numbers of Negroes have assumed most of the trappings of the white middle and upper classes and moved out

4. Even the other coloreds in the United States have never been singled out as the Negroes have. The Japanese, during the Second World War, were badly treated and Mexican-Americans are experiencing a caste problem too, but *no* group has remained at the lower levels of social distance as consistently as Negroes. (See, for example, E. S. Bogardus, "Changes in Racial Distances," *International Journal of Opinion and Attitude Research* (Vol. 1, 1947), pp. 55–62.) The social distances of whites from others seem to be highly related to the degree of visibility and the darkness of color. (Allport, *The Nature of Prejudice*, pp. 128–34.)

of the ghettos into white neighborhoods. But these successful Negroes have always been treated as exceptions, and their success has done nothing to remove the onus of caste. Blackness was still identified with low income, lack of education, high crime, and the other indices that characterize ghetto life. Furthermore, the majority of Negroes either remain in the ghetto, or at least are shut out of much of white society, and, as we have observed, it is likely that this will be a continuing fact of life.

The new pluralism, then, represents the determined effort on the part of Negro leadership to come to terms with a persisting fact of life. The Negro is segregated and separated from whites; he will probably remain segregated and separated from whites. What pluralism demands is that this separation shall not mean inferiority, but that black people as a group shall be able to function effectively as citizens in this country; that they shall share fully in the goods of this society; and that their distinctive contributions as black people shall be acknowledged as equally important as those of whites in the formation and development of a truly pluralistic American culture.

BLACK POLITICAL EQUALITY

The determination that Negroes shall function effectively as citizens requires in the first instance that they shall be able to participate fully in the decisions about the shape of the society in which they live. In other words, Negroes must develop political equality, and it is here that the major efforts of Negro leadership are presently being focused.

At this point Negroes are in the grandest tradition of American democracy, for political equality has been the primary focus of equality in America since its birth as a nation. What is the nature of political equality in this country? According to Hans Morgenthau, "political equality means equal access to political rule." [5] This means that no American citizen can be per-

5. Hans Morgenthau, *The Purpose of American Politics* (New York: Alfred A. Knopf, 1960), p. 19. Some of the material in this section is from

manently dominated by others. He may be ruled by them
today, but he may rule them tomorrow. "There were and there
are today, no permanent rulers and no permanent subjects in
America." [6] This is true because "American equality is equality
in freedom. . . . By making power equally accessible to all, it
makes all both potentially powerful and free." [7] Equality in
freedom, then, means that Americans are to be free from
tyranny because they are ensured the right of individual participation in the political decision-making process. This is the
ideal way of thinking about political relationships that has been
the inspiration of the American political experiment.[8]

But the ideal is not an empty one. If it represents a way of
thinking about how political participation should be ordered it
is also a method for implementing that order.[9] In other words,
the institutions that have been developed by Americans to implement "equality in freedom," are what gives the ideal its substance, and they are the means by which one can appreciate the
uniqueness of American political equality.

The primary political device to ensure equality is majority
rule. This is the foundation of representative government, for
without the consent of free men to abide by the will of the majority, representative government is impossible. However, majority rule in American democracy has a unique function. It
does not mean that a vote must be taken on every issue. And
there is no implied claim of the inerrancy of the judgment of
the majority in all things. On the contrary, majority rule, in
American democracy, is a device to ensure that the rulers are
responsible to the ruled. The power of the ruler to rule is both
established and restrained by the power of popular consent. The
government can rule as it sees fit so long as the majority has the

my unpublished dissertation, "Reapportionment in American Democracy:
A Critical Examination From the Perspective of Christian Ethics," pre-
sented to the faculty of Yale University in candidacy for the Doctor of
Philosophy Degree, Spring 1965, pp. 128ff.
6. Morgenthau, *The Purpose of American Politics*, p. 19.
7. Ibid. p. 20.
8. Ibid. pp. 22–3.
9. Ibid. p. 21.

"constitutional power to change the government and its policies by registering dissent." [10] In other words, majority rule is not founded on the belief that all wisdom and virtue belong to the majority, but upon the belief that power will be responsible only when it is checked or restrained.

However, there is more to political equality in America than restraint upon the government by the majority of the people. American political equality guarantees that certain basic ground rules of political competition shall apply equally to all citizens. Such provisions as freedom of speech, assembly, and petition are not subject to the will of the majority for their continued existence. They are the basis of the legitimacy of any particular majority ruling. Therefore, while the device of majority rule means that Americans shall be free from tyrannical rulers, the Bill of Rights and similar minority protections mean that neither shall dissenting individuals be subjected to unlimited tyranny of the majority. Each person is free to try to form his own majority through the exercise of the basic ground rules of democracy.

In summary, the institutional devices which Americans have developed in their quest for political equality represent an effort to distribute political power in such a way that the political process will reflect the ideal. On the one hand, the notion of majority rule is an attempt to distribute power between government and people in such a way that no government may remain in power without the consent of the people. On the other hand, the minority protections represent the attempt to distribute power among the individual citizens in such a way that none is denied the right to register his dissent.

If this description of American political equality were the whole story the situation for the Negro would be most encouraging, for this decade has been a time of great progress in expanding the Constitutional rights of Negroes and in extending individual Constitutional protections to them. This is not to say, of course, that today all Negroes can vote easily, but a whole series of Supreme Court decisions and legislative actions have

10. Ibid. pp. 245–6.

certainly made it possible for Negroes to vote more and to have their votes counted equally throughout the whole primary and election process.[11] However, when the basic rights of individuals are protected two problems remain.

The first problem has to do with the nature of the American political process. Since its founding the necessity of group organization has been a part of our system, and the development of the party system has been the institutional device whereby individuals could organize as groups around common interests. Within the party system itself there is also the formation of pressure groups and the bargaining of groups with other groups to form political coalitions.

Here the caste system complicates Negro political equality in an important way. The first badge of group identification for the Negro is his color. Because he is isolated by color caste, he represents a group with a wide range of common interests, and he has become increasingly discouraged by his attempts to bargain within the traditional party structure of the United States. Being fragmented within his own group, and being scattered among various political groupings, he remains at the bottom rung of power in all of his group associations. The exercise of his political power, then, is complicated by a double compromise. He compromises within the local interest group to which he belongs, and then his interests are compromised in the wider coalitions of power when his particular group joins with other groups of similar interests. As long as the Negro remains scattered in his group membership, then, he is at a doubly weak bargaining position. His interests as a Negro are watered-down at the local group level, and then again at the national coalition level.

The new pluralism represents a demand that Negroes be allowed to organize around distinctly Negro interests, because

11. It includes also campaigning, running for office, and the discussion of issues. (See Matthews and Prothro, *Southern Politics*, pp. 37 ff., for an excellent discussion of the various levels of political participation.) All of this has to do with the problem of intensity which will be discussed below.

Negro leaders are certain that this is the only way in which the unique Negro political voice can be heard. They are convinced that 19,000,000 Negro voices which exist throughout the various group organizations of American society will mean very little, while a united Negro group voice could become a very potent factor in the formation of ruling coalitions.

A second problem is what Robert Dahl calls "intensity." [12] Dahl argues that Constitutional forms do not provide any general protection against the deprivation by one group of the freedom desired by another. While the Constitutional forms do determine what groups in principle are to be included in the political process and under what conditions they are to be included, they cannot guarantee that the voice of the group will be heard in an effective way.[13] What guarantees the effectiveness of the group's participation is the intensity of the group's interest in the issues at hand.

Here again caste has complicated the problem of Negro political equality in a very direct way. One of the effects of caste that has already been noted is the apathy among the Negro people which is generated by despair and futility. This apathy is carried over into the political arena also, and until it is countered in some way, Negro political equality will be simply a dream. Hence, the appeal to black interests and black unity that characterizes the new pluralism is a conscious attempt to mobilize Negroes for political participation at many levels, so that their full political expression may come closer to being a reality.

The new pluralism, then, is attacking the problem of Negro political equality in a most realistic way. Negro leaders intend to take full advantage of the proximity of caste-segregated Negroes to develop unity and political strength, and at the same time to initiate programs and propaganda designed to maximize participation in the democratic process. In this way, they hope

12. Robert A. Dahl, *A Preface to Democratic Theory* (Phoenix Ed., Chicago: University of Chicago Press, 1963), pp. 90 ff. A clothbound edition is also available and was first published in 1956.
13. Ibid. pp. 134-7.

to turn the geographical concentration of the Negroes into an effective means of promoting Negro political power. Again, it is important to underscore the fact that the new pluralism does not mean that the Negro will withdraw from the political arena in any way. This should be obvious, but the undertones of separatism in the public statements tend to project a withdrawal or secessionist image. Therefore, I emphasize once more the fact that Negro leaders have rejected any "back to Africa" strategy, and they do not even agree to the Muslim suggestion for developing black states. While some talk of autonomous enclaves in the cities is part of current Black Power conversations, this does not reflect simply separatist sentiments. On the contrary, it is more a reflection of the very necessary judgment that if the Negro is to have political equality now, he must have it in the context of separation. The question then becomes: How, given the fact of segregation, can full political equality be achieved? The answer of the new pluralism is to begin where Negroes are to maximize political equality in the immediately effective way, and this points toward the development of an all-Negro party.

If the development of an all-Negro party in the United States is realized, another problem may emerge. The nature of the problem can best be stated by recalling one of the important points developed in the preceding chapter. There I argued that recent studies in intergroup relations give strong indications that the development of group unity under the pressure of vigorous competition nearly always meant a rise in the alienation of the group from out-groups. This meant that the growing Negro ethnocentrism was inevitably accompanied by increased anti-white feeling among black people. Furthermore, the phenomenon here described, "out-grouping," is by no means confined to one of the groups competing. This indicated that whites also would tend to develop a hostile response to the new Negro self-consciousness, and this, in turn, means that more and more the issues in American political life will be complicated by the growing division between black and white. All of this points toward the possible development of a rigid majority-minority situation in America in which Negroes would be established as the permanent minority. Thus, while Negroes might exercise to the fullest their own political rights, many of their political objectives would be unattainable simply because they are outnumbered ten to one.

Three things need to be said about this problem. In the first place, the gains already made are not likely to be lost in the new Negro quest for political equality. Even though there has been white retrenchment in some cases, it is inconceivable that the so-called "blacklash" would soon reach the proportions that would threaten the gains made by Negroes since 1940. Furthermore, it is likely that there will be *some* continued progress in the advancement of Negro opportunity irrespective of future Negro action. There have been and still are vast numbers of whites who will oppose discrimination for the same reasons that lay behind the fantastic support given to the Civil Rights Bills of 1964-5. The reasons are many and varied, but it is ridiculous to suppose that the mounting Negro pressure for equality now will automatically undercut all the factors that have altered the historical-cultural components of black-white relations in the United States.

Second, the Negroes are willing to gamble on "creative disruption." The Negro minority in this country as yet is not unified nor is it mobilized. When it becomes mobilized and unified, however, it will be further aided by strategic location. Negroes presently are the majority of population in one major city, and by 1980 they will probably represent at least 25 per cent of the population of all the major central city areas in the United States. Moreover, Negroes have less at stake in the continued maintenance of the status quo. None of this is unknown to Negro leadership, and it is no accident that Carmichael and others have responded to the threat of the 90 per cent against the 10 per cent with unmeasured hostility. I have quoted earlier his statement that if Negroes do not get what they ask for, we shall all go down together. This means, I think, that Negroes will gamble more and more on disruption if their legitimate aims are frustrated. And I believe that this will be a fairly effective countermove to increasing white rigidity. One severed power line, or one disrupted freeway, can create instant chaos more easily than we would like to imagine. It is likely that most of us, black and white, would rather avoid this kind of confrontation, but it is important for whites to realize that a minority continually frustrated by inaction on the part of a majority is not likely to be limited by the ground rules of the democratic process.

Finally, on a more hopeful note, it is highly unlikely that whites will ever confront Negroes as a rigidly united majority. There are simply too many lines of group affiliation cutting across the white community for this to happen. This is much less true of the Negro community, precisely because the years of segregation and discrimination have kept the vast majority of Negro people in much the same class and hence with much the same interests. But the American political scene as a whole certainly does not fit the pattern of *the* majority against *the* minority. This old Madisonian myth simply no longer conforms to the political facts of life. As Robert Dahl has argued, the American political situation today can be characterized as rule by minorities.[14] Even though a majority of voters do finally rule on policy questions, this majority is not constant and it changes from issue to issue. Therefore, the picture of a democracy in America that is or will be composed of all whites against all blacks is a highly inaccurate one today and an unlikely one in the future. It is probable, on the other hand, that Negroes will become a more self-conscious minority who will oppose whites on a number of issues, and it is true that most whites will oppose Negroes on some issues. What is not likely is that *all* whites will ever oppose *all* Negroes on *all* issues. The more probable possibility is that Negroes and certain white groups will tend to form coalitions on particular issues and that at later times other white groups will form coalitions with Negroes on other issues.

What is at stake, then, is not the danger of the white majority becoming completely tyrannical over Negroes as the permanent minority or the lonely 10 per cent. What is at stake is the possibility of Negroes' becoming effective enough as a minority to participate equally with other minorities in the coalition pro-

14. Ibid. Chap. 5, especially p. 133.

cess. Unless this happens, Negroes will remain permanently deprived as a political minority, for unless Negro negotiations in
coalition formation can be negotiation from strength, it is
highly unlikely that Negro group participation in the political
process will ever be on a par with that of most white groups.

In light of these considerations, the strategy of the new
Negro pluralism is both acceptable in the American political
tradition and realistic in terms of the facts of American political
life. The black leadership rightly recognizes that individual participation in the political process is meaningful only in the context of group affiliation, for American politics is above all a
struggle of interest groups, most of whom have traditionally excluded Negroes from any central position in the deliberation
about group aims. This very exclusion gives substance to the
constant assertion by Black Power leaders that the only road to
political equality in America for Negroes is through the development of an all-Negro political organization.

EQUAL OPPORTUNITY FOR NEGROES

The emphasis on political equality which presently characterizes the new pluralism does not reflect any diminishing interest in the concrete problems of discrimination. The purpose of
the political organization is to enable black people to put pressure upon the white power structures more effectively. That
pressure is aimed specifically at alleviating the abiding Negro
problems of poor housing, job discrimination, poor education,
low health standards, discrimination in public facilities, and discrimination in the judicial processes and law enforcement. All
of these remain targets of the Negro revolution today as they
have been in the past. If anything, the influence of Black Power
leaders has served to make Negroes *more* determined that
whites shall meet their demands on these issues. The talk of
"domestic Marshall plans" and "compensatory" hiring and education are certainly not calculated to give comfort to those who
would like to "solve" the race problem by suppressing Negro
demands or by having Negroes removed from sight. On the

contrary, the whole strategy of the new pluralism indicates that the presence of Negroes will become more and more troublesome for whites committed to the status quo, and it is a clear sign that Negroes no longer are in the mood to talk about gradual solutions involving the admittance of a few blacks at a time to the privileges of being white. In fact, Negroes are no longer interested in the "privileges of being white" but rather in securing the recognition that the privileges of being black include a full share in the goods of this society.

The Negro quest for equal opportunity, however, includes more than the addition of economic opportunity to political opportunity. They are seeking an equality that spans even more basic human concerns. We have seen that much of the talk coming from the new pluralism focuses upon the goodness of being black and the distinctiveness of black people. While it is true that this talk functions somewhat as a sloganeering device to effect political mobilization, it indicates more than this. The new pluralists are concerned with the problem of Negro identity. They are keenly aware of the fact that today blackness means inferiority even to Negroes themselves in many instances, and they are sensitive to the fact that simple racial balancing of institutions does not really get to the heart of this problem. When Negroes who have been disabled by years of caste existence are thrown into the open market of competition with whites, this situation may in fact serve to reinforce the sense of inferiority.

For example, if Negro children from ghetto schools are suddenly mixed with white children from the better suburban schools, it becomes immediately apparent that the quality of their previous education places them at a very serious disadvantage. What usually will happen is that Negro children will either remain at their present grade level and thus compete under almost impossible disadvantages or else they will be moved back to lower grade levels so that they can compete effectively. In either case, it is obvious that they are "behind" their white peers, and it is a short step from this kind of position to the inference of one's own inferiority.

This is how the caste system has always perpetuated itself. A disadvantaged minority is chided for its backwardness, and then the backwardness is utilized as justification for further discrimination, which in turn means that they remain disadvantaged. Soon the minority begins to accept their backwardness as "natural" or inevitable. It would appear, then, that the only way to counter this "vicious circle" of caste is to utilize the separation of the minority to an advantage. Then it is possible to concentrate on remedial programs to remove some of the disadvantages. This at least creates the possibility for a new self-understanding, for one way in which the self-image of a minority can be changed is to experience success in competition.

Again, it is important to remember that the whole problem of caste complicates the picture. The success of a few Negroes is simply no answer to the problem, because the few can always be looked on as exceptions. Furthermore, these exceptions no longer function to increase the pride of the masses of Negroes who view their successful brothers as tools by which the white man intends to keep the masses happy. In their view this simply means that whereas in earlier times, whites utilized the hope of heaven to keep Negroes placated, today they utilize the hope for an exception. In either case, the promise is not one of good faith.

Therefore, the new pluralists are convinced that the only way to deal with the problem of Negro identity is to remove the caste restrictions on the whole group so that the value and opportunity of Negroes can be weighed on the same scale as that of whites. Negroes are not so naïve as to request an equality which means "to all men the same thing in every way." Neither do they believe that all men are natively equal spiritually, physically, mentally, or morally. What they are insisting upon is that black men as a group *are* potentially equal in every respect to white men as a group, and their demand for equal opportunity is a demand that the caste onus be removed from American society so that no man is inhibited in his development or deprived of his sense of worth by the fact of his color alone.

Finally, the equal opportunity that is sought by the new

Negro pluralism includes the right to be distinctly black and to have the distinction acknowledged as important to American culture. Perhaps the closest analogy to the kind of pluralism that is sought here is the religious pluralism that has been developed in this country. Today very few Americans think that it is necessary for the good of the country to have all Jews become Christian or to have all Catholics become Protestant. We have at least begun to take seriously the fact that each of the major religious faiths has something to offer to the total religious life of the nation, and in spite of the persistence of prejudice,[15] religious assimilation is no longer held as an option by representatives of any sizable religious group in this country.

Negroes are just beginning now to develop some idea of the distinctiveness of black people with reference to their cultural heritage, and this must be understood in the total context of the quest for a true human equality. Viewed in this way, the emphasis upon cultural distinctiveness is an attempt to create a distinctive base for Negroes to participate not only in the exercise of power and the use of the goods of American society, but also to participate fully in the process of cultural formation in the years that lie ahead.

In summary, the new Negro pluralism is no longer content to have attention focused upon a few "instant citizens." Opportunity for the "talented tenth" is out as a strategy. Pluralism is a demand for some radical attempts in American society to establish the condition of equal humanity now, and Negro leadership is in no mood any longer to countenance gradual solutions involving only a few blacks at a time. In contrast to the previous acquiescence in tokenism which is the corollary of gradual assimilation, the Negro is demanding the right to be fully human on the same terms as the majority white color group, and this humanity spans the whole spectrum of human concerns.

This means that no longer shall a black child have to live in a society where he inevitably grows up feeling that he is inferior. It means that Negroes must be able to face the past with pride

15. Charles Y. Glock and Rodney Stark, *Christian Beliefs and Anti-Semitism* (New York: Harper and Row, 1966).

and the future with hope. It means self-determination, a sense of worth, a sense of being valued, and the right to creative development of one's potential—all of this and the many more things that constitute the real stuff of truly human existence. And as a first step, Negroes plan to move into the center of human activity—the political arena, where the shape of society is being determined. There, as black Americans demand the right to act, they will be able to create the conditions for true humanity by challenging the most inhuman vestiges of the political and social structures that so long have kept them isolated and humiliated in this land of growing promise. They shall feel the first ground swell of a new dignity as they demand the right to participate in decisions about what the nature of our new humanity will be.

VI

A Christian Ethical Response to the New Negro Pluralism

Negro-white relations in America have always been a kind of pluralism, the character of which has been largely the result of majority action. White men have effected this pluralism with a vengeance. They put the Negro "in his place" first as a slave. Then by law and finally by residential location they have kept him there. They have consigned him to separate and unequal chances in employment, public facilities, education, and housing. They have chided him for his backwardness and taught him that his distinctiveness made him inferior. When he aspired to be included, they have, for the most part, excluded him, and even when he was included it was clearly on the white man's terms.

Hence one cannot help seeing some irony in the fact that Negroes themselves are now moving toward a new pluralism of their own. White men have always dealt with Negroes as a distinct group, and now that the Negroes take the white community seriously, some whites have reacted with cries of alarm and anger while others show pique and resignation.

The reasons for these white reactions are not difficult to assess. It is not simply because Negroes want to be distinct as a group and hence a pluralistic minority. It is rather that the new pluralism demands respect for the distinctiveness of the minority and the removal of patterns of discrimination against them. Moreover, they are determined that the shape of Negro-white relationships of the future, unlike those of the past, will no longer be solely the white man's prerogative. Hence, some white men will be less and less able to exploit Negroes with impunity, and others with different leanings will find it more difficult to "help" him assimilate. In both cases, the new pluralism is threatening the familiar patterns of response.

Whatever the white responses to the new pluralism, however, they are crucial for the future of American race relations. Wirth and Wagley and Harris have cautioned us in their discussions of minority aims that the success of the minority aim is heavily dependent upon the response of the majority.[1] Even the most determined minority can be frustrated by a recalcitrant majority, and Wirth has argued that in the case of a pluralistic minority, the probable result of severe frustration will be a move toward either a secessionist or a militant minority aim.[2] Therefore, the full meaning of the changes in the Negro community that are symbolized by Black Power will be significantly determined by the white response, and it is to this important matter that I shall address the remainder of my discussion, particularly the response of white Protestant Christians.

There are at least two aspects of any Christian response to social problems. One of these is an articulation of the ethical resources of Christian faith which provide the motivation for and shape the directions of the response. The other aspect consists of specific actions that will give some concreteness to the Christian response. In the remaining discussion, attention will be given to both aspects.

THE DOCTRINE OF SIN AND POLITICAL EQUALITY [3]

From the perspective of Christian faith one major resource for understanding the Negro push for political equality is the doc-

1. Wirth, "The Problem of Minority Groups," in *The Science of Man* . . . , pp. 358–9; Wagley and Harris, *Minorities* . . . , pp. 288–9.
2. Wirth, "The Problem of Minority Groups," in *The Science of Man* . . . , p. 364.
3. Portions of this Chapter are from my unpublished dissertation, "Reapportionment in American Democracy . . . ," pp. 143 ff; and 165–273.

trine of sin. The various theological positions about the meaning of the doctrine do not concern us here. What is important for our purposes is that the doctrine always means that with respect to the judgment of God, all men are sinners. In contemporary Protestant ethics, this has been the primary basis for justifying political equality as a norm of social justice.[4]

Reinhold Niebuhr conceives of the justification of political equality on the basis of man's sin as pride of power. Sin as pride of power moves in two directions. In the first place, it is a refusal to admit the finiteness and contingency of all human existence. Thus, pride of power leads man to imagine that he is the master of his own fate, and manifests itself in great pretensions or idolatry. This aspect of the pride of power is most common to those who already are favored in the balance of power within the social order.

In the second place, the pride of power manifests itself as the lust *for* power. This form of the pride of power is based upon insecurity and it is common to those who are at a disadvantaged power position in the social order. But insecurity is common to all men. Therefore, those who hold the advantage in any balance of power fear the loss of their power, and those who are at a disadvantage try to gain power to increase their security.[5]

Since every man is functioning as a power agent in some way, the Christian understanding of sin as the pride of power means that the power struggle is the persisting fact of all human social life. What is necessary, then, for social life to be possible?

Niebuhr thinks that two kinds of power structures are necessary for any viable human social organization, a central organizing power and some institutional form of the balance of power. The central organizing power is necessary to prevent the lust for power from creating a situation in which all men

4. Aside from Niebuhr, below, see Emil Brunner, *The Divine Imperative,* trans. Olive Wyon (Philadelphia: The Westminster Press, 1947), pp. 467 ff., and *Justice and the Social Order,* trans, Mary Hottinger (New York: Harper & Bros, 1947), pp. 200 ff. Paul Ramsey, *Basic Christian Ethics* (New York: Charles Scribner's Sons, 1950), pp. 327 ff.
5. Reinhold Niebuhr, *The Nature and Destiny of Man* (New York: Charles Scribner's Sons, 1949), Vol. I, pp. 190–94.

war against each other. Though there is some "natural cohesion" built into human nature, the perversion of that natural cohesion in the absence of some ordering power inevitably leads to some form of anarchy. But the central organizing power will always be composed of sinful men too. If their power over others is too great and remains unchecked, their pride of power as idolatry and insecurity will lead them to consolidate their power and move toward tyranny. This means that alongside the central organizing power, some sort of distribution of power must also be institutionalized if sin is not to pervert the structures of the human community.[6]

In other words, Niebuhr's understanding of man as sinner means that the twin problems of society are those of justice and order. Order creates the possibility of community and justice ensures the order will not be bought at the price of oppression. In both cases the persisting problem of sin expressed as man's own self-interest keeps the existence of true human community on a very precarious "razor's edge." Attention to one of these requirements at the expense of attention to the other is fatal. Niebuhr thinks that the question of order is a prior question to that of justice, but his thought is equivocal. He qualifies the priority of order with the finality of justice. What he probably means is that attention must be given to both order and justice in society at all times if men are not to plunge into dehumanizing chaos or equally dehumanizing slavery, and there is no absolute rule of priority that can apply to every circumstance.[7]

In light of this understanding of man as sinner and the result-

6. Ibid. Vol. II, pp. 257 ff.
7. Reinhold Niebuhr "Limits of Liberty," *The Nation* (Vol. 154), Jan. 29, 1942, p. 87, quoted in Harry Davis and Robert C. Good, eds., *Reinhold Niebuhr on Politics* (New York: Charles Scribner's Sons, 1960), p. 174. See also, Reinhold Niebuhr, *An Interpretation of Christian Ethics* (Living Age Ed., New York: Meridian Books, 1956), p. 140; and "The Perils of Our Foreign Policy," *Christianity and Society* (Vol. 8), Spring 1945, p. 18, quoted in Davis and Good, *Niebuhr on Politics,* p. 174. Negroes believe the big question in American democracy is one of justice. The prevailing order is oppressive to them, and while Niebuhr would probably agree, his response to "creative violence" would be interesting.

ing problems of social life, it is not difficult to see why Niebuhr thinks that democracy is the ideal form of political organization. Within democracy the ordering power is subject to the consent of those whom it orders, and hence no oligarchy can finally make pretensions to ultimate power. Moreover, the institutionalization of political equality which we have discussed earlier represents a distribution of power among the individuals in society. The distribution of power on the equalitarian model means that ideally human self-interest is balanced against human self-interest in the political structures of democracy in such a way as to allow change without recourse to complete disorder. Therefore, democracy is seen by Niebuhr to be a "permanently valid form of social and political organization," precisely because it solves the problems of justice and order in such a way as to allow them to complement each other.[8]

Niebuhr is not unaware of the problem of group sin either. In an earlier work, *Moral Man and Immoral Society*, he described the problem of group self-interest as one of the most persisting realities of human sin. What is the inevitable struggle of self-interest with self-interest between sinful individuals is compounded when group loyalty enters the picture. Then, individuals are even less capable of transcending their own interests because of the pressure of group ideology. The result is that large human groups bound by both ideology and the natural need for cohesion seldom if ever can be expected to take account of other groups with whom they are in competition.[9] The only possibility for a group to transcend itself lies in the common loyalty of two or more groups to a higher loyalty such as the nation.

From one point of view, of course, it is ridiculous to talk

8. Reinhold Niebuhr, *The Children of Light and the Children of Darkness* (New York: Charles Scribner's Sons, 1944), pp. 1, 3; and *Christian Realism and Political Problems* (New York: Charles Scribner's Sons, 1953), p. 96.
9. Reinhold Niebuhr, *Moral Man and Immoral Society* (New York: Charles Scribner's Sons, 1932 [Rev. Ed. 1960]), pp. xi–xii. See also, *The Nature and Destiny of Man*, Vol. II, pp. 208 ff.

about the sin of groups. In every case, the sinfulness of groups is the compounded product of a plethora of individual sins, and the sinful actions of any group require the participation of individual agents at least as catalysts. Still, when the compounding has taken place and the time comes for the individual to act in accordance with his official position for the group, the pressure of the group sanctions and the history of the group's decisions can force a man into a position where his decision is not really his own. He could, of course, choose ostracism or death as an alternative, and in some cases this appears to be the only choice. However, the extent to which he can choose to free himself from group pressures is partially dependent upon the reference points that are available to him so that he can transcend the group norms functioning in the particular issue.

Certainly, the Christian faith is meant to provide just such a perspective. It is a faith that affirms the universal worth of human beings before an all-loving God, and this universalism should provide a higher loyalty than any other single loyalty. The truth of the matter, however, is that more often than not, faith in God does not function as the higher loyalty and at best functions merely to soften the effects of the loyalty to one's own group.[10] We shall see clearly in the next chapter that this has surely been the case with white Protestantism in America, for the position of the churches, and by far the majority of individual Christians, has been much more determined by the place and time of the institutions and individuals involved than by any unanimous or widespread affirmation of the universalistic nature of the gospel.

One might expect also that the pressure of the American creed of equality would provide a similar secular vantage point, and Myrdal is probably correct in his thesis that the democratic ideology of the United States has been one significant factor in what progress has been made in this country in the struggle for Negro rights. But one suspects that it has been more the pressure of the changes in the structure of American

10. H. Richard Niebuhr, *Radical Monotheism and Western Culture* (New York: Harper & Brothers, 1960), pp. 1–48, 100 ff.

society and the changed American position in the world that has pushed Negro rights to the fore rather than any conscious attempt on the part of Americans to square their practice with democratic ideals.

I am not so pessimistic as to say that neither Christianity nor democratic ideals have had any part in the changing character of race relations in the United States. In fact, one of the hopeful signs in the current crisis is the re-affirmation of both democratic and Christian ideals on the part of those who are committed to them. Yet, the loyalty of Christians and other Americans to their ideals is not alone a sufficient basis for hope that change can really take place.

In summary, the Christian understanding of man as sinner lends strong support to the demand of the new Negro pluralism. The intransigence of men in their loyalty to narrow group and personal interests will remain a problem because men will continue to be sinners. Hence, if there is to be any constructive attack made upon the caste barrier to justice in this country, it is necessary that a more equitable balance of power be achieved. That this is precisely what the new Negro strategy is attempting to do is already clear. We have already seen that Negroes are attempting to establish Negro group unity in order to mobilize political power to mount a frontal attack on caste. Since Negroes as a group are the target of discrimination and segregation in America, only unified action can really alter the balance of power sufficiently to bring about the end of caste. Color will remain the badge of deprivation as long as the blacks in this country are powerless in the political arena. When the power deficiency is corrected, one can expect that the interests of the Negroes as a group will find some more equitable balance in the coalitions and compromises that finally determine national policy. And this means that Negroes will have found a more effective way of placing restraint upon the sin of American white institutions.

The white Christian, then, more than any other white man, should understand the attempt on the part of Negro leaders to achieve a better balance of power. Knowing that men are sinners, the Christian also knows that sin must be restrained. And knowing that sin must be restrained, he should also support attempts to make that restraint possible.

The response of Christian ethics need not be cast purely in the terms of the restraint of sin. This negative understanding of the function of law simply does not capture the entire relevance of Christian ethics to the demands of the new Negro pluralism. The Christian response to the demands of Negro leaders goes beyond mere support of *their* strategy for restraining man's sin. It reaches into the whole claim the Negroes are making for the right to live a life that is more fully human than the caste system will allow.

I mentioned before the fact that the possibility of an individual's transcending the demands and norms of his own group is directly dependent upon his having a higher loyalty from which he can view as relative all other loyalties. This does not mean that I believe that any man can completely transcend his web of group affiliations, but I do believe that Christian faith provides the possibility of a center of loyalty from which other group loyalties may be put into proper perspective.[11] This would mean that *Christian* obligation ideally functions as the transcendent obligation which limits the authority of other obligations derived from lesser loyalties.

What then is the nature of Christian obligation? Paul Lehmann's excellent *Ethics in a Christian Context* is especially helpful in answering this question. Though Lehmann denies the imperative character of Christian ethics, it is clear that being a part of the *koinonia*, the reality of the church, gives a certain direction to the nature of the Christian's ethical task.[12]

The starting point of Christian ethics, for Lehmann, is the nature of the church. What happened in the Christian commu-

11. Ibid.
12. Paul Lehmann, *Ethics in a Christian Context* (New York: Harper & Row, 1963), pp. 45 ff.

nity was not the revelation of a new law, but rather the creation of a new fellowship within which the work of the Holy Spirit became a present and visible reality. Here in this fellowship the Christian becomes aware of what it is that God intends to do in the world and it is here also that Christian ethical reality takes form.

> We might, therefore, say that Christian ethics is koinonia ethics. This means that it is from, and in, the koinonia that we get the answer to the question: What am I as a believer in Jesus Christ and as a member of his church, to do? [13]

What I am to do as a Christian is dependent upon what I perceive to be happening in the context of the *koinonia*. From one standpoint, what is happening there is the creation of mature manhood or the new humanity.[14] This new manhood consists of

> the integrity in and through interrelatedness which makes it possible for each individual member of an organic whole to be himself in togtherness and in togetherness each to be himself.[15]

It is the recognition that each of us is dependent upon the other to be what he is and that none of us has any grounds upon which to think too highly of himself. It is, moreover, the presence of communication one with another, and this communication goes beyond the level of verbalization to a point at which one is able to give of himself to the other and the other is able to give of himself to you. When two or more are "in relationship" in such a way as this, mature humanity is more a possibility.[16]

If this happens in the church, (and there is no *koinonia* unless it does happen) then the church becomes the ethical reality, because what God is doing in the world is made concrete "in the transformation of human motivation and of the struc-

13. Ibid. p. 47.
14. Ibid. p. 53.
15. Ibid. p. 55.
16. Ibid. pp. 55, 64.

tures of human relatedness which are the stuff of human fulfillment." [17]

To give further illumination to the nature of the Christian
ethical context Lehmann calls attention to "God's political activity" as the criterion of what I as a Christian am to do.[18]
Utilizing Aristotle's understanding of politics as "the ideal form
of human association which is 'by nature' the precondition for
and the expression of the fulfillment of human life," Lehmann
concludes that God's political activity in the world consists of
doing all those things which are the preconditions for making
human life more human.

What Lehmann is saying about the nature of the Christian
context, then, is much more oriented toward an understanding
of what God is doing in the world than toward personal obligation. If a man is a Christian he is somehow already part of
this ethical reality, the *koinonia*. Being part of this *koinonia* he
is already free to do what he ought to do, and having experienced the reality of *koinonia* he knows what God is doing in
the world to make human life human. Hence, the answer to the
question of what to do lies precisely in the affirmation of what
one already is and has experienced—the making of human life
more human, or the creation of the conditions of human life
by which human fulfillment is really possible.

The character of this new humanity is very similar to the
kind of thing Protestants have become so familiar with from
Martin Buber's *I and Thou,* and from the various adaptations
of this insight that appear in the ethical writings of Emil Brunner, Reinhold Niebuhr and others. Perhaps one of the finest
statements of this type of human relationship appears in Karl
Barth's *Church Dogmatics.*[19]

Barth says that there are four levels of humanity on an as-

17. Ibid. p. 72.
18. Ibid. pp. 81 ff.
19. Karl Barth, *Church Dogmatics,* Vol. III, Pt. II (English Version),
T. F. Torrance and G. W. Bromiley, eds. (Edinburgh: T. & T. Clark,
1960), pp. 250 ff.

cending scale. These are (1) the "eye to eye" relationships; (2) mutual speech and hearing; (3) mutual assistance, (4) all of the other three levels together with a spirit of joy.

At the outset Barth argues that no man can possibly think of a truly human relationship that is singular. No man comes into this world alone; no man grows into maturity alone, and no man can exist in maturity alone in anything like a human fashion. The precondition of the humanity of the self is the co-presence of the self with the other. Man alone is man isolated and lonely, and of all things, isolation and loneliness can be the most de-humanizing.

According to Barth, the first form of this co-presence is "eye-to-eye" relationships. This "looking the other in the eye" is a very powerful metaphor. It is more than merely seeing someone pass by; it is catching his gaze, acknowledging his presence. It consists of seeing him as particularity rather than merely as one fleeting image upon a screen of humanity. It is the realization that not only am I seeing, but I am being seen by another. The eyes meet, and they really meet in the sense that two people really see each other and recognize their presence together. So long as we dodge this kind of eye-to-eye contact we either ignore the presence of the other or else acknowledge his presence with only indifference.

Beyond the look and the gaze there is speech and hearing. We do not become fully human until we tell others who we are and hear them tell us who they are. And the reverse is true also—I do not know who I am fully until I have heard from others who I am. Hence the possibility of my being myself at all is dependent upon the willingness of others to hear me and address me about myself and themselves. This level of humanity is not based upon politeness, upon "letting the other have his proper turn at speaking." Mutual speech and hearing is a matter of life and death itself. I am not human unless I am addressed, nor am I human unless the other will hear me. And not only does he have the "right" to speak, he has the "right" to hear what I have to say.

But speaking and hearing are not the only human needs. We have need of each other for a thousand other reasons. We need counsel when we are in trouble. We need money when we are broke. We need support when we are disabled. We need food when we are hungry, teaching when we would learn, recognition when we achieve, sympathy when we sorrow, joy when we are happy, and comfort when we are dying. Our mutual dependence requires mutual assistance at every phase of our existence. But when we really get to the heart of the matter, we need not only mutual assistance, but the assurance that that assistance comes not out of a sense of obligation and that it is not mechanically administered in an impersonal way. Human beings cannot really be human unless they can help each other and be helped by each other in a spirit of loving concern. Genuine loving concern, as opposed to any kind of sentimentality, is the real stuff out of which true humanity is fashioned, and when mutual assistance is done with joy and gladness, we have reached the full measure of true humanness.

Barth adds that when this kind of true humanness is enacted out of gratitude for God's goodness, it then becomes the meaning of true Christian love, *agape*.

What the Christian experiences in the community of believers, then, is the redemptive power of *agape* whereby men are made truly human. It is this revelation and the participation in the concrete reality of the community that is revealed here that form the context within which the Christian makes his decisions about what he is to do.

Returning to Lehmann, there are some problems with his description of what constitutes the ethical reality of the church. At the outset, there is a vast chasm between this description of the ethical reality of the church and what happens in the churches of the United States today. This is a very thorny problem for Lehmann himself, and he is never very clear about the relationship of the "ideal" church and the "empirical" church. Finally, he "solves" the problems by arguing that the empirical church "points . . . to the fact that there is in the world a *laboratory of the living word, or . . . a bridgehead of maturity. . . .*"[20] This kind of solution, however, does not resolve the problem. The inconsistency between what Lehmann describes the church to be, and what in fact the church is, still remains, and the problem began as early as the formation of the churches in New Testament times. This is a clear indication that the ethical reality of the church is experienced by the church in almost all cases as an obligation rather than as a description of its true experience, and the same will be the case with the experience of individual believers. What Lehmann has given us, then, is a description of the hope for the church that functions as a constant reminder of what our goals are and what Christian obligation is to be. The church ought to be that institution within which true humanness is really made possible, and it ought to function as the leaven that will make human life human in the world. When one cuts through the ambiguity, this is where we really are. The purpose of the church is to participate in God's redemption of the world. To do this is our individual and corporate responsibility. It may well be that the *koinonia* "in" the church is the place to "come in sight of the difference"[21] that God's activity in the world does make, but it is simply not the case that the "coming in sight of the difference" means that men who have seen and heard will now confess with their lives. This is why Lehmann must admit finally that there is in the *koinonia* "also an imperative pressure exerted by an indicative situation,"[22] and if *koinonia* has any relationship to the empirical church at all, that "pressure" will be the primary experience we have. In other words, the "what am I to do?" is most often "what ought I to do?" in the experience of most Christians.

That the ethical situation of the Christian is not simply indicative but always also imperative should not be surprising in light of our historical roots. It has certainly been true of the whole Judeo-Christian tradition that normative patterns have

20. Lehmann, *Ethics* . . . , p. 131; see also, pp. 50–51, especially note 1, p. 50.
21. Ibid. p. 112.
22. Ibid. p. 131.

been intimately associated with the reality of the holy community.

One clear example is the Sinai experience of the Israelites under the leadership of Moses (Exodus 19–24). The Sinai materials in their final form include the affirmation of the covenant. God declared that he would be the God of Israel and Israel committed herself to be his people. The cultic celebration that surrounded Moses' ascent of Sinai included the remembrance of what God had done and was doing in the world, and was followed on the mountain by the giving of the law. The point here is that the description of the conditions of the covenant and the remembrance of God's mighty acts were immediately followed by reflection upon the normative structures that would most adequately define the nature of Israel's obligation—to be a covenant people. Israel *was* the covenant people, that is true, but she was to *become* the covenant people, and this was the ground of her continuing obligation. Normative reflection answered for Israel the question "what ought I to do?" as the covenant nation.

Paul's letter to the Romans reflects a similar pattern. Throughout the first eight chapters, Paul literally sings a hymn to the goodness of God and the wonder of man's redemption in Christ. After he has made it clear that God will continue to form his covenant people even outside of Israel (Chapters 9–11), he then begins very practical normative instruction about the pattern of life that is characteristic of those whose "minds have been transformed" by those "mercies of God" which he has recited (Chapter 12). Again, the mighty acts of God are recounted—there is a description of what God has done and is doing. This is followed by a re-affirmation of God's steadfastness and then reflection upon the normative patterns appropriate to the Christian life.

Some sort of reflection upon the normative guidelines for Christian behavior is part of Christian ethical reflection. We simply do not go into every moral decision "wide open" precisely because that is irrational. Furthermore, to stop short of such a formulation is to forget one important lesson from the

Reformation—*simul justus et peccator*—Christian man is both justified and a sinner. Since sin is an abiding fact of the Christian life, ethical norms are part and parcel of the task of Christian ethics. The law belongs with the gospel so long as man remains in his ethically ambiguous situation in the world.

It would be unfair, of course, to say that Lehmann has failed to give normative direction for the Christian life. Though he does shy away from imperative sentences, it is clear that he certainly implies directives in his descriptive statement. Stated as directives, Lehmann's position would certainly include the admonition to be human and to act in such a way as to make truly human life more possible in the world. In general terms, this is a very excellent statement of Christian responsibility in the context of the present racial crisis. We have already seen that this is precisely what Negroes are seeking—the right to be fully human—and it is surely the Christian's responsibility to be the kind of person that will make the humanity of the Negro and the white more possible.

But when one recalls the specific content which Lehmann gives to maturity or true humanity, more problems arise. The terms like "openness to the other," "personal communication," and "interrelatedness" have a distinctly face-to-face flavor about them suggesting the intimacy of small groups. Moreover, they suggest a pattern of personal contacts extending over a period of time in which truly mutual understanding can develop.

What makes this way of conceiving a Christian ethical response immediately problematical in the current racial crisis is the persisting problem of segregation. The separation of Negroes and whites has always been a fact of American life, and the separatist implications of the new Negro pluralism will probably ensure that this will be even more a complicating factor in any face-to-face understanding of Christian obligation. How can a man be "open" to another man if he never sees him? And how can he really "see" him if he does not live near him? Truly human life cannot be carried on between persons whose relationships are fractured by persisting caste structures.

Before men can be "together" in relationship, they must be able to be present with each other in body.

Lehmann would answer, of course, that *koinonia* ethics supports desegregation for precisely this reason,[23] but this answer does not take seriously the new Negro pluralism. As we have seen, some Negro leaders are pressing for continued separation from their side as part of an over-all strategy to mobilize Negro power, and many of them view integration as irrelevant. Hence whites can no longer assume automatically that Negroes want "face-to-face" contact as an end in itself.[24]

I must emphasize again that this is *not* necessarily reverse racism, but it may be an effort to solve the very difficult problem of Negro identity. It takes no special insight to see that mutuality and openness between Negroes and whites have long been complicated by the Negroes' own self-image. As we have seen, Negroes have widely adopted the negative stereotypes about them as their own understanding of their group. Therefore it has been and still is difficult for many Negroes to think of themselves as equal partners in a relationship with whites. The speaking and hearing have been largely white speaking and Negro hearing, and the mutual assistance has been largely white paternalism. Even when whites sincerely intended that it be otherwise it was often difficult psychologically for Negroes themselves to accept the good intention.

Black Power leaders are especially sensitive to this fact, and, as I have noted previously, their sensitivity to this problem is one basis for insisting that the role of whites in the Negro community be limited. Face-to-face contacts with whites too often serve as reminders of an old identity that is inhuman, and before true mutuality can become a possibility between the masses of Negroes and whites in America, the problem of identity must first be solved.

23. Ibid. pp. 150 ff.
24. Cf. for example, Efrem Sigel, "Balancing Act in Boston," *The Reporter* (Vol. 30), May 4, 1967, pp. 22 ff. The author notes that even Negroes who support "busing" of Negro children to white schools are not interested in their children being with white children. What they want is better schools, and racial balance is irrelevant.

In light of the problem of identity, then, it appears that Lehmann could no longer argue with confidence that a policy of desegregation is a "sign" of God's humanizing action in the world.[25] If one takes seriously the new Negro pluralism, desegregation understood as broadening interracial contacts may at best be irrelevant, and it could even be de-humanizing. This, in turn, means that the focus upon face-to-face relationships over an extended period of time cannot be central in the Christian ethical response to the new Negro pluralism, for this response is tied to the conviction that desegregation is the primary goal of the Negro community.

How, then, can the Christian participate in humanization and thus participate in God's activity in the world? To answer this question, we need to begin by noting that the problem of Negro identity is not an isolated problem. If we follow Myrdal's suggestion, the problem of identity can be seen as part of a "vicious circle." [26] Whites exploit Negroes and Negroes are forced into the lowest economic status by that exploitation. This results in their having poor housing, high crime rates, high disease rates, and little ambition. Whites then point to these indices as evidence of the Negro's "natural" inferiority. Buttressed by a mythology of sorts, this conclusion then becomes the rationale for further exploitation and the circle continues. Finally, Negroes come to accept their backwardness as "natural" and adopt the mythology and stereotypes, and hence their blackness becomes a mark of shame. Myrdal also argues that an alteration in any one of the factors can cause a movement of the whole circle in the direction of the alteration.[27] For example, a significant rise in employment could slow exploitation and also indirectly enhance the Negro's self-image.

Seen this way, the problem of identity is related to a variety of social and political factors, the alteration of which could also help effect a change in the Negro's self-image. Therefore, if desegregation is irrelevant, social change is not. What is called for from the white community is a public policy concentrated

25. Lehmann, *Ethics* . . . , p. 152.
26. Myrdal, *An American Dilemma*, pp. 75ff.
27. Ibid. pp. 1065 ff.

on the abiding problems of ghetto life where the segregation of the Negro has resulted in the most stubborn external barriers to his full humanity.

If we are to understand Christian obligation in terms of making human life more human, then, the primary question for a Christian response to the new Negro pluralism becomes: Can there be a legitimate translation of Christian belief into a pattern of normative guidelines for political decision?

The answer to this question has not been unanimous in Christian history.[28] Some Christians have argued that faith has nothing to do with politics. Faith has to do with the salvation of souls, the preservation of the saints for the Kingdom of God that is removed from the world. Hence, a line of demarcation is drawn between what concerns the Christian and what does not. What is his concern is the fellowship of Christians and his own personal moral life, but his concern does not extend to the entanglements in which men find themselves in the world.[29] Even some of the more narrow versions of the modern pastoral care movement in the American churches seem to move in this direction. It is agreed that the proper meaning of Christian faith is accepting people, helping them to accept themselves, helping them to relieve their frustrations and organize their egos. This is the meaning of salvation—wholeness through mental health. The arena of faith shifts from the pulpits to the couch, but there is still the same kind of anti-political pattern as that represented by the ancient perfectionists and radical sectarians.

Another answer to the question of theology and politics has distinguished between the function of faith as such for the life of the Christian and the function of God's natural law in the world. This kind of answer does not deny God's activity in the

28. For a discussion of the various ways in which the church has approached political and social problems, see Ernest Troeltsch. *The Social Teachings of the Christian Churches*, 2 vols., trans. Olive Wyon (London: George Allen & Unwin Ltd., 1931). See also, H. R. Niebuhr, *Christ and Culture* (New York: Harper & Brothers, 1951).

29. H. R. Niebuhr, *Christ and Culture*, pp. 45 ff.

world, but it does make a clear distinction between God's relationship to the world in grace and his relationship to the world
in nature. Or the distinction might be made between God's action in the world as law and gospel. In either case, faith affirms
the action of God in the world through his natural law, but
faith as such has nothing to do with the ordering of men's lives
in worldly institutions. Faith provides the possibility for a new
fellowship, the church, and it may add the possibility of a new
kind of virtue or at least provide a new stance toward moral
action for the Christian. What it does not do is to provide any
real content for political decision as such. The natural law as
the criterion for political decision operates independently of
faith. It is universally cognizable. For example, the whole political approach of Aquinas bespeaks hope for a "Christian" civilization, but this hope is grounded in confidence in God's natural
law as his way of ordering the world.[30] In Calvin, the Christian certainly has an interest in and is related to politics, but his
concern is that religion be given a proper place in society and
that society be governed by the "laws of humanity." [31] There-

30. This is true of other aspects of the nature-grace distinction. For example, the theological virtue of charity carries with it the necessity for
performing new kinds of duties, but it is related to the "natural" forms
of love only as theological orientation or motivation. Charity adds no
content to natural loves. It merely confirms them. (See Thomas Aquinas,
Summa Theologica, IIa–Iab, QQ. 26–8; IIa IIab, QQ. 8, 19, 23, 24, 44, 45,
52, 121, 139.) Jacques Maritain, a modern Thomist, argues that the relationship of the gospel witness as charity to justice is both dynamic and
historical. It is dynamic because charity is the deepest foundation for the
belief in human worth, that is, the theological virtues arise from a direct
relation to the absolute who is the ground of human worth and dignity.
It is historical because only as the gospel awakened the "naturally Christian" potentialities of men did more democratic institutions emerge. Still,
there is no "policy of action" offered by charity for political decisions.
See Jacques Maritain, *The Rights of Man and Natural Law* (New York:
Charles Scribner's Sons, 1943), p. 4, and *Man and the State* (Chicago:
University of Chicago Press, 1951), p. 113.
31. *The Institutes*, Book IV, Ch. 20, Par. 1, 2, 3. Emil Brunner, one example of modern Reformation thought, argues that the witness of the gospel
(as love) and justice are "totally different" things. The gospel as such
really has to do with "personal" relations, a stance toward "official" rela-

fore, if one follows either Aquinas or Calvin, the natural law
plays an ethically significant role in the political decision-
making of the Christian, but neither "grace" nor "gospel" provides normative guidance for political decisions. Faith affirms
natural reason in its quest for higher justice, but it does not inform it.[32] Another way of putting it would be to say that
while Christian love may motivate a man to do justice, it does
not in any way inform him as to the content of justice.[33]

What is common to both the "anti-political" and the "natural law" answers to the question of theology and politics is the
separation of the gospel witness from the political life of man.
The grace announced by the gospel is confined to the life of
the gathered community. For Roman Catholic thought, God's
law is the foundation of the political order and the criterion of
political decision, but the supernatural grace revealed by the
gospel represents new virtues and special principles of action

tions and motivation for justice. Again, the gospel does not inform the
content of any rules or policy for making political decisions. (See Emil
Brunner, *Justice and the Social Order*, pp. 127 ff.)

32. There is, of course, considerably more pessimism about the capacity
of reason to direct man's quest for justice in the thought of the Reformation than there is in Roman Catholicism. One point at which this can be
seen is the doctrine of the *imago Dei*. See Brunner's discussion in *Man in
Revolt*, trans. Olive Wyon (Philadelphia: The Westminster Press, 1947),
pp. 82 ff. and 299 ff.

33. It is not clear that even Reinhold Niebuhr has succeeded in showing
that love gives content to justice. Neibuhr certainly thinks that one of
the "pinnacles" of love where love transcends law is universalism. (*Christian Realism and Political Problems*, p. 155.) The transcendence of love
exercises some "pull" on all justice and hence tends to move systems of
justice toward wider inclusiveness and a broader and more permanent
sense of obligation. (*The Nature and Destiny of Man*, Vol. II, pp. 248 ff.)
Yet, any justice is always a contradiction of Christian love because, for
Niebuhr, the uniquely Christian form of love is self-sacrifice. (*Christian
Realism*, p. 160.) This love is heedless and unprudential. Therefore it is
applicable only between two persons and it is "not even right" to ask
that political decisions involving the self and others conform to love.
(*The Nature and Destiny of Man*, Vol. II, pp. 81 ff., 88, 248.) All of this
is not especially clear as an answer to our immediate question about the
relationship of faith to possible norms of political decision.

for the Christian which are not related to political decision. For the Reformers, much the same is the case with the exception that there is considerably less confidence in "natural reason" and much more pessimism about the world.[34] For the sectarians, the world is really the devil's field and the witness of the gospel is for the faithful few who separate themselves from the world and prepare for heaven.

A third kind of answer to the question of theology and politics is represented by the English Puritans, particularly the Leveller Party. According to Woodhouse, Puritanism represented a "set of mind" or way of thinking about the world.[35] The methodology of the Puritan's efforts was distinctly theological. As Woodhouse says: "The Puritan turned to the theological aspects of a question as naturally as the modern man turns to the economic; and his first instinct was to seek guidance within the covers of his Bible."[36] While the Puritan might be accused of seeking rationalizations for his position rather than guidance, this does not in any way detract from the importance of theology for the Puritan's own understanding of his decision-making. The main characteristic of the "Puritan mind" was the dominance of dogmatic religion, and there was a prevailing tendency to carry the implications of this dogma over into secular life.[37]

Woodhouse believes that the Puritan method for carrying the implications of dogma to the secular world consisted of two main principles—(1) the principle of segregation, and (2) the principle of analogy.

The principle of segregation[38] meant that at first the Puritans separated the world into two parts, a scheme of nature and

34. Even Calvin's theocratic experiment at Geneva is a tacit confession that only the "church" can really redeem the life of the world. It is not to be seen as God's redemption of political institutions in the world, but rather as the church taking over the government of the world.
35. A. S. P. Woodhouse, ed., *Puritanism and Liberty* (London: J. M. Dent and Sons, Ltd., 1938), p. 37.
36. Ibid. p. 39.
37. Ibid. pp. 38, 39.
38. Ibid. p. 58.

a scheme of grace, and corresponding to these two schemes were two kinds of appropriate goodness. God, indeed, was the ruler of both schemes or orders, but he ruled them under different dispensations.[39] God ruled the community of believers under grace and the secular world under the law of nature.[40] Now within the order of grace, Puritanism manifested both a concern for liberty and a "sentiment" for equality. It must be noted that both these terms are qualified, to some extent, because the equality and the liberty that are the concern here are "Christian" liberty and "believers" equality. "The natural man can claim no share in these privileges, which belong to a higher order, the order of grace." [41] The various obligations and privileges appropriate to the order of grace were not, in the first instance, applied to the order of nature.

This principle of segregation could have easily meant that the English Puritans would despair of the world much in the same manner as had the earlier sectarians, but the activist bent of Puritanism prevented this from happening.[42] Unlike earlier Calvinism, however, the English Puritans did not try to develop a theocratic state.[43] In between these extremes the Puritans developed their own method for coming to terms with the order of nature. It was the method of analogy, a second Puritan principle of interpretation.[44] The spiritual equality of the order of grace was taken to mean analogously that the state should be composed of men of equal privilege.[45]

There is some question as to just how specifically this method of analogy was carried out. D. B. Robertson does not

39. Ibid. pp. 39–40, 58.
40. Ibid. pp. 92 ff. The law of nature, however, meant that reason which is common to all men. It is not "intellectualistic" at all. In fact, for Winstanley, this law of nature was interchangeable with the law of "universal love" (Ibid. p. 94).
41. Ibid. p. 59.
42. Ibid. p. 60.
43. D. B. Robertson, *The Religious Foundations of Leveller Democracy* (New York: King's Crown Press, 1951), p. 109.
44. Woodhouse, *Puritanism* . . . , p. 60.
45. Ibid. pp. 60, 69.

believe that there was really a methodology developed—at least not self-consciously.[46] What was really the case was very simple: "Life was . . . understood in terms of over-all principles applying to everyone and to every situation." [47] In any case, however, it is clear that the Levellers made inferences from their faith for political action, and Robertson, like Woodhouse, believes that it was their faith which gave impetus to their political endeavors. The Levellers were political men *because* they thought that their Christian faith demanded it, and they were political men whose understanding of proper political decisions grew out of their understanding of their faith.

Following this approach, the Levellers saw that the "levelling of all before the Holy Spirit," that is, the equal presence of the Holy Spirit with the members of the community and the priesthood of all believers, had democratic implications.[48] Moreover, the democratic organization of the church had implications for the organization of society, and there is a suggestion that the equality of man's sinfulness had democratic implications. At least it led the Levellers to see the need for the protection of the rights of the people, even from the people themselves.[49] With this kind of reasoning informing their political decisions, it is not surprising that they were the first men in history to advocate equally weighted votes for all voters.[50] This position was an understandable outgrowth from the theology which informed their political decisions. The Levellers, believing that the God they worshiped in faith was active in shap-

46. "Few, if any, of the intricate theological problems of social relevance were worked out. . . . Certainly there was nothing so self-conscious and rationalistic about Leveller procedure as a principle of segregation and a principle of analogy" (Robertson, *Religious Foundations* . . . , p. 11).
47. Ibid.
48. Ibid. pp. 13, 14.
49. Ibid. pp. 28, 73, 100–101; and Woodhouse, *Puritanism* . . . , p. 69.
50. "The English Levellers of the mid-17th century were, to my knowledge, the first to demand a . . . subdivision of the nation into election districts of equal population" (Alfred de Grazia, *Essay on Apportionment and Representative Government* [Washington: American Enterprise Institute for Policy Research, 1963], p. 26).

ing worldly life, found the extension of the implications of their faith to political matters to be as natural as it was necessary.

Some such method of analogy from the Christian gospel to politics is at the heart of the relationship between faith and political decision. Such an analogy presupposes that God's redemptive activity extends to the social and political institutions of the world and it raises the issue of criteria for pointing to his action. It also presupposes a commitment to obey God by participating in his action, that is, it presupposes a commitment to live in accordance with God's purposes as revealed by his action.

For Christian faith, the understainding of what God is doing in the world begins with the gospel. This is the point of reference for judging the adequacy of Christian action. Hence, if there is to be a direct translation of faith into political norms, two kinds of questions must be addressed. First, there is the question as to whether there *are* any ideas in the gospel which have political relevance. In other words, are there any guidelines for shaping political decision which are intrinsic to the gospel itself? Second, if there are such guidelines, is there any political language which can function as a reasonable and more concrete analogy for the gospel guidelines? The first question has to do with the transition from the gospel language influenced by the expectation of the imminent end of the world to broader sociological and political language. The second question involves what might be called the "analogical risk." By this I mean that the need for relevance and action requires some risk of reason in order to translate the language of the gospel into language which is more suitable for practical political direction here and now.[51] The element of risk can be minimized

51. The risk in making a translation of the gospel which has political relevance is very little greater than that involved in Rudolph Bultmann's translation of the message of the gospel into the categories of Heidegger's existentialism. The only respect in which this effort at relevant translation is more risky than that of Bultmann lies in the fact that the gospel seemed at first glance not to lend itself as readily to social transla-

A CHRISTIAN RESPONSE

by careful analogy, but man as sinner always risks self-justification or cultural justification in any translation of the gospel. Nevertheless, the risk is necessary because of the urgency of the Christian's task to express what God is doing in terms that are reasonably applicable to current political decisions. The analogical risk is intrinsic to the possibility of relevance, and for this possibility the risk is something the Christian must endure.

To develop the implications of the gospel for political guidelines, I rely heavily on Ernst Troeltsch's study, *The Social Teachings of the Christian Churches*. For Troeltsch the meaning of the gospel idea for all human relationships is that moral achievement is to be seen as participation in the work of God. Since God is active, creative love, then men are to manifest love toward each other in all their relationships. All virtues fall in line with this basic understanding of moral action. Troeltsch does not believe that the gospel yields a social ethic as such. Yet he does believe that certain social ideas are intrinsic to the gospel idea, and hence to the social meaning of "manifesting love toward each other." [52]

The first of these characteristics is individualism. It is an individualism which "removes all distinctions by concentrating entirely upon the differences in character in individuals, each of whom has his own value." In other words, it is an individualism in which "all earthly distinctions are swallowed-up in the Divine power and love which reduce all other distinctions to nothing." [53] The distinctions that do remain are "those which characterize creative personalities of infinite worth, each one of whom must trade with his 'pound' to the best of his ability." [54] Each man himself is related to God. Man in all his uniqueness is the object of the divine grace, and on the basis of the divine grace he is given value equal to all others.

tion. However, we shall see that there are very definitely social and political implications in the gospel message.
52. Troeltsch, *Social Teachings* . . . , Vol. I, p. 55.
53. Ibid.
54. Ibid.

Alongside this individualism is an idea of fellowship. The grace which is the ground of the value of individuals proceeds from the same divine center. The surrender and response to the divine grace, then, is a response to the same divine center, and this means that all who respond are united in God. The unity is characterized by a common sensitivity to the real values of life "through the manifestation of love." Though there is no humanitarian ideal here, Troeltsch believes that there is an absolute universalism which extends at least as far as the Gospel is known. Because the fellowship is conditioned only upon the "pure hearted self-surrender to God" by the individual, there is no limit except God's grace which can be placed upon the extent of the fellowship.[55]

When the permanent Christian community is established, the individualism and the universalism of the gospel undergo a transformation. What was a very general idea of individuality and a rather free idea of fellowship becomes more intensified.[56] The individualism becomes identical to the state of being "in Christ," and the fellowship becomes a brotherhood in Christ rather than a union of believers in God. The universalism of the gospel becomes both the revelation of the divine love toward the world and the impetus for the missionary task of the church.

Finally, as the community was formed and the members became mutually dependent upon each other, the Christian idea of equality emerged. According to Troeltsch, the idea of equality is intrinsic to the gospel, because it necessarily arises from any system of absolute value which is both universalistic and individualistic.[57] This idea of equality, like the other sociological characteristics of the gospel, was applied only to the religious community at first, but it is rather obvious that the idea could "venture on the most searching interference with the social order." [58]

55. Ibid. p. 56.
56. Ibid. p. 70.
57. Ibid. pp. 70–72.
58. Ibid. p. 86.

On the basis of Troeltsch's argument, then, there emerge three significant socio-political ideas. These are a radical individualism which takes account of the uniqueness of persons, a radical universalism based on the belief that those to whom God comes he comes fully in grace; and by implication, an equality which affirms that those who are related to God are related equally to him.[59]

One other characteristic of the gospel message is freedom. Although Troeltsch does not develop this notion, it is implicit in his conception of the gospel idea. He does say that God's activity in the world is creative love and that man's responsibility is to manifest that love to others. If God's activity is the coming of creative love, then freedom will be one of the relevant socio-political characteristics of love, because love and freedom are inseparable. Whatever else might be said about the gracious activity of God in Christ, this should be agreed: the divine grace coming to man means a freely loving God coming to a freely responding man. This freedom is also the basis of the Christian community. The mark of "belonging" to the community is the testimony that in faith man freely responds to God's love. Thus, the individualism of the gospel which rests

59. The term equality can be a confusing one because it can function in so many different ways. It will be useful here to note at least two ways in which equality can function to clarify what is meant by "equal before God." In the first place equality can be a descriptive term. One can say that X is equal to Y, meaning that they are identical in some respect. This identity may be absolute or partial, depending upon the components in the equation. Hence, if one says that all men are equal, he may be saying that with regard to some characteristics all men are identical. Second, equality can be an evaluative term. For example, the equation X is equal to Y may simply mean that the writer holds the value of both X and Y to be the same. Here it is not necessary that X and Y be similar in any descriptive way. One may be a horse and the other a fountain pen. The only thing that is equal about them is the value which they possess in relation to the one who states the equation. The difference between this use of equality and the first use is quite important. Whereas in the first case equality is something possessed intrinsically by the objects, in the second case, the equality is attributed to the objects by a third party. It is the second use of equality that is characteristic of the gospel idea.

upon God's gracious coming to unique persons means that they are free to respond to that grace in unique ways, and the universalism of the gospel means that the boundaries of the community of freedom cannot be limited by status, nation or ritual requirement. Every man is at least potentially a member of the community of grace, the fellowship of believers. One thing is very clear: no barriers constructed by man can limit the scope of the fellowship.

In summary, there are four characteristics of the gospel message which may have some socio-political significance—universalism, individualism, equality, and freedom. It is important that these characteristics be seen as a whole. They are integrally bound together. For example, Troeltsch argues that the individualism and the universalism of the gospel are inseparable. "They require each other." [60] The foundation of universalism is individualism and the implication of individualism is universalism. Therefore, any claim that is made by one man in the community is rightfully the claim of the other. Also, any obligation that falls upon one member of the community must be the obligation of the others. This means that equality is a norm of the gospel idea, for as Troeltsch has pointed out, equality is a necessary inference from an absolute universalism that is bound to an absolute individualism. This equality, however, does not mean "to all men the same in every single thing." Equality refers to status before God and value before God and not to the intricate details of individual response.

The equal value attributed by God in grace to men is attributed to unique individuals, and the valuing of them in their uniqueness confirms the freedom of their response. In other words, since God's love and man's freedom are inseparable, the individualism that is universalized is the unique freedom of each man to be what he is and still to be valued by God. Therefore, the gospel implies that God's grace creates the possibility of a community of men who are equal in their freedom. Equal because the coming of God's grace gives the value and in

60. Troeltsch, *Social Teachings* . . . , Vol. I, p. 57.

his grace there are no distinctions; free because grace comes to make man free for love of God and neighbor.

It becomes apparent, then, that any political analogy to the gospel message must take account of the notion of equality in freedom. The normative content of the message is not determined, but the characteristics of the gospel can function as guidelines for choosing an analogous political model that can give more concrete meaning to "Christian" political decision. This brings us to the second problem of a theology for political decision, the problem of a political analogy to the gospel message.

One political model analogous to the gospel idea is Albert Hofstadter's notion of "equal opportunity." [61] His conception of this norm is to be contrasted with the understanding of "equality of opportunity" characteristic of the early nineteenth century. The older notion was the idea that every man ought to compete under equal legal and political rules, but beyond that, the competition for the goods of society was an open game. Those with the most talent would win, and those without talent would simply be left behind. This notion of "equality of opportunity" was the product of the whole *laissez faire* position on economics, and the interpretation of the norm made no allowance for the importance of economic rights.[62]

Later in the nineteenth century and in the early twentieth century, men like R. H. Tawney and D. G. Ritchie began to insist that legal and political equality were rather meaningless in a society where extreme wealth and extreme poverty existed side by side. But so strong was Tawney's emphasis upon economic opportunity that this became the whole meaning of equal opportunity for him, and more especially for some of his followers. This was also true of the Marxists who saw economic equality as the basis of all equality in society.

61. Albert Hofstadter, "The Career Open to Personality: The Meaning of Equality of Opportunity for an Ethics of Our Time," *Aspects of Human Equality* (New York: Conference on Science, Philosophy, and Religion, 1956).
62. Ibid. p. 122.

Yet Tawney, and to a greater extent, Ritchie, T. H. Green, and L. T. Hobhouse, saw beyond simple economic equality to a broader notion of equality of opportunity which would be defined in terms of man's total interests and needs as a human being rather than upon any one given condition of his life.[63] Hofstadter is sympathetic to this development, but his own conception of equal opportunity centers more upon the creativity of individual human beings of equal worth. This does not mean that all men are creative in the same manner, but rather that all men are creative in individually unique ways. There is no common denominator of excellence or one simple creative avenue.[64]

Hofstadter's concern is for the development of the unique capabilities of each individual human being to the highest level possible. Implicit in this ideal of creative opportunity for individuals is individual freedom. Part of the notion of individual development is conceived as the opportunity for free choice about one's own destiny and freedom and the opportunity to participate fully in the choices about the shape of one's society.

> Creativity is no longer the mere unfolding of possibilities, the explication of the implicit, the actualization of potentialities. It is . . . more radically conceived: as involving novel decisions, individual responsibility. . . . Man is the being who makes decisions, takes decisive steps . . . as himself and for himself, as the radically creative and radically responsible individual person.[65]

Equal opportunity, then, means equal opportunity to exercise one's freedom with respect to one's own fulfillment and the means to that fulfillment.

From this general ideal of equal opportunity, Hofstadter proceeds to posit what he calls the conditions of this norm. In other words, certain kinds of rules or rights must exist if there

63. Ibid. pp. 122–6.
64. Ibid. p. 121.
65. Ibid. p. 131.

is to be any possibility for actualizing the ideal in the political life. These conditions are political equality, equality before the law, economic equality, educational equality, and social equality.[66] Each one of these rights or rules is based upon the recognition that there can be no equality of opportunity unless certain conditions prevail. Economic equality as a condition is based upon the recognition that without a minimum of economic necessities a person cannot have the kind of nutrition, housing, or education that is necessary for him to develop as a human being. It is also the recognition that wealth is power, that political equality is impossible in a society of vast extremes of affluence and poverty. Educational equality is based upon the recognition that in order to compete economically and politically in a society a high degree of understanding and comprehension must be developed.

The necessity for social equality can best be illustrated by the bitter experience of our own nation which had to learn from a "separate but equal" Court ruling that men cannot be *arbitrarily* separated by race or class without one man's inferiority being implied. Equality before the law means that my rights are bound by your rights, and both of us shall be given equal consideration in the settlement of our disagreements.

Political equality is based upon the recognition that many of the crucial decisions about my future and my destiny are made by the government. It is the recognition that the shape of my society thus determined is an important factor in specifying the limits of my own possibilities for free and novel choice. Also equal opportunity, as defined by Hofstadter, depends to a great extent upon whether or not such political decisions support a free society in which free choice can continually be made.[67]

Hofstadter's notion of equal opportunity with its attendant norms offers a striking analogy to the equality in freedom which is implied by the gospel. This is not an equality that levels all men to the same in everything, but rather one which

66. Ibid. p. 142.
67. Ibid. pp. 136 ff. I have tried to make specific here what is implied by Hofstadter.

focuses upon individual persons. The moving spirit of Hofstadter's discussion is concern for the unique individual. Equal
opportunity means equal individual opportunity as defined in
the rights he specifies. But if the opportunity is individualistic
in its focus it is universal in its scope. The goal of any society,
as Hofstadter sees it, is to secure the possibility of creative development for every person in the society. Nor are the standards to be imposed from without. They are to be freely
chosen in the concrete expression of political freedom. Moreover, the individualism inherent in the equalization of opportunity here is always to be seen in the context of free and creative choices by others.

Thus, Hofstadter's notion of equal opportunity preserves the
individualism and universalism that lie behind the Christian
idea of equality in freedom, and moreover, he makes a more
concrete translation of the ideal into specific kinds of rights
that should belong to all members of the society. This means
that the political norm here defined can function as a political
translation for the meaning of God's redemptive activity in the
world *if* the risk of analogy is taken. The strength of so doing
is that one is provided with a relevant image and a cluster of
guiding norms for political decision which ultimately rest upon
his theological convictions. This in turn means both a political
stance which is grounded in faith and a faith that is relevant for
political decisions.

Having taken the risk of analogy and having made a political
translation of Christian obligation, I should add that this translation is not meant to imply that every person who subscribes to
these political norms is a Christian. One of the worst forms of
Christian condescension is the "baptism" of all those with
whom one shares basic norms in spite of their disclaimer of
Christian belief. One must take seriously the self-consciousness
of an actor before he calls his total action Christian, for no description of an action is complete until an account is given of
the belief structure that informs that action.

For example, Stuart Hampshire has argued convincingly that
"action" does not have specific content, but like "event" or
"thing" it is indeterminate. Action must, therefore, be subject

to a description of what was actually done and an interpretation of the intention with which it was done.[68] Hampshire's argument will not allow that any interpretation of an action, whether past or future, is complete unless both aspects of the action are included in the description. Even though it is possible to talk about an "overt act" apart from the intentionality of the act, it is important to remember that intentionality is no less integral to the total concept of action than is the physical movement. In fact, Hampshire argues that intentionality is the *key* to the meaning of *human* action.[69]

If intentionality is the key to the meaning of human action, then it is self-evident that before we can be clear about the meaning of any action, the notion of intention itself must be clear.[70] It is not possible to elaborate all of Hampshire's distinctions here, but some of his comments will be helpful.

In the first place, intentions may be expressed or unexpressed. It is not a precondition of intentional action that one first give an ordered account of the propositons and considerations which led to the decision to act. It is not even necessary that one be clear in his own mind just how he would give an account of his decision. "Intentions, like beliefs, effortlessly form themselves in my mind without conscious and controlled deliberation. . . . Any human mind is the locus of unquestioned and silently formed intentions." [71] But Hampshire argues that the very condition of the existence of anything to be counted as intention lies in the "possibility of their finding an immediate natural expression both in words and in action." [72] The first comment, then, is that intention must at least be capable of being expressed if it is to count as intention at all.

68. Stuart Hampshire, *Thought and Action* (London: Chatto and Windus, 1960), pp. 92, 151.
69. Ibid. pp. 96, 98, 99.
70. "There are very great complexities in the concept of intention. . . . They cannot all be unravelled at once, even if they can be finally unravelled at all. Yet nothing else in ethics and the philosophy of mind can be made comparatively clear unless this notion is comparatively clear" (Ibid. p. 96).
71. Ibid. p. 101.
72. Ibid. p. 99.

Second, intention must be specific, but any specific intention must have a general reference. If one is asked the question, "What are you going to do?" he may reply that he is going to vote for a fair-housing law. This might be a legitimate expression of his intention to act in the future, and in some contexts, it may be all that is required. However, Hampshire argues that it is inconceivable that any *rational* man would not have some general pattern of intentionality or some policy of intention which serves as a background for specific intentions.[73] Thus, if one is asked why he will vote for a fair-housing law, his total explanation of his action will include some pattern of consistency or a "policy" of action over a period of time, if it is to be counted as a rational intention. This pattern usually consists of the norms and conventions to which one refers in justifying specific intentions. These norms may be culturally derived, but their cultural derivation does not in any way undermine their role in the formation of individual intention.[74] What is important here is that *some* pattern of intention must be a part of a total action if it is to be counted a rational action.

Third, patterns and rules do not form the only context for specific intention. There is also the expectation of what will be the effect of one's action, and the accompanying deliberation concerning whether one's action will in fact give adequate expression to one's intention.[75] This reflection has to do with the contextual integrity of one's total action seen as a unity of "what is to be done" and the intentionality with which it is done.

Fourth, intentionality always occurs in the context of belief. As Hampshire puts it, "every literate man can be said to have an ontology." [76] This "broader frame of reference" enters into and informs practical intentionality. To return to the previous example, a man might say that he will vote for a fair-housing

73. Ibid. pp. 148, 149, also p. 265.
74. "Every convention or rule that I accept is an intention that I declare" (Ibid. p. 99).
75. Ibid. pp. 109 ff.
76. Ibid. p. 205.

law. In giving an account of that action he might argue that he is following a religious conviction about what God wills in the world. In this case, no complete interpretation of the action is possible unless that reference to God is taken into account. It is obvious that an observer could contend that the frame of reference is false or irrelevant, but this would simply mean that the observer in accounting for the particular *overt* action on his own part would operate in a different frame of reference. To the extent that this is true, the actions would be different actions even though the overt action might be identical, or even if the pattern of norms or policy is identical.[77]

In summary, the concept of human action includes an overt action and an intention, but intention is the key to human action. Furthermore, an account of rational intention must be capable of including the expectations of a specific overt action as well as that specific action's relation to a policy of action and the belief pattern or frame of reference which informs it.[78]

What I have said about Christian action, then, implies nothing more than the fact that the pattern of normative principles I have suggested is a translation of Christian obligation. It is not my intention to demonstrate that *only* Christians can have these principles, but rather to argue that *any man who is a Christian ought to subscribe to these political norms.* If the Christian finds that others are in agreement with him on his pattern of normative judgments, this should surely be no cause for anxiety. From the standpoint of our faith, this can only mean that God is active in the world outside the holy community as well as inside the holy community. Our faith has always allowed us to view men outside the covenant community, like Cyrus of old, as the agents of the divine activity whether they

77. Ibid. pp. 204–6.
78. These components of action correspond roughly to some of the suggestions made by H. D. Aiken in his discussion of "levels of moral discourse." See H. D. Aiken, *Reason and Conduct: New Bearings in Moral Philosophy*, (New York: Alfred A. Knopf, 1962), pp. 65 ff. Some similarity might also be noted to the levels of reasoning in ethics suggested by Stephen Toulmin in his book, *Reason in Ethics* (Cambridge: Cambridge University Press, 1950).

self-consciously confess the name of Yahweh or not. In this sense, not only does the political translation of faith provide the Christian with guidelines for his own behavior, but it also provides criteria by which the Christian may in faith see the divine action taking place in the world. Hence the agreements of men of good will, both Christian and non-Christian, on the pattern of normative judgments about the social and political structures of the world become occasions for Christians to rejoice in the knowledge that God has been acting in the world and is still acting to humanize society wherever men dwell together.

Two further comments about the relationship of Christian faith to this political norm are necessary if the translation is to be made. In the first place, any Christian political decision which is based on an equalitarian norm does not rest on the self-evidence of the equality of men.[79] Equality is grounded in the gracious activity of God who values all men. It is God who gives all men their equal value, and it is their value to God signified by the coming of his grace to the whole world that is the basis of Christian commitment to equality in freedom. This means that any claim by the individual for equal rights based on the Christian foundation of equality in the gospel must be made humbly and gratefully in light of God's relation to man. Equality is never the Christian's possession by right. It is the gracious gift of God's love.

Second, the gift of God is also a claim upon the Christian. He is responsible to God. But his responsibility to God is also responsibility *for* his neighbor. Therefore, obligation to God and love for the neighbor are united in the one requirement that the needs of the neighbor should be the Christian's primary concern. This calls for a particular stance on the part of the Christian toward the norm, "equal opportunity for self-fulfillment." The struggle for "my" self-fulfillment will necessarily be a secondary concern for the Christian. His primary obligation will be to make those political decisions which will contribute to the possibility of universal self-fulfillment, but with

79. See Note 59, above, p. 155.

a particular emphasis upon those who are most deprived. As Karl Barth has said:

> The Church is witness to the fact that the Son of man came to seek and to save the lost. And this implies that—casting all false impartiality aside—the Church must concentrate first on the lower and lowest levels of human society. The poor, the socially and economically weak and threatened, will always be the object of its primary and particular concern, and it will always insist on the State's special responsibility for these weaker members of society. [80]

Still, the Christian's own self-fulfillment is not contradicted by his responsibility to God, because his own joy is made more full by God's claim upon him. Therefore, the Christian "fulfills" himself to a great extent by working for the self-fulfillment of the neighbor in need.

Thus the Christian's faith may inform his selected political norms as a limitation and as a stance. On the one hand, an examination of the gospel idea yields certain politically relevant characteristics which can be translated by analogy to political norms. In this way the Christian's commitment to his beliefs serves as a limiting criterion for commitment to political ideals.

On the other hand, the Christian's recognition of the ground of his value and the nature of his obligation will always mean that gratitude, humility, and joyful concern for others will characterize his political decision-making. Both of these observations together help to give more meaning to the total notion of "Christian" political decision which is the central problem of translating faith into a pattern of norms for Christian political decision-making.

On the basis of this statement of Christian obligation, the directions of a white Protestant response to the new Negro pluralism become clear. In the first place, white Protestants

---

80. Karl Barth, *Community, State, and Church,* intr. by Will Herberg (Garden City, N.Y.: Doubleday and Co., Inc.), p. 173.

ought to focus upon the political and social implications of our faith. We should insist that the church be political, for so much of our common humanity is shaped by public policy that an obligation to "make human life more human" necessarily involves political questions. In fact, political reform may well be one of the most viable goals of evangelism today, for if evangelism means bringing men together in a truly human fellowship, political and social problems are in the front line of obstacles which must be overcome.

Second, it is important that white Christians should take seriously the suggestions of the new Negro pluralism in regard to the white role in the Negro community, and it is already clear from the previous discussion that we should focus upon the white community in our action. However, this does not mean that *all* co-operation between whites and Negroes is impossible. On the contrary, most Negroes still welcome white allies in their struggle for justice, but Negroes themselves must define the terms of co-operation in the future. These terms will probably include insistence upon Negro leadership in matters of policy and strategy, and white leadership will be limited by this Negro effort to exercise full self-determination.

This is necessary for both psychological and theological reasons, and here especially, the resources of Christian faith converge. On the one hand, Negroes must have self-determination for the sake of their own self-esteem, for it is essential that they begin to see themselves as creative and free men who share in determining the future of our nation in order to destroy their negative self-image. Hence, the Negro's self-determination is an important step in his struggle for the true humanity to which our faith points us. On the other hand, the most morally sensitive whites are sinful men, not to mention those who have no moral constraint in their relationship to Negroes. Hence, Negroes must have self-determination in order to restrain the collective sin of the white community. In either case, the need for self-determination requires that whites take seriously the strategy of Negroes to effect political equality and not be discouraged by Negro exclusiveness.

Finally, whites should remember that while Christian political decisions are now necessarily the primary form of the Christian ethical response to racial crisis, they cannot be the total response. As Emil Brunner has pointed out, structures of justice can be further humanized by face-to-face relationships that are characterized by the true humanity of Christian love.[81] Though Brunner's sharp separation of personally humanizing love from the requirement of justice is mistaken,[82] he is correct in calling attention to *some* distinction between the Christian decisions about justice and Christian "personal" relations. Christian faith requires that both be humanizing and hence manifestations of the same love. What this means in the context of Negro pluralism is that Christians should not only engage in humanizing political activity, but that they should continue to be open to abiding human relationships with Negroes wherever they are sought by Negroes themselves.

I have already pointed to some of the complications involved in Negro-white personal relationships that will remain simply facts of life. Yet, while this is true for many Negroes, there are a number of others who may genuinely seek continuing relationships with whites, and for whom self-esteem is no longer a major problem. In *individual cases* where this is true, whites should certainly remain open to deep and abiding interracial personal relationships. These instances of personal relationship function as a "sign" of that time we all hope for, when Americans, black and white, may overcome caste and become fully mature humans together. However, the new Negro pluralism may even become a complicating factor here too. When this happens, whites should understand the tensions which are occasioned by the Negro's identification with all other Negroes, and we must remind ourselves that these personal relationships

81. Brunner, *Justice and the Social Order*, pp. 128, 129; and *The Divine Imperative*, pp. 220 ff.
82. Brunner, *Justice and the Social Order*, p. 127, where he says that justice is a "totally different thing" (referred to in Note 31 above, pp. 147–8). "Personal" love and justice are equal forms of Christian love which is a total humanizing process.

are "signs" and nothing more than that. Therefore, any concentration on contrived devices to effect "personal" interracial relationships is superfluous, and it may prove to be a hindrance at the present stage of the Negroes' move toward a more fully human existence.

From another point of view, however, the new Negro pluralism may itself be the beginning of humanization in interracial "personal" relationships as such. To clarify what I mean here, I return to the statement by Barth in which truly human existence is said to include several dimensions on an ascending scale. The first is "eye-to-eye" relationship in which two people *really* see each other. Now isn't this precisely what the new Negro pluralism demands? Whites must see blacks for what they really are—black human beings—and not as inferior men or potential copies of white men. Black men are *black* men, and Negroes are determined that their distinctiveness shall be acknowledged. They do *not* want us to become color blind; they want us to become color conscious, with an appreciation of what black color really means.

At Barth's second level also, the new Negro pluralism is humanizing. Negro pluralism is an attempt by Negroes to *speak*, to say a word about whites and a word to whites about Negroes. Furthermore, it is a demand that the white man *hear* the Negro's word. Too long we have spoken and they have heard, but humanity at this level is dependent upon *mutual* speech and hearing. This means that it is not only Negro humanity which is at stake but ours as well. Hence, we should be ever mindful of our own need to be human and of our dependence upon the words of Negroes for the co-humanity of us all.

After the second level, Barth adds the dimension of mutual assistance, and this is the level at which most of my ethical response has been focused. The Christian is uniquely required to attend to the need of his neighbor, and hence I have dwelt at length on the obligation of white Christians to support the Negro in his struggle for equal opportunity in ways that are acceptable to the Negroes themselves. I have also suggested that our response must be made in gratitude and joy over

God's action upon us. Therefore, our response must be partial, for our joy is made full in service to the neighbor in need. And our response can be neither condescending nor self righteous; for we know that all we do is possible only because God in his grace has favored us with his claim, and we know that whatever difficulties we face are predominantly the fruit of our own sinful labors.

VII

The Limitations of White Protestantism

The white Protestant churches are limited in their choices of a response to the new Negro pluralism. This is already apparent from the discussion of the previous chapters. The very nature of the new Negro pluralism places inherent limitations upon the role of all whites, and white Protestants will be restricted by these limitations too. In fact, white Protestantism as such may be under a special limitation in its response to the more ethnocentric elements of the Negro community precisely because we are white Protestants. Here I have in mind the very clear anti-Christian emphasis of the Black Muslims and the special indictment of white Christianity by Stokely Carmichael and Ron Karenga.[1]

As regrettable as this is, it is perhaps understandable because of our lofty pronouncements on race relations and our failure to implement these pronouncements. I have already noted the gap between our understanding of the church and the actual performance of the churches, but now I shall extend that discussion further from two standpoints. In the first place, I shall discuss the history of white Protestantism and the Negro in America. This will not only serve to illustrate the grounds for Negro criticism, but it may also serve to illustrate the depth of our responsibility for making some creative response. We have

---

1. Carmichael, "Speech at Berkeley," Nov. 19, 1966; Karenga, "Lecture," Feb. 16, 1967.

been party to the history of America that has created the current crisis in race relations, and in a real sense, we bear a special burden of responsibility as the dominant religious group during that history.

In the second place, however, our limitation is not only our history. The white Protestant churches of today share certain theological and sociological characteristics which in themselves may prove to be a limitation upon our response. It may even be the case that the prevailing theological understanding, the organizational patterns, and the sociological character of our institutions together are a more serious limitation upon any creative response than any of the restrictions which the new Negro pluralism might place upon us. Therefore, I shall follow the sketch of our history with a brief analysis of our contemporary profile.

Both our history and our profile are important at this point in our total response—important *at this point* because it is necessary to qualify with realism any ideal understanding of Christian obligation. Before we can give concrete expression to the "ought" of a Christian response, we must have some assessment of what we can expect from ourselves. In the final analysis, the "ought," if it is to have an important function in human behavior, must imply "can." [2]

WHITE PROTESTANTS AND RACE RELATIONS IN THE PAST

The problem of the Negro and the white Protestant churches began with the arrival of slaves in the United States in colonial times. This meant that there was a distinct difference in the character of the churches' response to the question of slavery in the North and in the South. The northern churches were,

2. My treatment of the history and profile of the churches will be admittedly sketchy, but this is appropriate because there are ample available resources for the reader who wishes to pursue these matters. For example, I shall rely heavily on David Reimers, *White Protestantism and the Negro* (New York: Oxford University Press, 1965), and Gibson Winter, *The Suburban Captivity of the Churches* (New York: The Macmillan Co., 1962), both of which are very excellent works.

for the most part, outspoken critics of the whole system of slavery, particularly during the early 1800's. While this developed in the North, the southern churches, many of whose members were slaveholders, were taking quite a different position. To be sure, there was opposition to slavery in the South. In fact, the South was the birthplace of most anti-slavery societies prior to 1830, but these societies were interested in colonization, for the most part, and they never thought in equalitarian terms as the later abolitionists did. By the 1830's, however, the southern churches had ceased any real opposition to slavery and many churchmen, including leading pastors, began to proclaim slavery as a positive good ordained by God.

After 1830, both the anti-slavery movement in the North and the pro-slavery movement in the South gained momentum. So great was the division over the issue, that beginning in the 1830's actual schisms were occasioned by differences on this issue alone. Hence, by the time of the Civil War, the Protestant churches of America were arrayed against each other on opposite sides of the most explosive moral issue in American history, and the divisions between the churches did not follow denominational or theological lines at all. They were internal denominational splits that were occasioned more by location and social and cultural milieu than any other factors.[3]

Though the record of the northern churches on the question of slavery was much better than that of the southern churches, the record in the North on segregation was not. Northern Negro Christians were segregated both within the white churches and in separate congregations. Like their fellow churches in the South many northern churches had special pews, Sunday schools, and sacraments. There was even segregation in northern seminaries. Church segregation in the South followed much the same pattern, except that it was even more carefully enforced than in the North.[4]

Thus, well before the Civil War, racial discrimination and segregation were part of Protestant church life in both the

3. Reimers, *White Protestantism* . . . , pp. 3–8.
4. Ibid. pp. 15–18.

North and South. The churches generally agreed that because Negroes had souls they were eligible for salvation, but this did not preclude discrimination and segregation within the religious community.[5]

By 1865, the southern churches were moving toward complete segregation. The few Negroes who had remained in white congregations were finally driven out by the repeated refusal of the churches to extend to them any semblance of equality, and by the early 1900's there were almost no Negroes at all left in the white churches.[6] Nor was this segregation in any way benign. The extremism *in* the churches actually helped to pave the way for the development of racism in the South. Such tracts as Carroll's *The Negro a Beast*,[7] gave theological arguments to support the most blatant stereotyping of the Negroes, and in some cases, churchmen actually were equivocal about lynchings. By and large, however, the churches did oppose lynching, but this in no way altered their position on segregation.[8] Approval of segregation followed the pattern of the approval of slavery. Southern churches simply substituted the former for the latter, and the southern churches accepted the pattern of segregation as necessary and good for all. Thus, was the problem of the Negro solved in the South.[9]

Segregation in the churches was also the most important issue facing northern churchmen after the Civil War. Many northern church leaders had argued that segregation was in violation of the will of God, and those who did support segregation never proclaimed that it was the will of God. The support was given rather on the grounds of some supposed immediate necessity or on the grounds that the Negroes really preferred their own separate congregations.[10]

The fact that segregation was rapidly expanding in the North in no way meant that the northern churches approved

5. Ibid. p. 18.
6. Ibid. pp. 30 ff.
7. Carroll, *The Negro a Beast*.
8. Reimers, *White Protestantism* . . . , pp. 25, 46–7.
9. Ibid. p. 46.
10. Ibid. p. 55.

of the manner in which the southerners handled the race problem. They attacked lynching with great vigor, and they were strongly critical of the developing legal and informal controls which were the basis for the southern pattern of forced segregation. However, even though the northern churches did not widely favor segregation and in almost no case thought it was the will of God, the post-war years were the time of increasing compromise. More and more church leaders began to accept the "second class" status of Negroes and their attacks upon the problems of the Negro in the South took the form of an enlightened paternalism. The Negro was a "white man's burden" at home, and Christians should manifest the same concern for these poor helpless people that he did for those in other countries.[11]

By the time of World War I, then, the churches, both northern and southern, had accepted the pattern of segregation in church life as either necessary or desirable or both. Furthermore, the separate Negro and white churches had very little formal relationship with each other at any level and almost none at the local level. And not only was church life segregated, but northern and southern churchmen had generally acquiesced in the second-class citizenship of Negro Americans.[12] Less than twenty years after the Supreme Court had formalized segregation, the Protestant churches of America had sanctified it, and church practice and preaching throughout the nation was increasingly in tune with the mood of the times.

The acquiescence of the church in segregation continued through the 1930's, although there were an increasing number of pronouncements dealing with various aspects of the race problem. Between 1930 and 1939, most of the major Protestant denominations began to urge some steps toward the elimination of segregation and discrimination in the life of the church. However, most of these pronouncements came from northern based groups, and the suggestions for desegregation were very halting ones aimed at the desegregation of conferences and

11. Ibid. pp. 75–80.
12. Ibid. pp. 82–3.

camp grounds.[13] It should be noted, moreover, that the most significant efforts at changing church attitudes and practices during this time were led by church women. Especially significant was the work of the Methodist women in supporting the education of Negro girls.[14] Still, for the most part, the churches were either silent about the question of race, or openly supported segregation.

Beginning in the early 1940's, however, some signs of change appeared. Like the American population in general, churchmen began to see that the "separate but equal" formula was nonsense in terms of justice, and that the separation of Christians within the community itself made absolutely no sense at all. Thus,

> During the 1940's and 1950's and early 1960's the northern churches expanded their pronouncements and sanctioned open housing, F.E.P.C. laws, the Supreme Court's ruling on desegregated schools in 1954, the sit-in movement of the South, and many other steps toward integration and equal rights.[15]

Even the Southern Baptists had passed a resolution of some good will by 1947.[16] By 1957, seminary desegregation had been approved, and the president of the Southern Baptist Convention had asserted publicly that there was no scriptural support for segregation.[17]

Within the life of the church, Negroes were given increasing recognition. Presbyterians, Congregationalists, and Episcopalians elected Negroes to high church offices, and most of the denominations began to attack the problem of all-Negro divisions within the church at the conference or synod level.[18]

With the mounting attacks on the problem of segregation in

13. Frank Loescher, *The Protestant Church and the Negro* (New York: Association Press, 1948), pp. 123–4.
14. Reimers, *White Protestantism* . . . , pp. 92–4.
15. Ibid. p. 113.
16. Loescher, *The Protestant Church* . . . , pp. 139–41.
17. Reimers, *White Protestantism* . . . , pp. 116–17.
18. Ibid. pp. 120 ff.

the churches there also emerged a tendency toward greater participation in the struggle for racial justice outside the church. Clergymen by the thousands joined individual Christian laymen in the March on Washington, the sit-ins, the Freedom Rides, and the March on Montgomery. In these dramatic protests and countless others that did not quite make the headlines in so spectacular a fashion, the presence of churchmen in the struggle for Negro equality in America took the form of positive support and active participation.

From a split over slavery to support of segregation to an attack on the color line in the life of the church and in American society—this has been the past history of white Protestantism and the Negro. The churches' actions have moved from active support of slavery and segregation to measured silence and then to a mounting attack on the problems of discrimination.

Theologically, it is very difficult to see why the churches take cognizance of race at all in their constituency. As Dr. Visser't Hooft of the World Council of Churches has argued, the church is "supra racial" in the sense that color is of no significance at all. The Church is the "people of God," and as such it is called together to "serve all humanity and . . . cannot become the monopoly of one race or nation." The Church is a "new people," and this new people is "to demonstrate the true universality of God's concern for all men." [19] At the level of resolutions the American Protestant Churches have officially followed very closely this understanding of church and race since the first quarter of the twentieth century. At the level of individual participation, the churches have provided a great deal of the leadership in the civil rights struggle. The most recent signs in the white Protestant churches, then, seem to point toward some closing of the gap between the preaching of the pronouncements and the practice of the institutions.

But this is not the whole picture. Alongside some remarkable changes in the thought and strategy of the churches on race, there remains the continuing problem of segregation of the

19. W. A. Visser't Hooft, *The Ecumenical Movement and the Racial Problem* (Paris: UNESCO, 1954), pp. 53, 54.

local churches. We have already seen that the post-Civil War years especially saw a virtual exodus of Negroes from the predominantly white Protestant churches. Due to segregated status within the churches and widespread refusal to allow Negroes in the white churches at all, Negroes rapidly formed their own denominational groups.[20] Much of the "desegregation" of the 1940's, 1950's, and 1950's consisted of some kind of affiliation of these independent bodies with white Protestant bodies, or else, as in the case of the Methodists, the incorporation of these bodies into all Negro subdivisions within the total denomination. In spite of this move at one level, however, not much has been done in the way of local church integration. For example, Frank Loescher discovered that by 1948, only 500,000 Negroes of the 8,000,000 in the United States at that time were affiliated in any way with predominantly white Protestant denominations. In addition, of these 500,000, the overwhelming majority were in segregated local churches. Further evidence led Loescher to conclude that the actual number of Negroes worshiping with whites on Sundays in local churches was less than 8000.[21] This figure is even more shocking when it is added that most of the Negroes who did worship with whites were in communities where few Negroes lived and hence where there were no Negro churches available for them to attend.[22]

Nearly twenty years later, Reimers found that this picture of the local church had not changed very much at all. This was true in spite of the fact that the whole attitude of the church had undergone rapid change, and denominational involvement at the national levels and within the National Council of Churches had gone beyond mere integration toward active support of Negro demands in the society at large. Still in 1964, no more than 10 per cent of the white Protestant congregations had Negroes worshiping with them. Even these 10 per cent had only a few members or occasional attenders, so that throughout

20. See H. R. Niebuhr, *The Social Sources of Denominationalism* (New York: Henry Holt Co., 1929, Living Age Ed.), pp. 236 ff.
21. Loescher, *The Protestant Church* . . . , pp. 76-7.
22. Ibid. pp. 77-8.

the United States probably no more than 1 per cent of all Negroes worshiped in integrated congregations on Sunday morn-
ings.[23]

This situation is not entirely due to the intransigence of
white congregations. As we have seen, the change in the aims
of the new pluralists among Negro leaders and the *de facto*
segregation that occurred in the cities is increasingly a problem
for white churches who might want to integrate. Yet, when all
this is considered, the local white churches remain the most
stubborn problem confronting Protestant moves toward integration.[24] There is ample evidence that the majority of local
white churches have not made any real effort to include Negroes in their membership, and in fact, many of them have
stubbornly refused to admit them at all.[25]

THE PROBLEMS IN THE CHURCHES THEMSELVES

Why does this anomaly of universal theology and the segregated church persist? The answer to that question certainly
could be discussed theologically under the doctrine of sin, but
sin has taken rather concrete form in the churches' relation to
the Negro, and concreteness is most important for our purposes here.

Prejudice and Cultural Dependence

In the problem of race, the most obvious manifestation of the
church's sin would be the persistence of prejudice among the
Christians. Studies on the relationship of religion to prejudice
have utilized a wide variety of methodologies, and general conclusions are somewhat risky. Still we can note some of the find-

---

23. Reimers, *White Protestantism* . . . , p. 178.
24. This critique is merely of the pretensions of Protestantism. It is already obvious that I have some question about the strategy of developing
interracial congregations in the context of the present racial crisis.
25. This is common knowledge. Any doubts can be dispelled by a
cursory reading of Reimers's study.

ings and draw a limited generalization from them. Some studies have found religion to be a negligible variable, either positively or negatively, in the development of prejudice.[26] Others have demonstrated a correlation between specific types of religious belief and prejudice,[27] and still others have found that prejudice and a high incidence of all kinds of religious belief and practice are significantly related.[28] Glock and Stark, in a recent study, found that the more orthodox the beliefs of a Christian, the higher the level of his anti-Semitism,[29] and Argyle found that agnostics and atheists are less prejudiced than Protestants who do not go to church, though the regular attenders were not so prejudiced as those who seldom attended.[30]

Even though this picture is confusing, it does seem safe to draw the conclusion that church members are probably no less prejudiced than other persons in the society at large. Therefore, one of the problems of the churches in their approach to race relations in the United States lies precisely in the fact that the members of the churches are beset with the same forms of prejudice that constitute a major problem for race relations in the wider American society.

When the persistence of prejudice among the members of

26. See Adorno, The Authoritarian Personality pp. 208 ff., and Bettelheim and Janowitz, Social Change and Prejudice, pp. 259-60.
27. See Clifford Kilpatrick, "Religion and Humanitarianism: A Study of Institutional Implications," Psychological Monographs (Vol. 63, no. 9); Else Frenkel-Brunswick and R. Nevitt Sanford, "Some Personality Factors in Anti-Semitism," The Journal of Psychology (Vol. 20, 1945), pp. 271-91; G. W. Allport and B. M. Kramer, "Some Roots of Prejudice," Journal of Psychology (Vol. 22, 1946), pp. 9-39. Gerhard Lenski isolated two kinds of religious orientation and found that they had different correlations with political and economic beliefs. He suggested further study in relation to such beliefs as prejudice. See The Religious Factor (Garden City, N.Y.: Doubleday and Co., Inc., 1961).
28. Frenkel-Brunswick and Sanford, "Some Personality Factors . . ."; Allport and Kramer, "Some Roots of Prejudice."
29. Glock and Stark, Christian Beliefs and Anti-Semitism.
30. Michael Argyle, Religious Behavior (Glencoe, Ill.: The Free Press, 1958).

the churches is known, then the public action of the churches is not surprising. The churches are culturally imprisoned, that is, the practices of the church with respect to segregation and integration are greatly determined by the prevailing group norms in the area where the church is located. Whatever else the local churches might claim to be, they are social institutions which share a common history with other social institutions within the cultural milieu where they stand. Therefore, as Reimers's excellent study so ably documents, the story of white Protestantism and the Negro is the story of America and the Negro. Churches located in the slaveholding sections of the country approved slavery. Many of those located in the North did not. Churches located in the South after the Civil War actively supported segregation as the will of God and rushed to segregate themselves. Churches in the North did not. When the North grew tired of conflict and began to acquiesce in segregation, the churches followed suit—and on and on the monotonous story drags.

In the late 1950's and 1960's, some churchmen, Robert Spike among them, began to foresee a new day in the church when finally the institution of the people of God would move out into the forefront of the struggle for justice.[31] But the objective eye of the historian had quite another interpretation. Reimers noted that the new flurry of activity in support of civil rights was no more than the old pattern of American white Protestants. They had always remained in the mainstream of American solutions to the problem of the Negro. If they were to continue to be in the mainstream after the fantastic revolutions of the 1950's and 1960's, they had to move very quickly. In other words, what else would one expect of institutions that had so long been the embodiment of the average American viewpoint on the problem of race relations? If they had not moved ahead in their own pronouncements and participation in support of the civil rights revolution, the churches would have

31. Robert Spike, *The Freedom Revolution and the Churches* (New York: Association Press, 1965), pp. 100, 106 ff.

found themselves completely out of step with the national consensus of the times.[32]

It is significant, however, that the churches in the South, like the South in general, remained behind the national mood. White Protestant churches were, in fact, often the most stubborn outposts of continued segregation. They were the one place where national governmental pressure could not touch the institutional life, and if my own experience in Clarksville, Tennessee, and Danville, Virginia, is any indication, I would suggest that the churches in the South will probably be the last institutions to fold the tents of segregation and steal into the present. My experience is confirmed by Liston Pope's observation that not only have the churches not led in the struggle for Negro equality in America, but they have, in fact, lagged behind most of the other major American institutions.[33]

Individualism, Localism, and Piety

Another problem in the churches is the persistence of a type of theological individualism. This is particularly a problem of the churches who have a frontier sectarian heritage like the Baptists and the Methodists, but it is not uncommon among the congregations of other large Protestant bodies who appear to be more "churchly." [34] The primacy of the individual's private relationship to God as over against any institutional or creedal obligations was built into the American Protestant churches early in our history, and it remains a problem.[35]

One important consequence of this individualism that is especially a problem for the churches' action in race relations is

32. Reimers, *White Protestantism* . . . , pp. 180 ff., especially 185.
33. Liston Pope, *The Kingdom Beyond Caste* (New York: The Friendship Press, 1957), p. 105. Pope noted, however, that the church is probably less segregated than other *voluntary* institutions (pp. 104–5).
34. This is obviously an allusion to Troeltsch's typology (*Social Teachings* . . . , Vol. I, pp. 331 ff.).
35. H. R. Niebuhr, *Social Sources*, pp. 137 ff. See also Will Herberg, *Protestant, Catholic and Jew* (Garden City, N.Y.: Doubleday and Co., Inc., 1960), pp. 105–7.

the complication of authority. In the first place, this type of individualism is certainly related to the emphasis in church polity on the authority of the local church. As Liston Pope has pointed out, despite a wide variety of official positions of polity, it is generally true that American Protestantism vests most responsibility in matters of faith and morals in the local church.[36] In other words, most American Protestant churches do not necessarily respond to the direction of national bodies at all. The most extreme example of this localism is, of course, the Southern Baptists. The Southern Baptist Convention has no authority either to speak for the churches or to enforce its decisions upon them. This polity arrangement has been a major problem in attempts to institute denominational-wide programs in race relations. The refusal of local churches to co-operate can break the back of such efforts, and on other occasions they can force the denomination to be equivocal in its stand.[37] Moreover, pronouncements by national leaders on questions of race can be taken with very little seriousness in the local churches, and this is especially true when the pronouncement is made by an ecumenical body.

Second, this localism is complicated in the local churches by the individualism of the members. After all, the "priesthood of believers" has long been interpreted to mean the equal access of every Christian to a knowledge of God's will by virtue of the presence of the Holy Spirit, and there is no reason even to submit to the judgment of a local church body, to say nothing of what "those guys in New York" might believe. In the churches where I have had experience, for example, it was not uncommon at all for individual church members to withdraw from the congregation if they did not agree with the direction the church leadership was taking. More often than not, this meant simply the withdrawal of financial support or inactivity, but on occasion it meant joining a church which more accu-

---

36. Pope, *The Kingdom Beyond Caste*, pp. 143-4.
37. The equivocation characteristic of the most recent Methodist General Conference (1966) is a good example. Of course, Southern Baptists are almost totally crippled by local church autonomy.

rately reflected the individual's own views on the question of race.[38]

This compounding of individualism and localism lies behind the very weak structure of authority in American Protestantism. When it is added that most of the pronouncements on race that have been consistent with the theology of the church have come from either national denominational bodies and agencies or ecumenical agencies, it is not too difficult to see why the gap between pronouncements and local church action has been so noticeable.

The moral aspect of theological individualism is the tendency to see moral questions almost entirely in terms of personal piety. It is expected that if individuals were converted from immoral practices, "social justice would naturally follow." [39] This view severs the nerve of corporate social action on the part of the churches and seriously hampers the local churches' attempts to deal with the socio-political questions that are so much the problem of race relations. Under the presuppositions of personal pietism it is utterly impossible to recognize the limitations which institutions place upon morality. The whole question of love's relationship to justice is seen more in terms of how one personally feels and acts toward his brother than in terms of any need for reshaping the structures of society. Such questions as desegregation of schools, economic aid to the poor, health services, and other questions of public policy and institutional reform are viewed as political questions which are not fit subjects for church discussion, and obviously, the whole question of race relations may be reduced to the question of whether one will love the neighbor person-

38. This is one of the major assumptions at which Campbell and Pettigrew arrived in their study of the Little Rock crisis. See Ernest Q. Campbell and Thomas F. Pettigrew, *Christians in Racial Crisis* (Washington: Public Affairs Press, 1959), p. 121.

39. Herberg, *Protestant, Catholic and Jew*, p. 116; H. R. Niebuhr, *Social Sources*, pp. 67, 68, where he discusses Wesley's conception of ethics, and p. 143 where one can note the similarity to the ethics of the American frontier. In both cases, the emphasis is upon personal piety rather than social justice.

ally or help individual Negroes who are in need. Hence there may be a flood of Christmas turkeys and tender attention to individual Negroes flowing from churches who would never countenance the minister actively supporting desegregation of schools. The former would be a matter of morals; the latter a question of politics. And the two are related only in the conscience of the individual Christian where they are neatly compartmentalized.

The Middle-Class Syndrome

Accenting the problems associated with this theological individualism is the increasingly middle-class character of the mainline Protestant denominations.[40] Protestants have always included large numbers of the middle class, and this has had some important effects. For example, Richard Niebuhr has observed that one of the most important features of middle-class psychology is the high development of individual self-consciousness.[41] This has been due to the fact that the whole rise of the middle class has been intimately associated with the doctrine of individual rights and liberties. Moreover, it has been supported by the nature of middle-class employment which generally places a great responsibility for success or failure upon the individual himself.

The development of individual self-consciousness has given to the middle class a tendency to think more in terms of persons than of institutions or forces, and in terms of personal merit and demerit as constitutive of the causal chain of events in one's life.[42] Carried over into one's religious life, the emphasis on individual self-consciousness results in the development of a religion that is likely to be "intensely personal in character," making the matter of individual or personal salvation much more important than the problems of redeeming society.[43]

40. Winter, *Suburban Captivity* . . . , p. 65.
41. H. R. Niebuhr, *Social Sources,* pp. 80–81.
42. Ibid. pp. 81–2.
43. Ibid. p. 82.

The emergence of the middle class as the dominant portion of white Protestant constituencies, then, has tended to pick up the main themes that were present in the sects and on the American frontier. Thus, the tendencies we have just discussed in American Protestantism will likely be given new impetus in contemporary church life by the increasing dominance of the middle class.

According to Gibson Winter, however, the increasing dominance of the churches by the middle class is not merely an emerging dominance of the same old middle class. Although the churches remain, to some degree, in contact with the old middle class, it is increasingly a new *suburban* middle class which forms the membership of the white Protestant churches.[44] As Winter puts it:

> From 1870 to 1950 the major denominations of Protestantism underwent a twofold transformation: (1) they decentralized their strong congregations to the suburban and satellite areas . . . (2) they changed the character of their constituency, since losses among the rural middle class and urban working classes were offset by gains among the new suburban middle class.[45]

As a result of this transformation, there has developed a set of problems in the life of the church growing out of the needs and pressures that are peculiar to the contemporary suburban middle class. Two of these are exclusiveness and active affability.[46]

The exclusiveness of the middle-class churches is occasioned by two important factors. One factor is the sort of "natural" exclusiveness that comes from dress style, form of worship, mutual interests, and other indices that form the marks of identification with the middle class. Most mainline Protestant churches in the suburbs today would find it disconcerting to have in their midst a person not wearing his Sunday suit and tie, and as a result, the person so "unsuitably dressed" would

44. Winter, *Suburban Captivity* . . . , p. 65.
45. Ibid.
46. Ibid. pp. 67-8.

himself be uncomfortable. The table talk of informal groups is also of a distinctive style. Suburban housewives certainly have created their own "Kaffee Klatsch" patois that is distinctive, and it is not a situation made for a person who does not share the interests and opportunities that are available to most of the group.

The coalescence of persons of similar life styles into homogeneous congregations is reinforced by the tendency of suburban churches to be residentially based. The flight to the suburbs has been peculiarly a journey into homogeneous housing. Especially in these days of "tract" building, class heterogeneity is almost ruled out by the price level of homes. Hence, when churches are residentially based, they tend to include persons who have the kind of employment that will enable them to purchase a home in a rather exclusive price range, and this usually means that the membership will be of the same economic class.

A second characteristic of the suburban middle-class churches is active affability. By this Winter means that a great deal of emphasis is placed upon the "friendliness" of the church and the warmth that is felt among the members and by visitors present. Winter thinks that this characteristic emphasis is tied to the general demand of middle-class existence for the ability to "get along" with others. In the world of the middle-class man, job promotions and hence financial security and social status are tied to the ability to operate smoothly within the organization setting and to be found "pleasant" by one's colleagues and superiors.[47] Carried over into church life, this means an emphasis on harmony and peacefulness in the church. Persons who are always raising issues are "troublemakers" and the minister expecially must have the gifts of keeping peace in the household of God. The presence of this "pop *koinonia*," as I have called it, tends to force the churches to avoid controversial subjects and the minister breaks this taboo only at great peril. All of this results in the witness of the church being reduced to the lowest common denominator of agreement among

47. Ibid. p. 68.

the church members. To do otherwise is to disturb the harmony and friendliness of the church and hence to undercut the real meaning of the church in the lives of many of the middle class.

The need for affability is not merely due to the occupational style of the middle class. It is also related to their residential mobility.[48] In contemporary suburbia people come and go with astounding rapidity. Relationships have to be established in a hurry, and they cannot become too involved, for the prospect of another move is just over the horizon. Churches serving mobile people are thus in the position of having to focus a great deal upon establishing pleasing relationships among the members and maintaining an atmosphere in which these relationships can develop rapidly and with a minimum of pressure. This being the case, one would expect a very low tolerance for controversy and conflict. Both of these require some degree of stability in interpersonal relationships so that some kind of corporate loyalty can be formed. If this does not happen, then, the controversy will tend to rend the congregation. In light of this, it is not difficult to see that residential mobility reinforces the emphasis on friendliness and harmony, and thus tends to keep the churches very shy of controversial issues.[49]

It would appear, then, that the "middle-class syndrome" of the white Protestant churches of America would result in a distinctly conservative position in regard to racial integration. This is not to say, of course, that middle-class people are inherently more prejudiced than other classes of people. It is to say, however, that there are factors operating in the whole middle-class style of life that would impede the growth of any kind of heterogeneity in the churches, including racial heterogeneity.

48. Winter has discussed this in relation to the function of organization in the church (Ibid. pp. 101 ff.). I agree with what he says and here I wish to relate it to the "pop *koinonia*" of suburban churches.

49. There is some question about this last paragraph. Campbell and Pettigrew in their study of churches in Little Rock concluded that the more *stable* the membership of a church the less likelihood that the minister of the church would oppose segregation (*Christians in Racial Crisis*, p. 124).

When it is recalled that the inclusion of most Negroes would require not only racial, but also economic heterogeneity in the churches, it is fairly plain that the problem of racial integration will continue to be a problem in white Protestantism.

The Pressure of the Organization

The factors we have mentioned already as problems within the churches coalesce and become a counterforce to the theology of the churches. As Campbell and Pettigrew put it:

> A basic dilemma is posed for every social movement that attempts to influence society—whether it be a political party or a religious organization. At one extreme, the movement can hold uncompromisingly to its principles even at the cost of alienating most of its potential and needed adherents. . . . Or at the other extreme, the movement can modify its ideals so sharply that it attracts a wide following but sacrifices its distinctive aims.[50]

We have seen that a variety of factors within the churches themselves exert very heavy pressure against the expression of the aims of the church in terms of racial inclusiveness. The institutions are composed of people whose prejudice is about average and thus whose eagerness to integrate is by no means to be assumed. Moreover, the bulk of the members of mainline Protestant denominations belong to a class of people whose whole style of life works against racial inclusiveness. Hence the membership and potential membership for American Protestantism is not pro-integration, and there is no reason to believe that they will soon become so. If the organization is to expand —indeed, if it is not to lose ground—it cannot afford to press for integration of local churches. The result would likely be the loss of membership to other religious groups who support segregation or ignore it, or else the withdrawal of members and funds from participation in church life.

In other words, the task of maintaining the organization of

50. Ibid. p. 127.

the churches will continue to run counter to the inclusiveness of its ideal aims, and this is a tension the church has long lived with and can expect to be a continuing part of its life. It would be comforting to believe that more appeals to be the true church would have a wide effect, but I am convinced that they will not. Most American white Protestant churches would become integrated only when American society had become integrated enough to allow Negroes free and full movement both socially and occupationally. And what is more, it is likely that the basic conservatism and voluntary membership of the churches will mean that the majority of them will not even match the pace of other institutions in society even as they have not in the past. The local church will continue to resist the implications of its theology.

Since the whole church bureaucracy rests upon the ability of its bureaucrats to secure funds and co-operation from local churches, the managerial level of the institutional churches will be of little help either. In fact, there are very few "reform-minded" ministers who have not at one time or another been given a friendly warning from their bureaucratic fathers. When the membership campaign lags and the building funds cease to come in, or when the contributions to the denominational programs are cut, there is usually some kind of pressure to "move the reformer to a more fruitful field of service," or if that fails, simply to remove him. As one of the young ministers in Little Rock said:

> To advance your career in the ministry today you must succeed in an organizational way. You must get for your church a bigger building, more members, and more money. But to do this you have to dilute the gospel enough to ensure its appeal for everybody. . . .[51]

This kind of pressure finally has its effect on many of Protestantism's preachers. It is no wonder that they think and talk about the validity of the pastoral role as opposed to the prophetic role. The reduction of their function to church man-

51. Ibid. p. 131.

agement and the severe reprisals that can result from prophetic action have created a real crisis for many of the men in the local parish. Therefore, they orient themselves more and more to the parish and less and less to social problems in the community as a whole, and as they do so, they are less and less likely to support desegregation.[52]

The deadly thing about this kind of orientation is that with the passing of years the silence seems to become more and more comfortable. As the minister develops his image as a non-controversial "loving pastor," his parishoners come to expect this role of him exclusively. Moreover, the years also take their toll of enthusiasm and adventure in the spirit of the man, and as he extends the time of his association with one congregation the likelihood of his supporting desegregation again decreases.[53]

What this indicates is a double peril for the Protestant clergy. If the clergyman is an innovator or a reformer, he will not likely be a success at his maintenance function. In addition, if he chooses to be a "success" at maintaining the institution as a preliminary stage of his ministry, it is unlikely that he will ever be a reformer. In either case, the influence of many of those who could press for any substantial integration on the part of the churches will not be very pronounced in white Protestantism.

We have already seen that the integration of the churches may well be irrelevant in light of the developing Negro pluralism. Still, this does not absolve the white Protestant churches from their responsibility. The fact still remains that our faith is incompatible with racial exclusiveness, and we are obliged to make it clear that at least we are open to persons of all races. If Negroes, in their freedom, choose their own churches, even this cannot relieve our consciences. The new Negro pluralism may well make interracial congregations a side issue, but it in no way reduces our obligation to counter the inherent exclusiveness that is so much a part of our churches.

52. Ibid. p. 124. This is one of the hypotheses advanced on the basis of the study.
53. Ibid. pp. 122, 123. These are two more of the authors' hypotheses.

Beyond the problem of integration as such, the problems inherent in Protestantism will also tend to keep us quiet on political questions where we could have some ministry. Of course, the average white Protestant minister will not be a bigot, nor will the average white Protestant church be blatantly anti-Negro. Both of them will simply be "apolitical" and not do much of anything by way of supporting the Negro struggle for political equality and social justice.

The sad part of it all is that to be silent and to be "apolitical" is to have a great deal to say in the political arena. Silence and non-involvement in the efforts to bring about change are really assent to *status quo*. To "keep the church out of politics" is, in fact, a very shrewd political move. It means that one of the agents that might help effect change in the society toward a more just distribution of power and opportunity will be disengaged, and this will apparently continue to be the state of most white Protestant churches. They will, as institutions, assent to the *status quo* and respond to change positively only when it is clear that such a response as they will make is indeed a "safe" one—one that will not pass beyond the limits of what is tolerable for the society at large.

The problem in the churches, then, is that they are conservative institutions in possession of a revolutionary gospel. They are exclusive groups founded upon inclusive ideology. Neither the history nor the character of the local church institutions gives us much grounds at all for hoping that the churches will move as a reforming force in the current racial crisis any more than they have in the past. In most churches, hymns will be sung and prayers will be chanted for brotherhood and peace, but the vast majority of churches will then be satisfied that they have done whatever is required to be Christian.

THE HOPEFUL SIGNS

The record of the white Protestant churches is not inspiring to say the least, and the prospect for their future role in American race relations is not very promising. Still there are a number of hopeful signs too, and these signs should deliver us from pessimism and resignation.

One indisputable fact stands out when one carefully reviews the history of race relations in this country over the last half-century. There *has been* great progress toward equal opportunity for all men, and there *has been* a significant move toward the affirmation of the equal value of all men. This is not to say that we have arrived at the gates of the New Jerusalem, nor is it to say that we should forget our past. Yet it surely indicates that utter cynicism on the part of Negroes and sheer pessimism on the part of concerned whites is inappropriate. The fact of the matter is that the nation has shown a remarkable ability to change. and the pace has significantly quickened in the last few years. Though there does seem to be a rise in bitterness in both the black and the white communities at the present time, our recent history indicates that it is possible for Americans again to respond creatively to the challenge of our ideals.

But what does this mean for the churches? We have already seen that the churches tend to be in the American mainstream. In fact, they even lag a bit behind other institutions in race relations, and this is indeed lamentable. Still our penchant for the mainstream does mean that we share all of the changes in American democracy, and the hope which I have for democratic institutions means also a hope for the churches. We, too, have the ability, as American institutions, to respond to change.

We have already observed that from the standpoint of Christian theology, this may well mean that the God who has always used agents outside the covenant community to purify his people is again acting on his covenant people in this same pattern. Perhaps the response of one Negro to the Supreme Court judgment on Alabama's segregation laws was more truth than poetry. Maybe "God Almighty *has* spoken from Washington, D.C." [54] Certainly our faith gives us grounds for the hope that God's action in the world is not entirely dependent upon the

54. Martin Luther King, *Stride Toward Freedom*, p. 140.

churches. He is the sovereign Lord of the world who has manifested his steadfast love for all men, and he will make his people to be his people.

A second hopeful sign that has been with us all along is the response of individual Christians to their faith. As Reimers has observed:

> If the white churches on the whole were slow in climbing to the high plateau established by their own social pronouncements, many individual Protestants over the years were ahead of institutionalized religion.[55]

Here even the strongly individualistic flavor of American churches has been redemptive. While the individualism of which I have written earlier tends to stand in opposition to the universalism of the Christian faith, there has been an individualistic response which has attempted to call the churches' attention to their inclusive obligation.[56] At times Christians even banded together in groups to challenge the stand of the churches in race relations.[57]

Moreover, individual Christians who have been frustrated in their attempts to make the church aware of its universal dimension have turned to channels outside the churches in order to make their witness to their faith. Countless numbers were active in the abolition movement, the civil rights movement, and other movements that have attacked the structures of segregation and discrimination. And finally, though difficult to assess, the power of the Christian faith has been felt in the political agencies of this country when individual Christian politicians and bureaucrats have responded to Christian obligations in their own consciences as they wrestled with the judicial and legislative decisions that have so vitally affected the course of race relations in America.

Obviously, this kind of response has never been characteris-

55. Reimers, *White Protestantism* . . . , p. 188.
56. I shall have more to say about the kind of individual response that is necessary in the next chapter.
57. Reimers, *White Protestantism* . . . , p. 188.

tic of the majority of persons in the local white Protestant churches, but it is well to remind ourselves at this point that there has always been internal criticism of the church as a whole and external individual expressions of Christian obligation that have been at the forefront of the struggle for justice. And there is certainly grounds for hope that the recent changes that have come about in the position of the church on race relations will mean that the number of individual Christians who feel led to forge ahead in the struggle for racial justice will increase.

A third hopeful sign is the new emphasis upon direct action agencies within the churches. As I have noted previously there have long been voluntary organizations in the churches committed to direct action, and most of the denominations have had official agencies engaged in education about race relations. But it was with the establishment of the National Council of Churches Commission on Religion and Race, that the church for the first time commissioned direct action agencies.[58] There are now direct action agencies sponsored and supported by the churches in most of the major urban centers in the United States, and some of the most creative projects in race relations have been developed under their supervision.[59] These agencies have the advantage of not being directly dependent upon the local churches for support, and they are not under the same organizational and sociological pressures that hamper local churches. Therefore, even though direct action agencies have no effect on the segregation in the churches, they are avenues through which the church can continue to express the social and political implications of the gospel and they can function through their connections with the local churches as some counterforce to the factors we have already mentioned, which tend to make the local churches and church bureaucracy very conservative.

Another hopeful sign has been the increase in the number of exceptional churches who have opened their doors to Negroes.

58. Spike, *Freedom Revolution* . . , pp. 85 ff.
59. Ibid. pp. 108 ff.

It is significant that some of these churches have appeared in the South where institutional segregation is still the rule.[60] Even though there does not seem to be a widespread movement toward developing inclusive local churches, the few exceptions are a "sign" that will continue to keep before us the ultimate goal of Christian faith. The same could be said for the attempts by the denominations to integrate bureaucratic staffs and for the developing movement toward Christian unity represented by the ecumenical movement. They do represent for Negroes and whites, who can overcome the barriers that separate them, a prophecy of that longed-for age to come which is the object of our common Christian hope.

Finally a hopeful sign for white Protestantism lies in the changes in the Negro churches. The new social relevance of the Negro churches means that it is just possible that Christianity will continue to be an important part of Negro self-understanding, and this, in turn, will provide an important resource for developing a future reconciliation between Negroes and whites if and when we can achieve racial justice.

Yet we must guard our optimism in the face of these hopeful signs. For one thing, we must remember that the hopeful signs for the white churches themselves represent merely the hope that a *few* more white Protestants will become directly involved in the struggle for justice and that perhaps there will be *slightly more* rather than less support for direct action agencies in their attempts to influence public policy and to address specific local issues. We still have *no* grounds for hoping that the majority of individual Christians and local churches will do any more than they have in the past, and recent reactions in the white community may well mean that they will do less.

Our optimism about the Negro churches as a resource for reconciliation must also be guarded. One of the reasons for the revival of the churches in the Negro community has been their increasing identification with Negro aims. We can expect that the developing Negro pluralism will force them more and more into the role of champions of the race, and Negro Christians

60. Reimers, *White Protestantism* . . . , pp. 160 ff.

will be increasingly under criticism about their connections with white institutions. In the immediate future this may well mean a further separation of Negro and white Christians from each other, and continued white recalcitrance could finally muffle the notes of reconciliation that remain.

VIII

Toward a Strategy for White Protestants

All of us have known that the creation of a truly integrated society was going to be difficult, and with the passing of time many of us have become more and more pessimistic. Still we have pressed ahead, for it became very apparent that the whole American "separate but equal" formula for race relations had been subverted and employed as a device for exploitation. The Negro leadership that has become more and more vocal in this century was focusing upon the desegregation of society as their central goal. They were convinced that the only way out of discrimination followed a path into white institutions. That was where the better schools, the better houses, the better hospitals, and the more lucrative jobs were located. If Negroes were to share in the advantages American society afforded, on any basis approximating equality, it seemed clear that the task ahead was to ensure them entree into white institutions. And so the legal work went on to change discriminatory laws, and the protests focused upon symbolic actions that illustrated how limited the Negroes really were. Whites fought the Negroes every step of the way, but increasingly northern, western, and some southern leaders joined the Negroes, and the caste shell began to crack. Impressive gains were made, and it cannot be denied that the last two decades have been times of great progress in American democracy.

Almost imperceptibly at first, however, the new shape of caste was arising. For one thing the increasing number of Negroes who were being "integrated" were discovering the subtle limitations of their integration. As one Negro lady put it, "I am an integrated teacher, and I attended integrated schools and universities. I am an integrated worker, an integrated church-goer, and an integrated consumer—I am *still* a *segregated* human being." Moreover, even the external types of integration had some limitations. For example, Hubert Blalock, in a study of Negroes in professional baseball, concluded that Negroes have not and probably would not be integrated into jobs that require social contact and which require a high degree of mutual dependence in job goals.[1] Or again, the pattern of residential integration has more often than not proved to be a way station toward further segregation and in the schools and the universities there is very often an informal segregation in terms of the formation of cliques and in social activities. Even in the churches, Negroes who attend, or even those who have conspicuous offices, have not generally been fully integrated into the informal fellowship of the group.[2]

The most serious aspect of the new shape of caste, however, is far from being informal. Like an evil phoenix, the ghetto arose out of the ashes of legal segregation, and the very freedom and mobility that allowed Negroes release from southern oppression became the means whereby they were funneled into the new and increasingly universal shape of oppression. Like all new migrants, they moved to the cities, and they went to the spot where housing was available in their price range. Like all fearful strangers coming to a new land, they began to concentrate in areas where there were at least some familiar surroundings. The rest of the story is well known. The whites who were there "flew," and they packed their institutions into the moving vans with them. More Negroes came, and more whites "flew" as the boundaries of the ghetto expanded. Thus arose the new shape of caste from the moment of the death of the old, and today the majority of Negroes are more segregated,

---

1. Hubert Blalock, Jr., "Occupational Discrimination: Some Theoretical Propositions," *Social Problems* (Vol. 9, No. 3), pp. 240–47.
2. Reimers, *White Protestantism* . . . , pp. 166–7, 178.

segregated than they have ever been.

In the face of the new shape of caste, Negro leadership was in a dilemma. While it was true that some Negroes, in fact more than ever before, could integrate, it was rapidly becoming evident that the masses of Negroes were more or less permanently isolated from white institutions by residential location alone. This, together with the newly apparent intransigence of northern and western whites, sent a shock wave through the leadership community committed to a policy of desegregation. In addition, the developing change in Negro self-consciousness meant that fewer and fewer ghetto-dwellers could be really "turned on" by the promise of desegregation. The black community, filled with frustration and self-hate, began to heave with the first birthpangs of fierce ethnocentrism. At first, it was simply a sense of common misery, but, as we have seen, there emerged and there is still emerging a shared sense of positive group identity and unity. And the self-hate began to be turned outward toward the long-endured symbol of oppression—"whitey." Thus, with the passing of time it becomes more and more apparent that white intransigence is not the only problem for a strategy of desegregation.

Most Negro leaders continued to push for desegregation, and the Negro community turned to the idea of "busing" school children out of the ghetto as one kind of specific action. However, this strategy itself has proved unsatisfactory, and even some of those Negroes who still support busing are not interested in desegregation for the sake of interracial contact.[3] Busing may in fact have contributed to the disillusionment of Negroes with desegregation, for as I have already noted, the moving of ghetto children into white schools may, in some cases, have served to reinforce their sense of being disadvantaged. In short, the masses of Negroes are not even touched by recent moves toward desegregation. The ugly cycle of deprivation in the Northern and western ghettos simply would not

3. See Efrem Sigel, "Balancing Act in Boston," *The Reporter* (Vol. 36), May 4, 1967, pp. 22-4, and Charles Silberman, *Crisis in Black and White* (Vintage Ed., New York: Random House, Inc., 1964), pp. 299 ff.

yield to the same solutions as southern segregation in which the
ghettoes were small, scattered, and accessible. And even the
South is rapidly developing urban ghettoes along the patterns
already established in the North and West.

Let us be clear—the ghetto is the key problem in race relations today, and this is where Negro leaders will focus in the
future. We need to keep this fact constantly in mind, for the
new Negro pluralism is precisely a response to this key problem. What the Negro leadership has done is to seize both horns
of the dilemma. If, in fact, Negroes are segregated and the
masses of them will remain segregated, then at least one can
fight to make the segregation more benign. Being aware of the
history of white opposition and exploitation, the Negro leadership is increasingly focusing upon the resources of the Negro
community, and we have already seen where their strategy de-
liberations are moving.

I have already suggested that this change in the Negro community is a problem for the traditional focus of white Protestant strategy in race relations, but we have known for a long
time that the efforts to create an interracial church by bringing
Negroes into our white churches were not working. We have
come a long, long way, to be sure, and I do not want to minimize the very excellent progress that has been made at the national level of white Protestantism. At the "official" level of
most of the mainline Protestant denominations and in the National Council of Churches, there has been a developing consensus about the nature of Christian obligation for quite some
time.[4] It is agreed that the churches *ought* to be racially inclusive, and that they *ought* to throw their support behind public
policy that will deal with discrimination and segregation in our
society—these have been the dominant themes of official agencies, church periodicals, convention resolutions, and books by
prominent Christian ethicists within the last two or three decades. Furthermore, Protestant theologians are almost unani-

4. Reimers, *White Protestantism* . . . , and the appendices in Loescher,
The Protestant Church . . . , and Campbell and Pettigrew, *Christians in
Racial Crisis.*

mous in their condemnation of racism and discrimination, and the vast majority of them also oppose segregation as inherently evil.

Though these are encouraging signs of a new ethical sensitivity at one level of the life of white Protestantism, the problem remains. With all the resolutions and the integrated denominational staffs; with all the new Negro bishops and the merging of heretofore separate racial church organizations; with all the marching, lobbying, and direct action by clergy and laity—with all of this, the stubborn reality of the segregated local white Protestant church remains; and it is painfully evident that the very character of those churches and the emphasis upon maintaining them as institutions combine to exert a pressure which runs counter to the position taken by denominational and ecumenical leadership. The character of our theological individualism undercuts the witness of denominational and ecumenical agencies to the local churches while, at the same time, the universalism of our evangelism is restricted both by the style of life of our membership and the relative homogeneity of the neighborhoods where we are located. Thus, at the local church level, neither the individualism characteristic of our "sectarian" heritage nor the universalism characteristic of our new "churchliness" is really providing us with an evangelism that points toward racial inclusiveness in the local churches.[5]

To this it must be added that we do have more interracial churches in "white" Protestantism today than we have had in the past, and I do not discount the importance of these churches. In addition, more churches than ever before are "open" to Negroes. Still, there is no really significant movement in white Protestantism in the direction of interracial churches, and even the Negroes who have "gained entry" are, in many cases, not fully integrated into church life.[6] The most serious problem with the interracial church, however, does not lie in the pace of change in white Protestantism. It lies rather in the

5. I refer here to Troeltsch's types. (Troeltsch, *Social Teachings* . . . , Vol. I, pp. 331 ff.)
6. Reimers, *White Protestantism* . . . , pp. 166–7, 178.

fact that the whole concept of interracial congregations cannot
cope with the fact of the ghetto, nor can it come to terms with
the stark reality of the new Negro mood of separatism.

Everything we have said, therefore, points us to the general
conclusion which I have been suggesting here and there all
along: There must be a change in the over-all focus of white
Protestant strategy in race relations today. Our energy must be
channeled away from the development of interracial churches
and token integration of predominantly white churches, and it
must be focused upon action which is more appropriate to the
crisis in race relations today.

The conclusion will probably come as no surprise to many
white Protestants, for the winds of change have been blowing
for quite some time. To chart the directions of the change, I
refer first to a very excellent book by Buell Gallagher, *Color
and Conscience*, which was written about twenty years ago.[7] At
that time, Gallagher wrote:

> As ministers and as church members, we can make the
> churches in which we worship and work inclusive rather
> than exclusive. There is nothing but human inertia and a
> certain fear of the unfamiliar to stand in the way of our
> making every congregation in this nation a cross section of
> the family of God.[8]

Gallagher was confident that segregation could be overcome "at
least within the churches, by virtue of inclusiveness," and he was
sure that by calling the churches' attention to their sin and seeking interracial congregations and ministerial personnel we could
"quietly get rid of segregation in our churches" in the near
future.[9]

In fairness to Gallagher, it should be noted that he suggested a
wide range of strategies for Christians with special emphasis on
influencing government policy toward minority groups. Hence

7. Buell Gallagher, *Color and Conscience* (New York, Harper & Brothers, 1946).
8. Ibid. pp. 222–3.
9. Ibid. p. 223.

there is a strong social action strain in his book. But when it came to the specific strategy for the churches, the one Gallagher suggested was desegregation; and what is more important, he exudes optimism of a very high intensity.

About ten years later, Liston Pope, a leading Protestant authority on race relations, published his book, *The Kingdom Beyond Caste*.[10] Pope differed very little from Gallagher in his stress upon the desegregation of the Protestant churches as a strategy, but he does not share fully Gallagher's optimism. Tempered by the study of Frank Loescher, published in 1948, Pope wrote:

> The fact remains that segregation is still overwhelmingly the pattern that prevails in local churches. . . . The present situation is a result of historical and social developments, reinforced by continuing fear and prejudice.[11]

He goes on to say that segregation in the churches is due to many factors, some of which are part of the sociology and the character of white Protestant churches in general, and this did not allow him to think that the integrated church would be an easy possibility that could be effected by simple strategies.[12]

In spite of this, however, Pope was still somewhat optimistic, and citing evidence of the recent progress of the local churches toward inclusiveness, he pressed ahead with his emphasis upon integration. Buttressed with insight from newly found allies in the social sciences, Pope laid down guidelines for increasing racial contacts in such a way that the problem of white prejudice could be overcome.[13]

Aside from the assumption that white prejudice was the main barrier to the integration of the churches, which is in itself not true about race relations today, there is a problem with the sociological model upon which Pope relied. He utilizes the suggestions supplied by Dean and Rosen in their book, *A Manual for*

10. Pope, *The Kingdom Beyond Caste.*
11. Ibid. p. 113; Loescher, *The Protestant Church.*
12. Pope, *The Kingdom Beyond Caste,* pp. 114 ff.
13. Ibid. pp. 84 ff.; John P. Dean and Alex Rosen, *A Manual of Intergroup Relations* (Chicago: University of Chicago Press, 1955).

Intergroup Relations, the cardinal principle of which is: "The more contact a person has with other groups, the lower is his level of general predjudice against them." [14] There is a heavy emphasis, therefore, upon providing a context within which intergroup contacts may take place. Moreover, the strategy calls for the involvement of "influentials" or "gatekeepers" in the community so that the possibility of community-wide progress in race relations may be enhanced. When more and more intergroup contacts are thus provided, the general level of prejudice will be lowered, and the implication is that once prejudice is lowered, interracial harmony can then be achieved in the mutual pursuit of common goals.

This strategy has been subjected to a penetrating criticism by James McKee, who argued that its chief defect lies in the authors' assumption that the power of the American Creed would make the "influentials" receptive to appeals for better intergroup relations and mutual progress. This, in turn, gives the whole strategy a conservative bias, for it clearly intends to operate within the existing power structures.[15]

While it is true that racial "harmony" may be preserved for some time in some locations in this way, such a biracial strategy has been found to be notoriously unproductive in effecting any radical social change.[16] Most of the "influentials" in a community owe their own power to the top power leaders who represent the *status quo.* Therefore, the "influentials" are basically committed to the preservation of the *status quo.* Hence their reaction toward Negro pressure for change is to contain it as much as possible short of precipitating the kind of Negro response that would bring undesirable publicity and the resulting economic loss to the community.[17] This means that the strategy

14. Dean and Rosen, *Manual* . . . , p. 8.
15. James McKee, "Community Power and Strategies in Race Relations: Some Critical Observations," *Social Problems* (Winter 1958–9), pp. 105–203, quoted in Killian and Grigg, *Racial Crisis in America,* pp. 23–4.
16. Killian and Grigg, *Racial Crisis in America,* pp. 72–3.
17. Ibid.

is not only conservative, but it reeks with gradualism and tokenism.

Therefore, recent developments in the Negro community as
well as the general picture that Relmers has given us of the
"progress" of white Protestant churches would lead me to conclude that not only was Pope's minimal optimism about the desegregation of the churches misplaced, but the methodology
which he proposed to effect desegregation is now irrelevant.

The first clear expression of pessimism about the possibility of
desegregating the local churches came from Will Campbell in
his book, *Race and the Renewal of the Church,* published in
1962.

> As social institutions, white Protestant churches are by
> nature conservative. Moreover, based on past performance,
> there is little likelihood that white Protestantism will play
> any significant role in preparing communities for true in-
> tegration or even desegregation. . . . The Protestant social
> action professional . . . is hardly considered a liberal by
> the new movements for desegregation. If Protestant social
> action does not shift its tactics for any other reason, it
> needs a new strategy to justify calling itself by that name.[18]

Campbell called for genuine contrition and repentance, "broken-
hearted" repentance over the alienation between white Christians as well as the sin against the black man. What has happened in America, Campbell argued, is first to be seen as the
judgment of God. He also called for the Protestant social action
professionals to get off the "social engineering" bandwagon, for
this is not the task of the church. It is the proclamation of the
gospel of reconciliation that is our main task, and we have utterly failed to communicate the forgiveness of God and the
power of God's reconciliation to people of all races. We have
deified man, and in this deification we have been seen as self-
righteous social reformers by those who most desperately need
the words of reconciliation.

18. Will Campbell, *Race and the Renewal of the Church* (Philadelphia:
The Westminster Press, 1962), p. 79.

Because the church is conservative, and because it has another task, it cannot lead the way toward desegregation and true integration. But there is one thing it can do—"clean up the mess." [19] By this Campbell means that the church can help to restore and keep law and order, and it can help to reconcile those who have been alienated in the conflict *after* the battles are over.[20] Though there are other minor directives for the church, this is Campbell's main strategy suggestion.

Obviously, Campbell's strategy is a radical departure from the previous focus of white Protestant strategy. It is unfortunate that Campbell's caricatured Barthian emphasis upon God's initiative in action leads him to overlook the very important and necessary emphasis upon the partnership of God and man in the world which I have suggested earlier. This might be the cause of his narrow and unjustified criticism of Protestant social action. Some recognition of the partnership of God and man might also have delivered him from some of his morbid preoccupation with guilt and thus, perhaps, qualified his somber pessimism. From another point of view, Campbell's extreme pessimism was probably a result of his experiences in the South just after the *Brown vs. Board of Education* decisions, at least in part. Still, our most recent history has validated some of his pessimism, for the confidence we had in the possibilities of the North and West has gradually yielded before the new national crisis in black-white relations.

It is this same crisis, however, which also undercuts Campbell's main suggestion for strategy to some extent. The church as the institution which will "clean up the mess" still makes a great deal of sense in the white community (and I shall have more to say about this later), but the white Protestant churches are so removed and so alienated from the ghettos that any role that they play in reconciliation must be largely that of reconciling whites with each other. It is true, of course, that the Negro churches are a very important resource for reconciliation between black and white, and they will continue to be. But as I

19. Ibid. pp. 78 ff.
20. Ibid. pp. 80 ff.

have said before, there is a strong anti-Christian strain in the more militant Negro leaders, and Negro churches are under attack because they are part of a "white man's religion." As a result, their role of reconciliation between whites and blacks will be complicated by the necessity to demonstrate again and again their independence from white institutions as well as their identity with the Negro cause.

This certainly does not mean that all communication between blacks and white Christians will suddenly or ultimately cease. What it does mean is that any strategy that focuses entirely upon the reconciling role of the church will be limited largely to the role of reconciliation within the group to which the church members belong. While in the time of rising conflict and heightening tensions which surely lies ahead, reconciling agents will be sorely needed in both black and white communities, any strategy focusing upon either intergroup or intragroup reconciliation is not likely to be very significant as a total approach to race relations.

THE FOCUS OF THE NEW STRATEGY

In 1965, the late Robert Spike finally pointed white Protestants beyond pessimism toward the new directions in race relations.[21] Picking up on Campbell's emphasis upon reconciliation, Spike suggested that the churches have an important role to play as a "third force" between an alienated ghetto and a rapidly solidifying white power structure. Spike was not so much talking about the reconciling function of the churches here as he was pointing to their role as channels of communication. If the alienation is left to develop without any communication, the only result would be a head-on collision.[22] In addition, the churches' role as a "third force" must be implemented by direct action, for Spike was convinced that it was absolutely necessary for the churches to assume the role of both partner and critic of government action in order to effect the kinds of changes in Amer-

21. Spike, *Freedom Revolution.*
22. Ibid. pp. 113–16.

ican domestic policy that would enable the problems of the ghetto to be met.[23]

To implement this latter function, Spike suggested that the churches should encourage the development of "para-church agencies," that is, church-supported and church-related agencies that would be free to make certain critical tactical decisions that would be impossible for traditional denominational agencies to make under the pressure of local church criticism.[24] Obviously, Spike had in mind the very important model of the National Council of Churches Commission on Religion and Race. That agency has had an extremely important role in making the power of the churches felt upon government policy as well as providing a channel through which the corporate church could support projects that would have been impossible for the denominations alone. One example of the work of the Commission under Spike's leadership has been its co-sponsorship of the "March on Washington" in 1963 and its direction and planning of the subsequent lobbying by churchmen in support of the 1964 Civil Rights Bill. Perhaps the finest tribute to the Commission came from Senator Richard B. Russell of Georgia who said that the Civil Rights Bill had passed because "those damn preachers had got the idea that it was a moral issue." [25] Another example of the work of the Commission has been its support of civil rights organizations, particularly SNCC, in planning an extended program for community development in Mississippi which was called the "Delta Ministry." That project continues to this day in spite of repeated harassment by local officials and the opposition of most of the Mississippi churches.[26]

The focus in the white Protestant strategy of the future must be precisely where Spike has pointed us. Not only the National Council of Churches, but the denominations as well, must be willing to take the kind of risks necessary to become involved in shaping public policy and in developing projects within the

23. Ibid.
24. Ibid. p. 94.
25. Ibid. p. 108.
26. Ibid. pp. 108–11.

Negro community itself wherever this is possible. Moreover, Spike was right in insisting that this witness must be made through relatively independent church-supported agencies whose funds are supplied from the general budgets of the denominations and hence will not be as easily cut off by local churches who oppose some of the things they will and must do.

An encouraging sign of progress has been the development of departments of Urban Ministry in some local denominational structures. For example, in Los Angeles much of the credit for creative action in the city must go to a group of denominational officers whose primary responsibility is to develop ministries for the city. Through the co-operation of these executives, there have been some significant developments of grass-roots ecumenicity involving both black and white churchmen, and the cardinal principle of this interracial co-operation has been a focus upon *issues* rather than interracial contact as the occasion for interracial meetings.

Another significant channel of the church's ministry in the current racial crisis in Los Angeles has been the Southern California Council Commission on Church and Race. Under the excellent, creative leadership of John Pratt, the Commission has been instrumental in establishing within the Negro community a leadership training center for the young Negro leaders, and it has provided a setting for community gatherings and celebrations at the Watts Happening Coffee House. The Commission was also active in securing the support of 36 churches to support 37 Head Start centers. This literally saved the program, for without this help most of the centers for the Head Start program would have been closed because of their failure to meet the requirements set down by the Los Angeles Department of Building and Safety. In addition, the Commission, through grants to the American Civil Liberties Union, has provided legal assistance to hundreds of persons, and Pratt has more than once played a vital mediating role in some of the more explosive issues that have erupted in the minority community.

The Commission has not only given attention to the minority communities in Los Angeles, but it has also played an important role in the surrounding churches as well. There has been a continuing effort to interpret to the churches what was happening in the ghetto, and through Project Equality, the Commission joined with six Protestant denominations and four Jewish organizations in an attempt to encourage the local religious leaders to review their own employment practices and to bring pressure upon those employers who supply religious institutions with a variety of products. Finally, the Commission has begun to develop a program for interdenominational co-operation at the local church level in the center of Los Angeles. With a grant from the Church of the Brethren, the Commission was able to secure the services of James Donaldson, and under his vigorous leadership already nineteen local pastors have come together to begin what promises to be one of the most exciting ecumenical experiments in community organization and planning yet.

Another type of agency that can be very important to the church's ministry in the new era of race relations is exemplified by the Interreligious Committee on Goals for Los Angeles. Working in close co-operation with the Los Angeles City Planning Department, the staff of the "Goals Project" has helped to bring the resources of the religious community to bear upon the very vital discussion about criteria for a "human" city which would be more than new buildings and planned communities. Under the leadership of John Wagner and with the support of the National Council of Churches, the Committee has already made significant headway toward involving local religious communities in the dialogue about the future of Los Angeles. It is too early to assess the full impact of the project at this point, but I am certain that sociologists, political scientists, urban planners, and politicians must be in dialogue with the religious community if there is to be any solution to the problems of subgroup alienation and urban blight that are plaguing the cities of America.

To help build support for direct action agencies as well as to increase the understanding of the racial problem in the cities, the churches should provide the funds and the support necessary for the development of urban training centers. These centers can become the agencies through which new urban pastors can be given some kind of orientation to their city, and they will also provide opportunities for interpreting the churches' mission in the city to pastors and laymen in the suburban churches. Here, too, might be a place where the seminaries could focus urban training internships for theological students, who in turn could provide some of the much-needed personnel for the urban ministry as part of their internship experience. This could provide a growing number of Protestant clergymen who are interested in the church's mission to the city, and whether they actually become involved in a city ministry or not, they could certainly play the important role of interpreting the church's ministry to the city in the suburban churches they serve.[27]

Finally, the churches should begin to develop channels through which direct grants can be made to non-church Negro direct action organizations. This is especially needed in light of the criticism directed at the churches for their policy of channeling all support to Negro communities through white-controlled "middle man" agencies. Such a strategy would both express the faith and respect of white churches for black leaders and allow for full Negro self-determination in projects relating to the black community.

This, then, is the general focus for the future white Protestant strategy in race relations. It is a focus upon church-related agencies which can be the tactical arm of the churches by participating in projects within the Negro community and by developing support for local, state, and national government policies that deal creatively with the problems of the ghettos in

27. This section is based upon some of the planning done by Robert Ryland, the director of COMMIT, the urban training center in Los Angeles. As chairman of the board of directors, I have an excellent opportunity to observe this venture. It is still too much of a fledgling organization to see what directions it will finally follow. There are numerous other similar attempts in the country, such as the urban training center in Chicago, and the project sponsored by the Methodist Board of Missions in New York, Metropolitan Urban Service Training (MUST). These are older and further along than COMMIT.

the city. Moreover, these agencies can also be the institutional channels for interpreting the ghetto to the churches and for training laymen in the task of mission to the city.

These agencies should be developed nationally and locally, and both Councils of Churches and denominations should be involved. Wherever possible, the work of the agencies should be closely co-ordinated to avoid duplication and competition for available funds, and interdenominational co-operation must be the keynote of planning. In this way perhaps, the moribund councils could get some new life, and the denominations might get some experience in grass-roots ecumenicity which would help to prepare them for genuine unity in the days that lie ahead.

The whole strategy in a plan for direct action, and the focus is upon the city. This is appropriate, because the chief internal problem of the nation today is the city, and the chief problem of the city is the Negro ghetto. Furthermore, as the Negro population expands, more and more cities will become part of the total problem, for the pattern of migration leads the Negro directly to the heart of cities. Therefore, a Protestant ministry to the city will, in a very real sense, be a strategy for race relations, for as we have already seen, the Negro ghetto is the center of race relations in the future.

A NEW STANCE TOWARD PLURALISM

No white Protestant strategy for race relations will be relevant or even mildly successful for long unless it is based upon an understanding of the new Negro pluralism. On the basis of our past history, one of the most serious problems the churches face may be precisely at this point. Almost without exception, recent white Protestant leadership has lambasted the pluralism of the past, and this is understandable in light of the nature of previous American pluralism as a majority policy. Both Negroes and whites understood that the pluralism of the past was white-enforced and that it was utilized to exploit Negroes under the pretext of a "separate but equal" formula; and we were right to expose that subterfuge. It is understandable also that whites and Negroes alike opposed the "back to Africa" emphasis of Garvey and the black racism of the more extreme Muslim teachings. This is especially understandable from the Christian community, for no racism or hate ideology is compatible with Christian faith. The new Negro pluralism which I have described, however, presents quite another problem, and it requires something more than universal belligerence as a white Protestant response.

In the first place, the new Negro pluralism requires repentance. By this I mean the recognition that the pluralistic move of the Negro is not only self-determined, but it is partly a response to the sin of American society which has repeatedly provided new forms of caste as soon as the old ones are destroyed. I do not mean a morbid preoccupation with our own guilt, nor do I want to suggest that the Negroes are guiltless. In fact, it is one of the failures of white Protestant liberals that in their earnest desire to advertise their own guilt, they tend to describe the Negro in terms that would make Francis of Assisi look like a villain. This, in itself, is de-humanizing, for it really says that the Negro is not really man, *humanum*, in the eyes of the Christian. If he were really man, he would be a sinner, and a number of Negroes with whom I have talked have indicated that the refusal of many white liberals to allow the Negro any guilt is viewed by them to be another form of condescension.

Second, the stance of white Protestants toward the new Negro pluralism must be one of listening. Negroes are demanding the right to say to themselves who they are and what they will be. No longer will they allow white men to tell them who they are; they have heard that news already too well, and far too many of them have taken it seriously. The white Christian, however, does not listen because he must; he listens because he wants to hear. This is as necessary for our own humanity as it is for the Negro speaker. It is our interest in the common humanity of white and blacks, then, that calls for listening, and it is this interest that prompts us to take the risk that what we hear may not be the word we would speak about the Negro, and what he says about us may not be what we want to hear.

Throughout this book, I have tried to relay what I hear the Negro leaders saying about themselves and about white men, and one thing is very clear. Negroes are talking about their freedom—their freedom to say what blackness means; their freedom to have a voice in government; and above all, their freedom to determine how that voice can be spoken. Therefore, if participating in God's humanizing activity is a fair statement of our obligation, and if part of that humanizing is the development of mutual speech and hearing, then we must take seriously the Negro's right to say his word about himself and his destiny. And we must take seriously our obligation to hear and honor what he says before we speak in response.

Third, the stance of white Protestantism toward the new Negro pluralism must be realistic. Knowing what we do about man's sin and being aware of the gigantic problems Negroes face, we know that pluralism makes sense. On the one hand, a powerless minority always will find it difficult to make its voice effective in the nation's policy. On the other hand, the Negro minority with its problems of identity and lack of unity will never have power until these problems can be overcome. Therefore, even though we know that all men ought to be part of the church as one fellowship, our understanding of sin provides us with the flexibility to see various possibilities for interim strategies in a sinful world.

THE TASK OF THE WHITE PROTESTANT CHRISTIANS

At the conclusion of Chapter VII, I suggested that in spite of the gloomy picture I had painted of white Protestant churches, there were considerable grounds for hope. Already one of these has provided us with our general focus for a new strategy, that is, the new emphasis upon direct action agencies in the churches. I mentioned also that one of the redeeming facts of white Protestant history had been the constant witness of individual Christians who are far ahead of the churches in general. On the basis of this, I now suggest several guidelines for individual white Protestants who are anxious to be a part of the solution of the race relations crisis.

At the outset, what I have said about the stance of white Protestantism not only applies to the direct action agencies, but it is the presupposition of all our action—both individual and corporate. Hence the new stance toward pluralism provides the beginning point for all the suggestions that follow.

Interpretation

One of the very crucial tasks of white Protestants will be that of giving some interpretation of the whole Black Power phenomenon to their white communities. This is especially important for white liberals, for one of the distressing things about the current racial crisis has been the withdrawal of support that has been coming from white liberals to Negro civil rights organizations. It is extremely important for the future of American race relations that white liberals shall not now become completely alienated from the Negro community. My concern here is partly based on my own assessment of the Negroes' need of support in the white community. But it is also based upon the realization that alienation of whites from blacks is finally destructive to the humanity of whites, too. Therefore it is very important that it be made clear that the racists and the haters do not yet dominate the Negro community, nor do they dominate the new Negro pluralism.

Of course Negroes are angry at most whites, and in a public pep rally one does not pause to make all the distinctions between good and bad men in the opposing group. Understanding this, the white liberal must be capable of accepting the pro-black movements of Negro leaders that are required by the stubborn problems of the ghetto and he must undertake the task of interpreting these movements to the broader white community in a proper perspective.

Countering White Racism

I hardly think I need to document the revival of white racism. None of us have ever thought that racism was dead or even dying in Mississippi or any of the other deep South states, but we had hoped that it might be dying in the border states. However, no one is that naïve anymore. The revival of the Ku Klux Klan in North Carolina, the vicious white attacks upon the SCLC demonstrators and white clergymen who supported them in Louisville, Kentucky—and many other signs, all point to a reviving monster who had only been lulled to sleep. What is more, we can no longer rest in the North and West either. If anything, the racism of Chicago, New York, and Los Angeles may be worse than that encountered in the South because of its subtlety.

All of this is simply to say that racism as an ideology is not dead, and the white Protestant should plan programs in the churches using films, lectures, and study materials that counter racist ideology, and he should make every effort to see that antiracist materials are introduced to the broader community through school programs, club programs, and other appropriate channels.

Co-operation in the Negro Community

Some white Protestant liberals will still want to get involved in interracial co-operative projects, and this is still quite possible on a very broad scale both in and out of the ghettoes. As Kenneth Clark has pointed out, the various civil rights organizations will continue to function, and they will continue to provide some of the same patterns of co-operation that have been possible in the past.[28] The NAACP will still rely on interracial co-operation in many areas. The SCLC will still sponsor interracial protests where they are needed, and the Urban League will still provide the opportunity for interracial projects focusing on local and national issues.

Without a doubt, however, the possibilities in general of the traditional patterns of co-operation are diminishing, and this is already true within the ghetto. Even here, however, broad co-operation with whites is both accepted and needed under cer-

28. Kenneth B. Clark, "The Civil Rights Movement," *The Negro American,* pp. 622 ff.

TOWARD A STRATEGY FOR WHITE PROTESTANTS 217

tain conditions. The capital condition is that Negroes must be seen in positions of leadership. This, in turn, means that whites must remain in the background in planning sessions or they must be willing to provide skills for particular jobs that must be done. This kind of interracial co-operation is not as "heart-warming" as marching arm-in-arm in a demonstration, but in the long run it may be more effective. White Protestants who are interested in co-operation on these conditions can work through church-related direct action agencies, or they may find it possible to work directly with Negro organizations.

Worthy of special mention is the work of the white minister who is pastor of an all-Negro church in the ghetto. This is still fairly common in some denominations, although it is probably a passing thing. One of the most impressive jobs I have seen done in this kind of situation has been the ministry of the Reverend Speed Leas of Immanuel United Church in the Watts section of Los Angeles. Though Leas is white, he has learned to think black, and he has transformed a dead church into a center of community activity involving more than ten staff persons. None of the activities are traditional. Most of them are community-focused rather than church-focused. Leas has succeeded in becoming a part of a black community in spite of his white skin. As one of his members said to me, "Speed may have a white skin, but he has a black heart."

Yet, Leas himself thinks that the possibilities for a white minister to lead a black congregation are diminishing, and he is convinced that even the white minister must remain out of the leadership spotlight in the ghetto if he is to maintain his rapport with the people.

Finally, white Protestants should become politically involved. We should be informed about the political aims of candidates in local elections as well as any particular initiative measures. Furthermore, we should discuss these issues in our communities, campaign for politicians who support the kind of policy that will deal with ghetto problems, and perhaps even run for office. Our attention should not only focus upon local elections but national ones as well, and we should demand that minority representatives have some voice in any party structure of which we are a part. In other words, we should support the Negroes in their quest for justice by political action of all kinds, and we should support the Negro demands for their voices to be heard in shaping both local and national government policy.

This action is absolutely crucial, for though the possibilities of white co-operation with Negroes may be diminishing, the faith of the white Protestant can be given legitimate expression in the kind of political action that I have suggested in Chapter VI. In fact, for most white Protestants, this is probably the most promising avenue for participation in the new strategy for American race relations. Here again, we can work as individuals in our white communities, or we can co-operate with the direct action agencies in the programs they might suggest to white Christians for influencing both local and national policy.

The Local White Protestant Churches

The picture of local white Protestant churches which I have already drawn is discouraging, but this was a general picture that needs some modification. White Protestant churches have never responded to the problem of race relations in a monolithic fashion. Some denominations have responded more creatively than others, and churches in some regions have responded more openly than those in other regions. Therefore, it is appropriate to draw some distinctions between several types of churches and then suggest what might be appropriate strategy for each of them.

At the outset, there would be a group of churches that would be of a distinctly liberal type. By this I mean that there are white Protestant churches in which a majority of the members would be interested in becoming involved in political action within the white community as well as co-operation with Negroes in the Negro community. For these churches, the kinds of strategy I have suggested already for individual white Protestant Christians would apply. They could either attempt church-sponsored projects of their own or co-operate with the direct action agencies of the church in the programs they might sponsor. Moreover, the church could give substantial financial support to direct action agencies if possible, and support to Negro organizations within the ghetto. Since these churches are very rare and also very poor in many cases (most of them seem to be around college campuses and composed mainly of students and faculty), I am not very optimistic about their impact as institutions. Moreover, much of their witness will probably be made through agencies other than the church on an individual basis.

The main core of white Protestant churches is the "apolitical" type. As I noted in the previous chapter, most white Protestant churches will not be blatantly anti-Negro, and most of the clergy will be sympathetic to the Negroes' struggle for justice. In both cases they will be alarmed by "extremists" and will generally support some symbolic actions of good will, such as "Race Relations Sunday," interracial pastoral exchanges once a year, and perhaps an occasional interracial conference. In these churches it is also possible to have fairly widespread and frank discussion of some of the issues in race relations, especially among the members who are interested.

It would appear, therefore, that some important action might be possible and appropriate for these churches that form the largest core of white Protestantism. I suggest the following: (1) The churches should organize discussion groups centered upon the fallacies of racism, particularly "Christian" racism. This will give support to those who are anti-racist, and it will provide them with evidence which they can use when they encounter racists in the white community and in the church. (2) The churches should organize discussion groups which focus upon the problems of the Negro in the ghetto.[29] This is really the root of the contemporary racial crisis, and unless we understand that the ghetto is the problem, we too easily fall prey to a false optimism based on the recent giant strides we have made in our national life. Such an understanding will help to counter the

29. Kenneth Clark, *Dark Ghetto*, and Claude Brown, *Manchild in the Promised Land,* are two excellent books which I have already noted.

developing white opinion that Negroes are moving "too fast," [30] and it could give support to the sympathy for the Negroes' cause that is already present in many white Protestant churches. (3) The churches should discuss the nature of the new Negro pluralism. One of the real dangers of the current racial crisis lies in the possibility that the present trend in Negro leadership will be interpreted by whites simply as extremism, and some understanding of what is involved in the changing mood of Negro leaders might prevent a precipitous hardening of racial lines in those churches whose main concern is harmony and peace.

Even though I am fully aware of the limitations of "talking groups" who are not "involved," I see this kind of discussion in the church as important in three ways. In the first place, any creative white Protestant action in the current racial crisis will require funds, and it is important that those who have some understanding and sympathy for the Negroes' effort to improve their life chances be encouraged to support those church agencies which are involved in a more direct way. Therefore, even if most white Protestant local churches themselves will not become directly involved, it is possible that those who are not blatantly anti-Negro will be more inclined to give the needed financial support if they are aware of the nature and scope of the needs. Second, direct action projects require personnel, and many of the persons now involved in creative direct action have come out of white Protestant churches that were not "involved." Hence, it is possible that wide discussion of the problems in race relations today will encourage more individuals to become directly involved and thus provide some of the needed personnel for direct action agencies. Third, even if many of these churches finally prove to be incapable of financial support, and even if many of them never produce a person willing to be directly involved (and I for one am not *that* pessimistic), it is still crucial that white Protestant churches shall not become centers for opposing direct action through independent church-related agencies. Therefore, the very least that I hope for from

30. See *Newsweek*, Aug. 22, 1966, pp. 24–6.

the strategy I have suggested is that open and frank discussion might possibly keep the white Protestant churches "apolitical."

Unfortunately, there are still white Protestant churches in America that are not merely "apolitical" in their stance toward race relations, but they are avowedly white supremacist.[31] Hopefully these churches are a small minority in white Protestantism, but this is by no means certain. In any case, these churches are, quite frankly, part of the problem, and the most that can be expected from them is that they will not do anything at all about race relations but will continue to focus upon the personal religious experience of individuals in the congregation. This I say in all seriousness, for I am confident that God is active here, too. Any of us who have known churches like this are aware of some remarkable individual transformations that have occurred in the racial attitudes of some individuals within them. Certainly the history of Protestants in this country allows us to hope that God will continue to work, even in a church that is racist, to redeem individual Christians and to free them from their prejudice by the power of the gospel.

It is absolutely necessary, however, that these churches be confronted by a prophetic witness to their sin, for it is utterly clear that Christianity is incompatible with racism,[32] and the larger Christian community must continue to counter biblically rationalized "Christian" racism wherever it is found.[33]

31. I noted in Chapter VII that the level of prejudice in the churches is probably about the same as that in society in general. Hence when one finds racism in the society, there will be *some* racism in the churches as well.

32. See George D. Kelsey, *Racism and the Christian Understanding of Man* (New York: Charles Scribner's Sons, 1965).

33. "Christian Racism" is not dead. As late as 1959, I received a privately published document from Woodward Kimbrough, who argued on the basis of the Bible that God willed the races to be separate and that the Negro is from an inferior line. (*Man in Light of the Scriptures*, Ethel, Miss.: Woodward Kimbrough, 1958). The author is a Christian layman who appeals to the guidance of the Holy Spirit in his writing (Preface), and who bases all of his conclusions on a literal reading of the Bible (pp. 19 ff.) Everett Tilson's *Segregation and the Bible* is an excellent refutation of this kind of argument (Nashville, Tenn.: Abingdon Press, 1958).

If the liberal Christian community is to address the white supremacist church, we must bear in mind at least two things.
First, we are sinful men addressing sinful men. Too often the
"prophecy" of the liberal Protestant community comes off as a
blatant self-righteousness. And when this happens, it is impossible to address the white supremacist with the gospel. It will
neither be spoken nor heard, and the result will only be a widening alienation. This may happen anyway, of course, but at least
the non-racist Christian should not precipitate the alienation
with a sin of his own. Second, the point of contact with most
racist churchmen is the Bible. This is the source *they* use to jus-
tify their own racism. Liberals have never been noted for their
familiarity with the Bible, and especially this is the weakness of
some of the young "reformers" in the churches. With the resources now available for interpreting the Scriptures there is absolutely no excuse for not grounding what we say biblically.
The answer to biblical literalism is not anti-biblicism. It is biblical literacy.

With these reminders, then, my suggestion is that strategy in
race relations today with respect to this type of church simply
means that they are to be addressed as part of the problem by
the larger Christian community.

The Effect of the Current Racial Crisis on the Churches

The suggestions I have offered to white Protestant churches
were primarily based on my understanding of what one could
reasonably expect from the churches themselves. Realism de-

There is still some "scientific" support for racism too. (See Carleton Putnam, *Race and Reason* [Washington, D.C.: Public Affairs Press, 1962].)
Putnam's book was endorsed by a number of active social scientists. Furthermore, a student of mine at the School of Theology in Claremont,
Calif., recently interviewed an anthropologist who said that there is increasing evidence for racially determined differences in various kinds of
abilities. (I cannot use the name of the professor involved at his request.
He is anxious that his findings not be used by racists.) Still the vast majority of social scientists hold to the view I suggested in Chapter III.

mands, however, that we now turn to the possible effects of recent changes in the Negro community as a significant factor in
white Protestant strategy, for it is now impossible to discuss
strategy in any meaningful way without taking account of these
changes.

The churches that are white supremacist in character will
likely respond by a hardening of the lines. We have seen that
increasing competition usually increases the antipathy of the in-
group toward the out-group. Therefore, those churches which
are primarily composed of white supremacists will likely become even more anti-Negro in their response, and they will
probably utilize Negro riots and widely publicized Negro
racism as a basis for insisting that the only way to deal with the
race problem is to demonstrate power and toughness. Moreover,
they will continue to point to the depravity of the ghetto as an
evidence of Negro inferiority, and they will be likely to interpret unrest as an indication of the Negro's closeness to savagery
and his inability to be a "civilized human being." This, in turn,
will probably result in some revival of biblically based rationalization of discrimination and segregation.

For the "apolitical" type of the white Protestant churches,
however, two kinds of response to the current racial crisis are
possible—the one hopeful and the other tragic. One tragic thing
that could happen would be a hardening of the lines in the main
core of white Protestantism. As I have said before, most white
Protestant churches are strongly opposed to "extremism" of any
kind, and if the pattern of Negro unrest continues and expands
to include violent action and destruction in the white suburbs,
there is a strong possibility that the so-called "genteel conservatism" of the churches will yield to a policy of power and
toughness also. While the majority of the churches now would
support some social change, such a hardening of the lines could
mean that all support for any further changes could be killed. In
the South, particularly, where segregation has been all the more
damaging because it is softened by a dependency-creating paternalism, it is possible that any remaining opportunities for "per-

sonal" relationships between whites and Negroes would be considerably narrowed,[34] and even what Waldo Beach has called "unconventional tasks of tenderness" required by Christian *agape,* may begin to disappear [35]—this from the white side of the picture. From the side of the Negroes, it is already apparent that many of the "unconventional tasks of tenderness" have come off as ill-disguised paternalism, and without some evidence that the institution represented by the bearer of tenderness is supporting the kind of changes the Negroes demand, this will be more and more the Negroes' interpretation.

To turn to the more hopeful possibilities, I believe that some of the constructive action I have suggested for "apolitical" white churches are possible. In addition, however, one other possible effect of the current crisis might be what I label the "stretching of the extremism spectrum." This can best be illustrated by referring to a series of conversations I had had with a friend in the South.

About 1953, I had my first conversation with this person about race relations, and he and I agreed that while the Negro deserved a better chance in America, we must be careful to oppose two kinds of extremists—the NAACP and the Ku Klux Klan. In 1955, we had another conversation, and again we agreed that Negroes ought to be able to attend desegregated public schools, but that we should oppose two kinds of ex-

34. Frankly, I find James Sellers's description of the South a bit overdrawn. The so-called "personalism" of the southerner is more agrarian trait than anything else, and it is rapidly disappearing. Moreover, I am a southerner, and I love the South, but I have seen quite clearly that the "person," black or white, can quickly become a despised "object" if he dares to raise a serious challenge to the "Southern Way of Life." When this happens, the South does not distinguish between her own sons and the Yankees, nor is the white skin any protection from her wrath. See James Sellers, *The South and Christian Ethics* (New York: Association Press, 1962), pp. 53 ff. Sellers does say that differences between North and South are disappearing, but I submit that they were "gone" for all practical purposes long before he wrote his book.
35. Waldo Beach, "A Theological Analysis of Race Relations," in Paul Ramsey, ed., *Faith and Ethics, The Theology of H. Richard Niebuhr* (New York: Harper & Row, 1957), pp. 223-4.

tremes—White Citizens Councils and Martin Luther King. In 1966, this same friend said to me, "If we could get the good whites and the good Negroes to support Martin Luther King, perhaps we could put the brakes on these SNCC and CORE people and also put a stop to this ridiculous revival of the Ku Klux Klan." I submit that this is evidence of some progress, and I hope that now it is possible for white Protestants in general to realize the urgency of supporting the new Negro pluralism in its objectives. If we respond with power and toughness, we shall undercut even those Negro leaders who see a small possibility for Negro-white co-operation in the future—and this includes many of the new militants of the Black Power movement. This, in turn, might assure the dominance of racists and black supremacists in their ghettos, and the result of that is not a pleasant thing to contemplate.

Up to this point, I have not referred directly to the separatism that is inherent in Negro pluralism. It has not seemed necessary to do so, for the types of churches I have been discussing in this section will not be especially affected by Negro separatism. White supremacist churches, of course, could not be happier. In addition to their usual rationalizations about segregation, they can now add Negro separatism to the repertoire. It is important for us to realize, however, that Negro pluralism itself does not create white supremacist churches. It may simply provide some of those who are a bit uneasy with a clearer conscience.

The "apolitical" type will be only mildly affected, for most of these churches are and would remain segregated anyway. It is possible, though, that most Protestant churches will find it more difficult to have racial exchange programs, and it will perhaps be somewhat more difficult to find Negro participants for "Race Relations Sunday." In some cases, too, the more liberal clergy and laity of these churches will find themselves increasingly frustrated in their search for "instant Negroes" to "integrate" their churches. This, however, will not be the serious problem for the core of white Protestant churches. The most serious problem will be the danger of allowing Negro separatism to

obscure the clear obligation of all of our churches to be open-
membership churches, and without individual Negroes to make
the issue concrete, it will be very easy to forget that our exclusiveness is our own doing.

Conclusion: A Final Word to White Liberals

The churches of liberal persuasion and liberal white Christians
will be under the same kind of dangers that I mentioned before
concerning the total white liberal community, and I am convinced that the danger will be greater before it eases. We will
be tempted to quit or withdraw.

The conflict will rise in intensity and white resistance will get
tougher and tougher. There will be more violence. Violence is
always just over the hill from frustration, and the more Negro
frustration increases the more violent will be their response. In
addition, it is clear that many Negro ghetto leaders follow
Frantz Fanon's view about violence. In his book, *The Wretched
of the Earth*, Fanon argues that violence has a double operative
role for a minority without power. On the one hand, the majority or dominant group does not want violence and the threat of
violence and chaos will produce changes more quickly than any
other single strategy. On the other hand, a call to violence is a
rallying cry to gather support for a revolutionary movement.
Men who will not respond to calls for organized political action,
men who are too apathetic to move for any other reason, will
respond to the call for violence. This is true because violence,
more than anything else, is a cleansing of frustration.[36] Hence it
is likely that less and less of the future violence in American
cities will be spontaneous eruptions of mass frustration like the
riot in Watts. They will be more in the organized pattern characteristic of Detroit, where the later stages of the uprising ex-
hibited evidence of strategic planning. Moreover, it is highly
likely that some planned violence will be moved out of the ghettos into white suburbs.[37]

36. Fanon, *The Wretched of the Earth*, pp. 27 ff., pp. 55 ff.
37. Morris Renek, "Whistling in a Very Lively Graveyard," *The New
Republic* (Vol. 156), May 13, 1967, pp. 14–15.

Furthermore, the hatred for whites will become more evident in the speech and action of some Negro leaders, and that hatred will distinguish less and less between the good white and the bad white, as is always the case with stereotyping of the out-group. In other words, white liberals will be less and less appreciated and more and more hated.

At the same time, however, many of the leaders of the new Negro pluralism will be searching for alternatives to violence and they will be seeking the support of the white community to bring about the kind of changes in American society that will make violence a less attractive alternative to the masses of Negro people. Yet it must be remembered at all times that the very pressure of black extremists upon more moderate Negro leaders will force them toward the most militant alternatives available short of violence.

It is already evident what will be the white racist response, and so what is crucial is really the liberal response. White liberals must not withdraw from the conflict, because those whites who are willing to take the risks of involvement form the most important resource for communication during the time of intensifying conflict, which surely lies ahead.

It is an irony, in a way. We white liberal Protestants have long professed our love for all men, and we have especially professed our love for the Negro. Can we love those that curse us, who revile us and spitefully use us? That is the question, and a tremendous portion of any hope for Christian reconciliation in the future rests upon that question. We have long been tested by our white racist brethren on this question, but then we always had the Negro community to give us succor and appreciation. Perhaps the racism and violence, the curses and the denials of militant Negroes will put us to the test—the Christian love of the enemy when we are catching it from both sides.

Finally, we have our continuing human interracial relationships and those of the past as reminders that there is some hope left for men. At times, however, it appears to be a very slim hope in the face of mounting conflict and talk of violence. The response of the ancient wise man in a situation like this is surely understandable. "Vanity of vanities, all is vanity, says the preacher," [38] and it might well be. But the Christian's hope has never been hope in himself or any other man alone. His hope is in God, and our hope now is finally based on a conviction that "in everything God works for good with those who love Him, who are called according to His purpose." [39]

38. Ecclesiastes, 1: 2 (R.S.V.).
39. Romans 8:28 (R.S.V.).